Church, Gospel, and Empire

Church, Gospel, and Empire

How the Politics of Sovereignty Impregnated the West

ROGER HAYDON MITCHELL

WIPF & STOCK · Eugene, Oregon

CHURCH, GOSPEL, AND EMPIRE
How the Politics of Sovereignty Impregnated the West

Wipf & Stock
An Imprint of Wipf and Stock Publishers
199 W. 8th Ave., Suite 3
Eugene, OR 97401
www.wipfandstock.com

ISBN 13: 978-1-61097-744-9

Manufactured in the U.S.A.

Contents

Acknowledgments vii
Introduction ix

PART I: THEOLOGICAL DISLOCATION

1 New Bearings: The Origins of Modernity and Their Ongoing
   Impact, Critical Themes 3

2 Conduits of Christendom: Eusebius of Caesarea 28
   The Church as Instrument of Eschatological Progress
   The Strategic Function of the Cross
   The Necessity of Sovereignty
   The Christological Controversy of the Council of Nicaea
   Impulses of Christendom

PART II: A GENEALOGY OF SUBSUMPTION

3 Conduits of Christendom: Innocent III and His Seminal
   Contemporaries: Frederick II the Hohenstaufen,
   Joachim of Fiore, and Francis of Assisi 63
   The Papacy of Innocent III
   The Rise of Emperor Frederick II the Hohenstaufen
   The Inversion of the Body of Christ
   The Innovations of Joachim of Fiore and Francis of Assisi
   Currents of Medievality; Impulses of Modernity

4 Conduits of Christendom: Church, Sovereignty, and Money
   in the Genesis of the Modern World 96
   Gilbert Burnet and the Development of a Latitudinarian
      Approach
   William III and the Multiplication of Sovereignty through
      Diplomacy and War
   The Founding of the Bank of England
   An Alternative Vision
   Currents of Modernity; Impulses of Biopower

5   Conduits of Christendom: Biopower and the Century
            of the Spirit 131
      Biopower
      The Century of the Spirit
      *The Potential Power of Immaterial Labor and Living by
      Faith*

PART III: RECONFIGURING THE DIVINE

6   Kenotic Theology 171
        Kenotic Christology
        Kenotic Love: Weakness or Strength?

7   Towards a Kenarchic Hermeneutic 196
        Initiating a Fullness of Time
        A Hermeneutic Suitable for a Fullness of Time
        *Historical and Archeological Indications of a Counterpolitical
        Jesus*
        Towards a Kenarchic Theopolitics

      Conclusion 233
      Bibliography 241
      Subject/Name Index 249

Acknowledgments

To begin with I must thank my two able academic supervisors at the University of Lancaster, the late Dr Paul Fletcher, for his extraordinary insight and encouragement, and Dr Gavin Hyman, for his insistence on clarity of argument and the avoidance of unsubstantiated opinion. My thanks also go to Professor David Clough and his colleagues in the theological texts seminar at the University of Chester. Their relational approach and affirmation have been more significant than perhaps they realize. I am extremely grateful to Professor David Brown of the University of St Andrews, who graciously allowed me free access to the manuscripts of the relevant chapters of his book *Divine Humanity* prior to its publication. Then I cannot fail to acknowledge the collaborative support of a network of wonderful friends, some of whom are academics but most of whom are committed practitioners in the various spheres of society, who agreed to walk with me throughout this project. The inspiration is theirs, the end product is mine. I thank them all. Finally I thank my wife, Sue, whose quick brain and deeply prophetic perspective have been a vital complement to my own dogged determination to pursue the issues to the end.

Introduction

THE THESIS PRESENTED IN this book emerges from a conviction of the pertinence of particular questions relating to the contemporary zeitgeist, which may be set out as follows. Why has the assumption of progress towards peace and prosperity persisted throughout the history of the West despite the prevalence of war and the continuance of poverty? Given Western democratic institutions, why do the politics of power and the commodification of human worth increasingly characterize society? And given that the church has had such a central role in this history, why is it now so politically marginalized as to be seemingly incapable of remedying these problems? And how is it that the best of church experience in both traditional and radical expressions tends to relapse to hierarchical domination and control? The central claim outlined here is that these questions can best be understood and answered in relation to a posited historical capitulation of the church and originary gospel principles to dominant political configurations of sovereignty, which, throughout this book, are denoted by the term "empire."

1. EMPIRE

In its etymology "empire" is the noun developed out of the Latin *imperare* from *perare* (to prepare or order) and *im* (in, into), which the Oxford Dictionary defines as "supreme and wide (political) dominion; absolute control (over); government in which sovereign is called emperor; territory of an emperor." While it may be claimed that such dominion is intended to be for the benefit of the people thus ruled, the common experience of the multitude in these circumstances is that expressed by Matthew Arnold's famous nineteenth-century poem "A Summer Night," where "most men in a brazen prison live."[1] Giorgio Agamben continues this imagery when he depicts the postmodern West as a biopolitical empire in which the motif of the prison camp describes "the hidden matrix

---

1. Watt, *Matthew Arnold Selected Poems and Prose*, 85.

and *nomos* of the political space in which we still live."[2] For the purposes of the proposed discussion, this dictionary definition and poetic characterization sustain a working definition of empire as "the domination of the many by the few for the benefit of the few in any conscribed territory or political structure, where political is used in its generic sense of relating to the ordering of the *polis*."

From this beginning, adding to it aspects of neo-Marxist analysis, together with a specifically kenotic, incarnational gospel perspective, the book seeks to develop a neo-Christian view of empire as a dynamic political and economic construct empowered by sovereignty and undergirded by law and war. While this view preferences the exercise of sovereign power as the *telos* of empire, it recognizes the ownership of property and the extraction of tax as the necessary means to its function. In this way empire is positioned over against the supposed initial gospel and *ecclesia* where love and gift are the means to cooperative relationship.

The viewpoint that ensues presents empire and sovereignty in a close correlation where empire depicts the overall shape of a totalizing entity in which sovereignty is consolidated through economic means secured by juridico-political force. This latter phrase specifies the active means by which empire is constituted through law and war, while sovereignty is used to signify the ongoing operation of empire in relation to the *polis*. In this way sovereignty is viewed as the whole governmental mechanism for the subjection and exploitation of the multitude to the primary benefit of a ruling social hierarchy of individuals, families, *ethnae*, cities, classes, or nation states in the various economic phases of empire whether feudal, property, capital, or life.[3] All three expressions are characterized as modes of imperial power: empire as consolidated power, juridico-political force as the means to power, and sovereignty as ongoing governing power in action.

With the help of the neo-Marxists and in particular Michael Hardt and Antonio Negri, it is possible to track the trajectory of empire as thus understood through medievality and modernity to the postmodern present. This posits an ontological dualism throughout the medieval world from the fourth century onwards that framed desire and order by the legitimation of a transcendent authority to which the multitude was obliged to submit. The neo-Marxists see this as succeeded by a modern

2. Agamben, *Means Without End*, 36.
3. Wood, *Empire of Capital*, 47.

era, which they describe as consisting of two modes. They see the first mode as a radical revolutionary attempt to sever links with the perceived ontological dualism of transcendence and sovereignty expressed by empire and emphasize instead the importance of human knowledge and freedom of expression on the immanent plane. The second mode is then viewed as a counter-revolutionary process that rose up within the modern renaissance to divert its direction, transplant the new image of humanity to a transcendent plane, occupy the capacities of theoretical reason, and, above all, to oppose the reappropriation of power on the part of the multitude and reassert the authority of church and government. The functional dualism that emerged with this second aspect of modernity manifested in a reconfiguration of empire and sovereignty that developed through two historical phases separated by the Thirty Years War and continues to the biopolitical empire of the present day.[4]

From the beginning of this genealogy, transcendence is exposed as an ontological partner with empire, and church and empire are seen to be no longer opponents but bedfellows. The thesis set out in this book posits a fourth-century fall or *lapsis*[5] in which this tendency for sovereignty to subsume transcendence was consolidated. However, the neo-Marxists regard the partnership of sovereignty and transcendence as a complete identification rather than the consequence of a secular penetration. As a result, transcendence is consistently regarded by them as an expression of empire rather than the victim of subsumption by it. In consequence, although neo-Marxists expose a trajectory that illuminates the progress of church and empire, they posit substantive transitions between the medieval world and modernity and again between modernity and the biopolitical empire of capital that, from the perspective of the thesis configured here, obscure the potential power of transcendence to re-empower the multitude. In the first transition they see transcendence as the necessary partner in a dualism that must be rejected, and in the second they see it as the reconstituted partner in a transfigured dualism that may yet be surpassed by the immanent power of the multitude.

The nature of these transitions is central to the genealogy explored in this book. The neo-Christian standpoint synchronized here asserts a persistent partnership of transcendence and empire from the fourth

---

4. Hardt and Negri, *Empire*, 74–75.

5. A word derived from the Latin *lapsus*, meaning error or fall, as contained in the familiar theological terms prelapsarian and postlapsarian.

century and continuing to the present day. It will be argued that the Renaissance, while containing a revolutionary aspect, did not succeed in breaking with the interpenetration of theology and sovereignty. It will then be proposed that the so-called functional dualism contended by the neo-Marxists was choreographed by the ongoing partnership of church and empire as they configured the nation state to conserve their own power by means of multiplied sovereignty. As a result, the empire of capital that characterizes modernity may properly be understood as the progeny of the partnership of church and empire. So while a new form of empire is growing up that appears to marginalize the church, the church necessarily remains responsible for it. The final chapters will make the case for a different configuration of transcendent power from which empire and sovereignty can be thoroughly distinguished. Consequently the characteristics of sovereignty become even more clearly discernible as empire, and its trajectory throughout the stages of Western Christendom to the present can be the more obviously demarcated. The thesis therefore puts forward the view that, while it evolves in the course of time, empire maintains a consistent character, the genealogy of which constitutes the medieval, modern, and now postmodern worlds.

2. ORIGINARY CHRISTIAN PRINCIPLES

It is, of course, acknowledged that there is a variety of hermeneutics available with which to approach the connection of church and empire. One of the most recent of these is the straightforward stance taken by Linda Woodhead who simply recognizes that the Christian repertoire has always contained two main trajectories, the one sponsoring, supporting, and legitimating modes of power from on high, the other affirming and supplying possibilities of support from below.[6] However, the unapologetic standpoint taken in this project regards the second of these trajectories with its humble identification with the poor, as seen in the Magnificat's pulling down of the mighty and the Beatitudes' love for one's enemies, as the radical Christianity of the gospel testimony. The orientation of the thesis, therefore, is to seek out answers as to how this lowly stance was subverted into support for the higher power and suggests that it happened as the result of an invasion and colonization of the concept of transcendence by sovereignty. As a result, what was originally

6. Woodhead, *An Introduction to Christianity*, 406.

a single identity for Christianity has been divided through the development of ecclesiastical structures and theologies that have colluded with empire.

The book attempts to show the development of this bifurcation by tracing the genealogy of the supposed subsumptive invasion through history. While it proceeds from the standpoint of a displaced originary Christianity, its insights are not exclusive to this perspective. Rather it offers a story of the development of a Christianity supportive of the higher power that it takes to be the nature of Christendom from the fourth century to the present. This has the advantage of providing a genealogy of church and empire that can at least in part contribute to the corpus of knowledge of both trajectories of Christianity, while offering an explanation of the displacement of the supposed originary principles. This means that the status of the genealogy developed here is not simply conditional upon its provisional standpoint but utilizes it to shed light on the interpenetration of church and empire that Woodhead has termed its trajectory of support for the higher power. This is by no means to claim that the perspective provided is a neutral one. As will become clear, the very idea of a rationally objective unearthing of the events of history is itself considered to be a consequence of a quasi-transcendent view of human reason that the subsumptive genealogy traced here helps to expose.

The attempt will be made to trace this genealogy as it develops through the various generally recognized movements of history. The most influential explanations for these historical movements tend to focus on a perceived shift from religious to secular perspectives rather than from egalitarian to hierarchical ones and to focus their investigation of the location of such a shift on the transition from the middle ages to the modern world. It is the view of the thesis, however, that the loss of an originary egalitarian orientation to the needs of the multitude occurred in the much earlier fourth-century partnership of church and empire and that this provides a deeper explanation of the trend to secularism. In line with this, hermeneutical positions adopted in respect to the genesis of modernity are presented in Part I and the proposal for a much earlier origin for the eventual secularization is evaluated within the contours of those arguments.

3. CONDUITS OF CHRISTENDOM

The method chosen to expose this genealogy is by means of a number of specific synchronic case studies or *conduits* of Christendom. The symbol of a conduit, more than say a window or a picture, lends itself to the possibility of selecting a time period within the diachronic passage of events and, focusing on it in a synchronic study, to identify particular people and institutions in order to examine the interplay of relationships, choices, and actions. This has two distinct advantages. Firstly, it carries the idea of a period in which a specific current or impulse was effecting events and which could be investigated as one might test for live power or drill down looking for oil or water. Secondly, it resolves the difficulty posed by the desire to bring into focus a trans-historical connection in order to evaluate the relationship of church and empire as a whole. Instead of attempting the inadvisable task of covering vast tracts of history within a single research project, the idea of a conduit delineates a way forward that can be applied to various appropriate periods in history, which can be similarly mined and together used to build up a genealogy of church and empire.

In this way four key turning points have been selected that provide graphic illustrations of the collusion of church and empire. By making the lifetime of Eusebius of Caesarea the first such conduit and depicting the contemporary biopolitical empire of capital as the last, it has been possible to take a bearing on the relationship of church and empire, viewing the whole not as a provable theory of cause and effect, but as the narrative of a relationship. With this in view, although many moments in history between the two points could lend themselves to this treatment, two specific intervening moments have been chosen and are explored in Part II of the book. These focus on the interrelated lives of Pope Innocent III, Emperor Frederick II, Joachim of Fiore, and Francis of Assisi at the turn of the twelfth century, and the partnership of Bishop Gilbert Burnet and King William III and the founding of the Bank of England at the end of the seventeenth century. While the first and last conduits lend themselves relatively easily to exposition and interpretation, precisely because they form supposedly beginning and ending points, the intervening two are necessarily the more overtly functioning conduits. In them the impulses and currents exposed in the first study and experienced in the last are more completely traced in movement from the supposed inception of the fall to its consummation. In consequence they contain more narrative detail through which the developing genealogy is pursued. While the endeavor is made to show precisely how the genealogy is choreographed by the sovereignty consequent on the supposed subsumption, the intention is to avoid imposing a preconceived process on the events of the conduits. These intermediate conduits therefore require more participation by the reader in the movement of the narrative as it attempts to follow the trajectory of church and empire through history.

4. AN ALTERNATIVE VIEW

In the course of these investigations it will be shown that the originary gospel principles did not disappear from view. Each conduit takes note of evidence of ecclesial behavior and thought that continually returns to disrupt the dominant theological order at each point in history where the collusion of church and empire is the most decisive. These consistently present a counterpoint theme, which in turn functions as a resource for the explicit development of a kenotic configuration of contemporary ecclesial and theological forms.

This configuration of a contemporary theology and praxis of kenosis consonant with the supposed early gospel testimony is the explicit task of Part III. Although a fully developed theology is beyond the scope of this study, the final part of the book points towards ways in which church and theology may be reconfigured to challenge the historical collusion of church with empire that will have been exposed in Parts I and II. It will be argued that, if church and theology were to develop along these lines, the church might yet recover its originary principles and rediscover its political potency, thus being better able to address and confront the questions raised at the outset of this introduction.

PART I

Theological Dislocation

1

New Bearings

The Origins of Modernity and Their Ongoing Impact, Critical Themes

THE INTENTION OF THIS initial chapter is threefold. Firstly, it places the thesis in the context of contemporary theology. It does this by affirming a general sense among many theologians that there has been a serious dislocation of theology from contemporary life. It identifies a common methodology among theologians who are investigating the cause of this dislocation, which is to posit and search out some kind of fall in the history of the Christian faith. The thesis is then introduced within these same methodological contours. The way in which theologians commonly locate this lapsis in a shift in the apprehension of the divine at the onset of modernity is noted, and the attempt is made to show that the much earlier dislocation posited here contributes to the field of enquiry by qualifying, expanding, or questioning the arguments propounded by the theologians concerned. Secondly, the chapter aims to highlight a problematic tendency for modern and postmodern thinkers to predicate their analyses on immanence and positions the thesis as a possible explanation and antidote for this trend. Thirdly, the chapter aims to prepare the ground for the ensuing exposure of the genealogy of church and empire by introducing key themes central to its ongoing development in the conduits that follow.

In line with this intention, this chapter is in three parts. Firstly, it provides a brief overview of contemporary theologians who recognize the theological dislocation and posit a fall in the genesis of modernity to explain it. Particular reference is made to the proposals of John Milbank,

Michael Allen Gillespie, William Cavanaugh, and Paul Fletcher. The work of Michel de Certeau, building on the ideas of Henri de Lubac, is seen to indicate that all these perspectives can be read in terms of the loss of a body. The implications of proposing an earlier lapsis are then contemplated. Secondly, Paul Fletcher's recognition of the tendency of responses to modernity to predication on immanence and the relevance of this to the dislocation of theology from the Western intellectual and political arena is examined. The possible rooting of this tendency in the identification of divine and imperial power consequent on the proposed fourth-century fall is then considered. Thirdly, themes crucial to the proposal of a fourth-century subsumption of the church by sovereignty and its subsequent genealogy are indicated and explored, in preparation for the ensuing conduits of Christendom where the supposed lapsis and its subsequent genealogy are investigated in detail.

It is anticipated that the initial presentation of the thesis in relation to contemporary responses to modernity and questions about the nature of sovereign power and its status in the medieval world will undergird the overall argument and shed light on the challenges faced by contemporary theologians in hope of a renewed theopolitical vision. For if imperial sovereignty is necessarily subversive of originary gospel and *ecclesia* and has been embraced by the church, then the primary theological formulations and ecclesial institutions that make up the Christian tradition may well have been misconstrued and deformed in consequence. And if the era of medievality known as Christendom was the outworking of a secular intrusion into an initial Christian orientation, then it will be important to reconsider and revise theories of modernity that have been predicated on what was already an era of covert secularization. This is particularly to be welcomed, given that the current understanding of modernity as the response to a representative Christian mindset tends to render permanent the marginalization of the church and its contribution to contemporary society. As will be indicated, theological responses to this predicament are themselves often predicated, at least in part, on a diminished view of transcendence vouchsafed by modernity with the result that they fall short of providing a sustainable practical theopolitical alternative. If however, as the coming conduits will suggest, the conflictual sovereignty of church and empire that modernity was in part a reaction to is evidence of an earlier dislocation of originary Christianity, then an alternative theopolitical mindset might yet be reconfigured.

A. THE ORIGINS OF MODERNITY
AND THEIR ONGOING IMPACT

1. Lapsarian Perspectives

The classic view of modernity generally regarded the modern era as a period in European history from the beginning of the seventeenth century onwards. It was seen as a time when, through the adoption of rational methods of intellectual enquiry by such as Galileo Galilei in physics, René Descartes in epistemology, and Thomas Hobbes in political theory, religion played a lesser part in life than in the medieval era, people prospered economically, and conditions improved across the board.[1] Late twentieth- and early twenty-first-century approaches, however, in response to the exigencies of the modern world such as the persistence of poverty and the prevalence of violence and war, or the perceived marginalization of Christian faith, tend to reject previous more positive analyses. Instead they concentrate on modernity's ambiguous affirmation of human potential alongside the oppressive sovereignty of its juridico-political constructs and rationalistic approach to knowledge. Stephen Toulmin, for example, affirms an early positive root to modernity in a literary or humanistic phase represented by the work of Montaigne, Machiavelli, and Shakespeare, and predating a more pretentious philosophical and scientific phase by a hundred years.[2] Hardt and Negri propose first the emergence of a radical plane of immanence, embodied in the writings of such as Duns Scotus and Dante Alighieri, succeeded by a counter resurgence of transcendent sovereignty as depicted by Michelangelo on the ceiling of the Sistine Chapel.[3]

These approaches to the early Renaissance disclose a problem with the medieval world that early expressions of modernity were an attempt to address, while at the same time calling into question the theoretical and political direction of the later modern worldview that succeeded it. It is the endeavor to understand how these positive and negative aspects arose and their perceived tendency to depose the church and its theology from the public sphere that has provoked the lapsarian analyses of

1. Stephen Toulmin cites Lawrence Stone, *The Crisis of Aristocracy*, as exemplifying this view. Toulmin, *Cosmopolis*, 213.

2. Ibid., 22–30.

3. Hardt and Negri, *Empire*, 70–83.

contemporary theologians. That is to say they posit some kind of specific fall after which Christian faith is estranged from the socio-political and cultural-intellectual mainstream. For John Milbank the lapsis is ironically Hardt and Negri's perceived moment of breakthrough in the late thirteenth-century work of Duns Scotus. In Hardt and Negri's neo-Marxist approach, Scotus' concept of the univocity of being establishes immanence as the sphere of human freedom by making the apprehension of the transcendent a component of temporal thought. Milbank's radical orthodoxy, on the other hand, sees this as the manifestation of a foundational metaphysic of modernity, which he describes as "ontotheological idolatry regarding God."[4] The problem with univocity from Milbank's perspective is the way in which it posits being independently of the divine and then describes God by means of it. This might be termed an intellectual fall because of the way it renders ontology and metaphysics supra-theological by creating a theoretical human grammar, or what Catharine Pickstock calls a *mathēsis*,[5] to which language about God is subjugated. For Milbank this is "the turning point in the destiny of the West."[6]

Michael Alan Gillespie postulates a nihilistic crisis in late medieval thought brought about by the impact of the nominalists and in particular William of Ockham. Building on Blumenberg's conception of the origins of modernity as a proto-Nietzschean self-assertion that reoccupied the scholastics' need to show the hand of God in all events,[7] Gillespie contrasts the Thomistic attempt to reaffirm the notion of the ultimate reality of universals with Ockham's assertion that all real being is individual or particular and universals are thus fictions.[8] Whereas for the scholastics creation itself was regarded as the embodiment of divine logic, and man, as the rational animal and *imago dei*, was seen as the pinnacle, the nominalists asserted that God could not be understood by human reason but was only accessible by biblical revelation or mystical experience. From Gillespie's perspective this implies that creation is radically particular and thus not purposeful. Human beings have no natural or supernatural end or *telos* and God is presented as "frighteningly omnipotent, utterly

---

4. Milbank, *The Word Made Strange*, 44.

5. Pickstock, *After Writing*, xiii.

6. Milbank, *The Word Made Strange*, 44.

7. Gillespie, *The Theological Origins of Modernity*, 11–12.

8. Ibid., 14–16.

beyond human ken, and a continual threat to human well-being."[9] This position presented an ontological shift "that shattered every aspect of the mediaeval world."[10]

William Cavanaugh proposes a political fall, in which the church acquiesced to the separation of Christian faith from the public sphere on the conviction that the violence of the post-Reformation wars was the inevitable result of variant theological ideas and opposing ecclesiastical structures. He suggests that this perspective was in fact a basic creation myth of modernity, fundamental to the legitimation of the nation state as the guarantor of the modern world.[11] He supplies a plethora of convincing arguments to show that no so-called religious war of the sixteenth or seventeenth century was fought solely between the exponents of conflicting doctrines or representatives of different churches. He argues that the concept of religion is itself a modern theory relegating faith to internal values without external disciplines in a way unique to the emerging Western nation state.[12] Paul Fletcher posits a more distinctly theological fall, which he identifies as a dislocation of theology that took place in consequence of the Copernican revolution. As he sees it, this had universal theological implications because it displaced a metaphysical cosmology and thereby disavowed an analogy of being that was basic to the general understanding of church and society "in which concepts such as hierarchy, gradation and participation make perfect sense."[13] As a result, since that time, any theology that wishes to be relevant and accessible, or speak to the social and political needs of a society consequent on modernity, tends to direct itself towards the immanent plane. However, this ultimately renders any such theology captive to the mores of modern temporality with the result that it falls short of providing a sustainable, practical, theopolitical alternative.

Finally, Michel de Certeau, focusing on the mystics from the thirteenth century onwards and drawing on the work of Henri de Lubac,[14] posits behind them an inversion in the traditional understanding of the *corpus verum* and the *corpus mysticum* that took place during the latter

9. Ibid., 15.

10. Ibid., 14.

11. Cavanaugh, *The Myth of Religious Violence*, ch. 3.

12. Ibid., ch. 2.

13. Fletcher, *Disciplining the Divine*, 139.

14. See de Lubac's *Corpus Mysticum*.

part of the twelfth century and that is considered in detail in Part II of this dissertation. Describing the mystics' writings as a "mystical body" of alternative doctrine, he claims that they represent the intended goal of a journey that moves towards the site of a disappearance. Their discourse lacks a body and, whether it relates to the question of reforming a church, founding a community, or discovering a new personal spirituality, the production of a body plays an essential role.[15] He depicts two intertwining movements, the first of which he identifies with Ockham and the nominalists, as "the critique of the sign," by which he refers to the insinuation of particularities in place of universals that deliberately transcended the limits of a tradition that time seemed to have corrupted and occluded. The second is exemplified in Hieronymus Bosch's famous *Garden of Delights*, which he refers to as the complementary substitution of a problematics of production for that of deciphering mysteries, by means of which a new alternative cosmos of messages could be heard.[16]

In summary, Milbank regards the proposed fall as the subjection of God to human reason while Gillespie sees it as the reconception of reason so as to exclude the mediation of transcendent certainties. Cavanaugh ascribes the lapsis to the reduction of faith to internal human values and Fletcher assigns it to the disavowal of an analogy of being between God and human society. In each case the supposed lapsis is reckoned to have disconnected the proper relationship of knowledge and the divine transcendent. The thesis argued here is that in order to come to a proper understanding of the significance of this, and in order to consider how it may effectually be corrected, it is necessary to look back much earlier to a fundamental shift or fall that created the conditions that made these later shifts inevitable. The proposal of a fourth-century lapsis suggests that the heart of the problem was the interpenetration of transcendence and sovereignty consequent on the acceptance of imperial power as the means to the temporal fulfillment of the eschatological peace. Without this conflation, divine transcendence might itself have provided a corrective to the dominating characteristics of political sovereignty. In this way de Certeau's recognition that the occlusion of the body of Christ lies behind nominalism and mysticism can be seen to make sense in the light of such a lapsis and can be applied equally meaningfully to the configuration of univocity, the supposed conflicts of religious certainty, and

15. de Certeau, *The Mystic Fable*, 79–80.
16. Ibid., 59.

the Copernican disavowal of being. In each case, had the incarnational possibilities remained intact, recourse to its counterpolitical properties might have corrected the extremes of sovereign power. However, the configuration of the divine being in ontologically sovereign terms obscured the potential of an alternative radical Christ and left the genealogy of Christendom endemically entangled in the operations of juridico-political power. This helps explain both the negative climate from which the late medieval and early modern thinkers were attempting to escape and the enduring assumption of ontological sovereignty in the analyses of contemporary theologians.

From this perspective it is possible to draw on these theological genealogies of modernity to shed light on the proposed earlier lapsis. Eusebius's presentation of God as imperial sovereign, from whom worldly emperors such as Constantine mirrored their power, might be termed, utilizing Milbank's language, an ontotheological misrepresentation, which provided another earlier but decisive fulcrum for the destiny of the West. Or, to use the phrase with which Gillespie characterized Ockham and the nominalists, it represents an ontological shift that altered every aspect of the interpretation of the gospel testimony. Similarly Eusebius's identification of the *pax Romana* and the conversion of Constantine as evidence of the success of the church and gospel supplied a creation myth for Christendom analogous to Cavanaugh's treatment of the theory of religious violence in the advance of modernity. Just as Fletcher positions Copernicus as representative of a transformation that issued in a comprehensive theological dislocation that gave way to an inundation of immanent power, so Eusebius's choice of imperial sovereignty as the means to universal peace overwhelmed the counteractive potential of eschatological hope and affirmed an apparently unassailable political world order.

De Certeau's prescient disclosure of the loss of a body focuses the heart of the matter, the occlusion of the incarnational *euaggelion*. But while these genealogies shed further light on the supposed fourth-century lapsis, it in turn serves to question them in several important respects, by rendering them responses to the earlier fall. Such a fall substantially questions Milbank's defense of the divine from its apparent subjection to human reason and Gillespie's resistance to the individualized revelatory experiences of the nominalists. Similarly the conflictual and territorial aspects of deity's perceived authority as displayed in the thought and practice of Innocent III and Frederick II in the second conduit may reinvigorate the ascription of violence to the supposed outworking of the divine will, despite Cavanaugh's indications to the contrary. The potential reintroduction of the incarnational identification of deity with a mortal body may overcome the impact of the disavowal of the analogy of divine being perceived by Fletcher and reaffirm the centrality of the earth to divine transcendence, notwithstanding its relationship to the sun's orbit or the dynamics of the solar system.

The common difficulty disclosed by each of these lapsis propositions and affirmed by the proposal of an earlier fall, is the rendering of transcendence problematic as the source of certainty and the resultant preferencing of immanence as the only safe ground for knowledge. For however the various lapsis viewpoints are understood, they all disclose an attempt to disconnect human knowledge from divine transcendence. The occlusion of the *corpus verum* meant that there was no alternative recourse to the connection of divine being and the temporal world apart from imperial sovereignty, and it was this that the modern era was at pains to escape. Consistent to all these views is the centrality of immanence to modernity and the connection of this to sovereignty. The embrace of the immanent plane eventually resulted in faith, as Fletcher puts it, becoming "beholden to the force of law."[17] As this consequence will be central to the analysis at the heart of this book it will be worth explicating it in more detail. To this end the next section provides a brief overview of the salient components of Fletcher's argument as to how this predication on immanence came about.

2. Disciplining the Divine

According to Fletcher's analysis, the theological dislocation of the accepted Christian world order with the loss of the medieval analogy of being consequent on the Copernican revolution issued in two cultures of immanence. These developments, in Fletcher's view, separated "the book of God" and that "other book of God—the world."[18] The first culture emphasized those truths that could be theoretically obtained from the biblical text, and the other, those aspects of faith that impinged directly on the practical individual life of Christians. As a result "the Christianity

17. Fletcher, *Disciplining the Divine*, 178.
18. Ibid., 12.

that is bequeathed to the post-Reformation world is established on those truths which can be 'scientifically' garnered from the text and the author's intention or that which is relevant to the practical, individual life of Christians within a strictly demarcated cultural sphere."[19] While these developments were not exclusively properties of the Protestant Reformation, and similar emphases may be found in Roman Catholic theology, the Reformation was their primary vehicle. Fletcher argues that the dislocation consequent on the loss of the medieval analogy of being thus seriously limited the expression of Christian faith and became "the pretext for the relocation of truth in the favoured spaces of faith, trust and voluntaristic decision."[20] The thesis presented here, however, posits that the medieval analogy of being was already supporting an understanding of transcendence subsumed by sovereignty. As already stated, it was an analogy in which hierarchy and gradation made perfect sense.[21] So rather than consign "faith, trust and voluntaristic choice" to the sphere of personal devotion and private behavior, this thesis will seek to reclaim and develop them as a means of re-accessing the originary testimony of a God who embraces human mortality and wholeheartedly affirms creation in the kenotic love-gift of Godself to the world. This has the effect of recovering the *ecclesia* as a people of faith and choice to re-invade the imperial world of both church and *saeculum* with a totally different kind of power to sovereign law, as Part III will begin to explicate.

Without this recognition and potential retrieval of the ground of being, lost by the supposed fourth-century *lapsis*, theology became, as Fletcher perceives, predicated on immanence and obligated to its methods and means.[22] This rendered ensuing attempts at relevant theological response to the problems of modernity subject to the utilitarian "juridical schema of practical reason."[23] Theology allowed the reified human self to take the place of the divine, and left the world at the mercy of the enduring sources of imperial power. Fletcher notes the connection between modern absolutism and modern self-assertion in the lives of late medieval and early modern monarchs[24] as evidence of the colonization

19. Ibid., 12.
20. Ibid., 13.
21. Ibid., 139.
22. Ibid., 13.
23. Ibid., 22.
24. Ibid., 101.

of monotheistic theology by sovereignty, which he acknowledges to be rooted in Eusebius,[25] and points out that "the manifestation of monarchical power in its sacred and mundane semblances is not concluded at the threshold of modernity."[26] This will be further evinced in the case of Frederick II in the second conduit. Fletcher quotes Carl Schmitt and Erik Petersen to the effect that this was still manifesting itself in the totalitarianisms of the twentieth century.[27]

He explains that the cosmological shift, embodied symbolically in Copernicus, lost the Aristotelian recognition that "because man is not the highest being in the universe" the theoretical takes precedence over the moral and political.[28] This resulted in the loss of hierarchical transcendence and in turn issued in the primacy of the immanence of personal human selfhood, which then reduced institution, doctrine, and tradition to expressions of negative heteronomy. From this perspective modernity appears consequent upon the apotheosis of the subject and the quest for freedom from all restrictions on the autonomy of the human ego.

Fletcher uses the example of Jürgen Moltmann and a rainbow coalition[29] of other proponents of a social trinity to expose the consequences of this ongoing operation of immanence at the heart of contemporary theology. As he painstakingly exposes, their theology functions as the carrier of sovereignty in two ways. Firstly, by focusing on the social, relational, and political rather than resorting to the primary revelation of the transcendent, they bring the ongoing impact of the reification of the human into the very heart of theological and doctrinal discourse.[30] This both furthers the autonomous importance of the self and colludes with the burgeoning biopolitical empire. He shows how their predication on immanence leads to the trivialization of patristic theology as manifest in the over-pleading of differences between the trinitarian theology of the Cappadocians and that of Augustine of Hippo,[31] and results in the

---

25. Ibid., 98–99.

26. Ibid., 103.

27. Fletcher cites Carl Schmitt, *Political Theology: Four Chapters on the Concept of Sovereignty*, and Erik Petersen, *Der Monotheism als politisches Problem: Ein Beitrag zur Geschichte des politischen Theologie im Imperium Romanum*. Ibid., 103–4.

28. Ibid., 27.

29. Fletcher lists twenty theologians across a spectrum from Roman Catholic through Lutheran, Reformed, Anglican, Methodist, and Orthodox, to liberation and feminist standpoints. Ibid., 39.

30. Ibid., 97.

31. Ibid., 52–62.

anachronistic import of modern concepts into the developing doctrine of the trinity, such as that of personhood.[32] Fletcher also shows the political implications of predication on immanence. First highlighting Hegel's ontological subjugation of the divine to the modern state,[33] Fletcher then indicates from a twenty-first-century perspective how the modern tendency to predication on immanence leads to the same move being made between social trinitarianism and the so-called political "third way" of a neo-liberal capitalism tempered by the aspiration for social justice.[34] In this way the divine is ongoingly submitted to the state and the increasing subsumptive power of contemporary biopolitics, a detailed analysis of which forms part of the subject of the fourth conduit.

Fletcher thus argues that while the submission of transcendence to the immanent plane is the result of the loss of the medieval analogy of being, immanence soon displays its own kind of sovereignty. From the perspective being developed here, as will emerge in the next section and be explored in the fourth conduit, this resurgence of sovereignty was an understandable reaction in order to maintain the newly gained freedom from the perceived thrall of transcendent power. However, while the oppressive impact of imperial power was the reason for the rejection of divine transcendence, the oppression was not the necessary property of transcendence but of the sovereignty with which it had been identified. It was the earlier lapsis that had secured this identification of transcendence with sovereignty. This being the case, the rejection of transcendence was no guarantee of an escape from sovereignty, and the latter's ongoing operation, albeit on the immanent plane, soon introduced quasi-transcendent theories and practices. As a result, despite the constraints of immanence, the modernity that Fletcher describes exhibits profoundly transcendent exterior properties, what Michael Dillon and Arthur Bradley describe as "the sacralization *of* the secular."[35] This eventually manifested in a biopolitics in which the human body replaces the lost body revealed by de Certeau and de Lubac and "material, naked existence . . . has now become everything, and the body alone is the 'substance' of politics and power."[36] Fletcher suggests that in this way the immanent assumes the fullness of

32. Ibid., 69ff.
33. Ibid., 123.
34. Ibid., 123.
35. Ibid., ix.
36. Ibid., 127.

transcendent status. It is in this context that Capital has emerged as a Religion that "defiantly engulfs the futures and horizons of Christianity"[37] and even acquires eschatology as the means to instantiate consumption as the fulfillment of promissory hope.

Fletcher's discussion of the theological tendency to continue in modernity's predication on immanence paves the way for an interrogation of the juridico-political coercion that results, on his argument, from a political system established to preserve the sovereignty of the self in freedom from the negatively perceived heteronomy of a past ontocosmological unity. However, it is the argument of this book that beneath the modern predication on immanence that he exposes, lies the deeper ontological shift that calls into question the priority of the transcendent theoretical over the moral and political. This helps explain the negativity demonstrated towards institution, doctrine, and tradition. For if the penetration of imperial sovereignty into the calling and identity of the church imported the concept of hierarchy and theoretical knowledge and ascribed it to divine transcendence for the purposes of using the resultant ontology of divine being to legitimize imperial rule, then this has serious implications for Fletcher's argument. It would suggest that the oppositional attempt to liberate the human individual and multitude is not primarily the desire for the glorification of the individual or corporate self. It can also represent the attempt to escape the consequences of the colonization of church and theology and reverse an earlier ontological larceny in order to restore the primacy of love between the divine and the human revealed in a fully incarnational gospel perspective. This renders modernity as both the negative attempt to acquire individual sovereignty and the positive attempt to escape the hegemony of imperial domination. It thus affirms Fletcher's argument that the attempt to acquire personal sovereignty is a negative quest but contends that the attempt to assign imperial sovereignty to God is similarly negative. Not only is the assertion of human sovereignty from this perspective a form of domination, but so is the assertion of divine sovereignty. Fletcher, nonetheless, proffers three steps out of the contemporary theological predicament that delineate a way forward for the development of the thesis proposed here. The first is an eschatological reconception of time as a means of freeing theology from the bondage of modern

---

37. Ibid., 155.

sovereignty;[38] the second exploits the eschatological "instant" to make a reconnection with the counterpolitics of Jesus;[39] and the third calls for an interrogation of the process by which faith became "beholden to the force of law."[40] The first two of these will be explored and developed in the third part of this book. But it is Fletcher's final step out of contemporary theology's complex predicament that takes us to the core of this project. In it he calls for the interrogation of "how it was possible that faith became beholden to the force of law, and how the historical development of juridico-politics brought theology to a point beyond which it survives only as a parasite."[41] The proposal of a fourth-century *lapsis* attempts to contribute to this interrogative task, by seeking out the origins of a subsumption of originary Christian principles and tracing the interpenetration of *ecclesia* and empire in order to uncover the genealogy of faith's obligation to the force of law.

B. CRITICAL THEMES

The proposal that the fourth-century ecclesial embrace of imperial sovereignty embodies a fall lying behind faith's eventual subjugation to juridico-politics, gives considerable prominence to the themes of sovereignty and medievality and their related semantic families. This next section of the chapter attempts to delineate provisional definitions and anticipate seminal questions that attach to each of these themes by opening them up and exploring them in preparation for the historical investigations that follow.

1. Sovereignty

There are four important questions that attach to the topic of sovereignty in this context.

(A) Is all sovereignty necessarily imperial?

The word "sovereignty" derives from "sovereign," which, in its original use according to the Oxford Dictionary, denotes "a supreme ruler, especially a monarch." "Sovereignty" refers to the expression of the rule of

38. Ibid., 159.
39. Ibid., 162.
40. Ibid., 178.
41. Ibid., 178.

such a sovereign and is associated with the terminology of power, dominion, and authority. As has already been noted in the introduction, it is closely linked in its etymology with the word "empire." "Sovereignty" emphasizes the character of rule as supreme while the word "empire" identifies the nature of rule as ordered. Together they carry the idea of hierarchy under a supreme rulership. In the course of history this has come to include the corporate exercise of power as well as monarchy. For, as is argued later in this section, a republic is dependent on the subordination of the rights of the individual to the sovereign rule of the people and remains a hierarchical configuration of power. While it may be possible to use the word "sovereignty" to refer to the simply accidental or neutral possession of power, because of its close etymological association with dominion and empire, it is difficult to separate the word from its connotative loading. One may refer, for example, to "the kenotic sovereignty of the gospel Christ" to mean something very different from imperial sovereignty, and Part III will intimate that the ascription of lordship to Christ signifies something like this, but it has surely to be regarded as a marked or ironic use of the word.

While there are examples of sovereignty being exercised in a non-hierarchical way, the idea of supreme power is inevitably still in place to some degree. This can be expressed anecdotally with reference to the directors of a contemporary charity. As trustees they have the legal power to insist on their own way and could dominate their staff team accordingly. However, in the light of current practice they have established a culture of team decision-making. They have sovereignty but they choose to give it away to others. Nonetheless, by the law of the land they still retain the overall sovereignty. They have established what might be called a permissive sovereignty, but the supreme power still remains intact in the background. As directors they can suspend or share their supreme power, but it is theirs to decide. It is something like this covert aspect of sovereignty that Giorgio Agamben recognizes as contained in the power of the exception, which is discussed in the section below and in more detail in the fourth conduit and Part III. The central proposal of the thesis presented here is that an interpenetration of church and empire took place in the genesis of the medieval world on the supposition that the hierarchical domination of the many by the few was the means to universal peace. This assumption greatly increased the connection between sovereignty and empire by making sovereignty the chosen means of both the fulfillment of the eschatological task of the *ecclesia* and the legitimation of the imperial system of Rome. From this perspective the argument of the thesis itself offers an explanation of the way in which the word "sovereignty" has come generally to connote, if not denote, hierarchical domination.

(b) Is transcendence necessarily denotative of sovereignty?

It is the contention of this book that transcendence is not denotative of sovereignty in the general imperially linked sense. The subsumption of transcendence by sovereignty, embodied in the proposed fourth-century lapsis, is seen as the source of an early secularization. It is further argued that the attempt to transfer sovereignty from transcendence to immanence is definitive of the transition from the medieval to the modern world. This was because sovereignty and transcendence were seen to be equated and the initial phase of the enlightenment aimed to throw off the shackles of sovereignty. The counter-revolutionary phase then attempted to reconfigure sovereignty in immanent terms but, as indicated in the previous section, could only do so with recourse to a reconfigured secular transcendence. Nevertheless, it suited the secular authors of renewed sovereignty to identify transcendence with universal sovereignty, along with their opponents, in order to present the new order as freedom. As a result both parties continued to conflate sovereignty with transcendence and it remained distinctive of modernity to do so. This conflation is examined in more detail in the fourth conduit.

The word "transcendence" as generally used carries both the sense of surpassing excellence, and having existence apart from the material universe. For the purposes of this discussion it is being limited to its use in reference to deity and in regard to that aspect of deity that, while not necessarily incompatible with immanence, refers to and includes the existence, qualities, and character of the divine life outside and beyond it. While the concept of transcendence as commonly understood includes the characteristics of otherness and superiority, the definition posited here is a deliberately limited one. This is because the focus of the thesis is, particularly, divine transcendence, and specifically the transcendence of the Christian God. In this context it is possible that at least some of the characteristics of otherness and superiority, especially those that imply hierarchical ranking, are properties of the imperial sovereignty with which the understanding of transcendence has supposedly been subsumed. The subject of otherness will be returned to in more depth in Part III. At this point it will suffice to say that it is the suggestion of the thesis that such a subsumption has indeed taken place.

So the question formulated here is whether the possession of this more concise view of transcendence by deity necessitates the operation of sovereignty. The proposition being made is that the answer depends on the character of deity. This has many possible implications, the discussion of which may be abbreviated in the following two ways. Firstly, if the concept of a supreme authority operating without hierarchical sovereignty were to be rejected on the grounds of rational logic, it would seem to be evidence of predication on immanence, and could itself be cited as an example of a covert imperial authority operating to colonize knowledge. Secondly, the whole contention of the thesis is that the gospel testimony directly challenges the correlation of sovereignty and transcendence, and attempts to show that the non-imperial kenotic character of God is the substance of the originary good news. However, these considerations, in simplifying the central thrust of the question, fail to penetrate the entanglement of transcendence and sovereignty in contemporary thought. In order to probe this admixture it is necessary to explore the relationship between sovereignty and transcendence more carefully.

While the avoidance of modern rationality and the assertion of gospel testimony allow for the possibility that sovereignty is not a necessary corollary of transcendence, it has to be recognized that if it does not denote it, a strong connotation is carried by it. When, for example, Michael Hardt and Antonio Negri put forward the radical proposal that the premodern Judeo-Christian concept of love might yet configure the constituent power to resource a new social solidarity, they find it necessary to disavow any return to transcendence. As they put it, "There is really nothing necessarily metaphysical about the Christian and Judaic love of God."[42] From this perspective the eschatological potential of the gospel testimony is lost to the neo-Marxists because they perceive constituent power as entirely separate from the transcendent sovereignty they reject as the source and nature of the constituted power of empire. They regard institutionalized power as a property of sovereignty, and sovereignty as synonymous with transcendence. Agamben's position identifies sovereignty and transcendence even more closely because he regards constituent power as ultimately indistinguishable from constituted power,

42. Hardt and Negri, *Multitude*, 352.

and specifically challenges the supposed difference between constituent power and sovereignty that is basic to the neo-Marxist view.[43]

This perspective of Agamben's is dependent on an ontological exposition of sovereignty as the power of the exception necessary to open up the space for all juridico-political order, including the operation of constituent power, thus binding it, too, to sovereignty. He proposes that the connection between power and sovereignty is an altogether transcendent one that irrevocably absolutizes the sovereign order, potentially reducing the contemporary biopolitical world to a prison camp and the sacred to the status of a human being who can be killed but not sacrificed. The thesis being developed here recognizes the genealogical connection between the progression of sovereign power and the Western biopolitical order, while challenging Agamben's opinion that constituent power is inextricable from it. Rather, it regards this ontological conjunction and its consequences as the result of the subsumption of transcendence by sovereignty and its configuration in legitimation of the partnership between *ecclesia* and empire represented by Eusebius. If sacrifice is not the appeasement of divine sovereignty as Eusebius supposes, but is the necessary substance of divine love, then the ontological result of the progression is not "sovereign is he who decides on the state of exception" as formulated by Carl Schmitt,[44] with its consequential "sacred is he who can be killed but not sacrificed,"[45] but something like "sovereign is he who annuls law with grace" with the resultant "sacred is he who sacrifices his sovereignty for the sake of love." It is the contention of the thesis being proposed here that God is not in the generally accepted sense sovereign at all, and sovereign government, dependent as Agamben incisively indicates on the state of the exception, is ontologically illegitimate. An originary theopolitics is indeed impolitical. The implications of this are further explored in the fourth conduit and Part III.

(c) Is sovereignty necessarily subversive of originary gospel and ecclesia?

If the meaning carried by the use of the word "sovereignty" could be disentangled from imperial power, and only used of deity with reference to its potential power, then it could be said that it is not necessarily

43. Agamben, *Homo Sacer*, 43.

44. Ibid., 11.

45. Ibid., 82.

subversive of originary gospel and *ecclesia*. But if sovereignty remains semantically and culturally connected to empire, then its penetration of the *ecclesia* is tantamount to an invasion. The thesis of this book suggests that originary Christianity and imperial sovereignty subsist in a subalternate relationship. That is, if the gospel testimony affirms or is consistent with imperial sovereignty, then a particular manifestation of empire, be it Roman, British, or biopolitical, may or may not be Christian. However, if the testimony can be shown to indicate the rejection of imperial sovereignty, then no expression of empire can be Christian. As already indicated, Part II of this book considers to what extent those theological doctrines and ecclesial formations that have legitimated or become characterized by sovereignty are examples of the imperial subsumption of church and gospel. Part III then attempts to develop a kenotic Christology and an eschatological hermeneutic sensitized to the central proposal that the institutional expressions of church carry the genes of empire, in order to show that originary Christian testimony and recent historical anthropology indicate that no empire can be Christian.

(D) IS MULTIPLIED SOVEREIGNTY PROPERLY CONTIGUOUS WITH IMPERIAL SOVEREIGNTY?

Part of the focus of the thesis is the genealogy of sovereignty in its transformation from the absolute forms of monarchy, polyarchy, and tetrarchy that it took in medieval church and empire, to its multiplication and limitation into what may be described as "multiplied sovereignty" and "limited sovereignty." These last two phrases are used to characterize the modern nation states as configurations of sovereignty contiguous with the monarchic expression typical of the medieval period. The phrases identify the continuity between the two eras as the attempt to retain as much power for the few over the many as possible, while allowing a degree of perceived sovereignty or rights to an increasing number of the many. It is argued that this development led eventually to the supposed negotiation of the maximum amount of potential imperial power for all while still continuing to maintain the hegemony of the relative few. There are three main issues bearing on this. The first is the already mentioned proposition of a deep structural synonymy of monarchy and republic. The second is the difficulty of sustaining the definition of multiplied, limited sovereignty when the domination of the many by the few appears to have ceased or decreased. The third, as Paul Fletcher's exposition of modernity's assumption of immanence has already indicated,[46] is the supposed primacy of personal human selfhood and the configuration of sovereignty as the quest for freedom from all restrictions on the autonomy of the human ego, with the countercultural conclusion that human rights themselves are expressions of imperial power. The following paragraphs indicate some of the implications of these three issues, which are developed further in the third and fourth conduits.

To begin with, the fundamental synonymy of monarchy and republic is rooted in the shared purpose of exercising political power. In the genesis of modernity this manifests in response to the crisis of universal sovereignty and the various attempts to resist it. The need to maintain power by alternative means, what the neo-Marxists regard as a counterrevolutionary move, was provided by its multiplication. This occasioned the development of non-universal monarchic structures and the formation of republics. Although the root meaning of hierarchy is simply order itself, republican order continued to contain the fundamental ranking of the people under the sovereignty of the People. As Jürgen Habermas argues, with the shift from royal to popular sovereignty, the rights of subjects were transformed into human and civil rights. Although ideally and in principle this seemed to guarantee political autonomy to everyone, it only worked in the context of what he terms the *Volksgeist*, a unique corporate spirit of the people that constituted the modern form of corporate identity. In his view this could only have arisen from the consciousness of a people defined by subjection to state power. In this way rights were predicated on a primary conscious acquiescence to the idea of the nation. The sovereignty of the people was thereby mediated through the political structures of the city or nation state.[47] The depths of this perception are further signified in the ambiguous semantics of the Latin word *populus* that has been carried over into the European languages and carries both the referent of people as the general population and the People as a corporate identity. As Agamben makes clear, this tends to reinforce the ontological subjugation of the people as the excluded multitude, by the People as sovereign power.[48] This question of

46. Fletcher, *Disciplining the Divine*, 27.

47. Habermas, *The European Nation-State*, 404.

48. Agamben, *Means Without End*, 28–34.

the relationship of people and multitude is taken up again in the fourth conduit.

The second issue surrounds the difficulty of sustaining the definition of multiplied sovereignty when the domination of the many by the few appears to have ceased or decreased. The question is not simply the specific one of how the working definition of the domination of the many by the few for the benefit of the few operates in a republic, but it includes the general, wider issue of how it operates as both monarchy and republic continue to concede power. It raises the question of the nature of human rights, particularly when established as civil rights. Two further important observations relate to this. The first is that the process to republicanism at this stage was characterized by an eking out of power commensurate with its minimum loss. The configurations of sovereignty in the ensuing republics favored the ongoing influence of the personages wielding power as representatives of the people. Hierarchy as ranked order thus remained embodied in the republican shape. The tendency to default to monarchic figures in the initial phases of these transitions rather than the antagonism later directed at monarchs who held on to universal pretensions to power, can be seen in the emergence of the Dutch Republic and the English Commonwealth and Restoration. The concession of power was gradual and the persistency of monarchic leaders remained strong, as the third conduit narrates.

Finally, two further points apply to the multiplication of sovereignty into the apparent freedom of human rights. Firstly, and simply, as seen from Habermas, human rights are inseparable from civil rights, which consisted of the same substance as the imperial sovereignty from which they arose. This presents human rights as individual manifestations of imperial sovereignty. Secondly, there is the important related consideration that such rights, derived or acceded in this way by sovereign power, in either monarchies or republics, are necessarily incompatible with kenotic grace. So in a republic an active response to contingency makes a way to act through violence to see that power is captured and maintained, whereas the political question in the monarchic context is divine right, not contingency. It is dependent on God's plan and heredity. The republican, however, cries freedom and representation. Given that both forms of power are attributes of subjects, they are therefore possessions not gifts. Human rights derived from these monarchic and republican multiplications of power are likewise viewed as possessions, and as such are similarly at variance with kenotic grace.[49] They belong therefore to the genealogy of empire and not to the donation of God's life as revealed in creation or incarnation. There is, however, a different kind of freedom of human being that kenotic grace itself provides. This consists in the donation of the divine freedom to choose to give oneself to the world in mirror image of God's gift of himself to the world. From this perspective the problem of power is the spirit or manner of the choice by which it is held. Kenotic power is freely given whereas sovereign power manifests as domination whether universally applied or simply related to personal space and bodily territory. Civil rights as derived from sovereign power simply re-empower individuals to be both dominators and the dominated. In this way a continuity of sovereign power can be traced from the origins of medievality in the ecclesial embrace of imperial sovereignty, through bifurcation and conflict and into its multiplication and limitation in modernity, and to the heralded human rights of the apparently unabated biopolitical empire of the present day.

2. Medievality

The concept of medievality developed and utilized here impacts a thousand years of Christendom, offering an explanation for the persistent and intransigent problem of the dilution of an ecclesial political imperative due to a continuing alignment with mundane politics, sovereignty, and imperial power. In so doing it makes sense of the theopolitical shift that Ellen Meiksins Wood describes as the transition that the Christian religion had to undergo in order to be "transformed from a radical Jewish sect which opposed the temporal authority of Empire, into a doctrine amenable to, and even encouraging, imperial obedience."[50]

(A) A SIMPLE CONCEPT

The idea of medievality being put forward here is a very simple one. It is not offered as the means to a reassessment of the medieval world, although it could conceivably provide a starting point for such a project. It offers no detailed description or evaluation of the human impact of the politics of the era and makes no assessment of the pastoral care, concern for the poor, or degree of devotion to spiritual exercise in the practice of

---

49. I am indebted to Paul Fletcher for remarks made in conversation for this point.

50. Wood, *Empire of Capital*, 35.

the medieval church. It simply discloses that the controlling motif of the era was the choice of imperial sovereignty as the means to eschatological peace and that this had a formative impact on the development of theological tradition and the structural formation of both *sacerdotum* and *regnum*. It is this alone that is being proposed as differentiating the era from the initial years of gospel testimony. The reading of the initial character of the gospel era supposed in this thesis is the pursuit of peace through kenotic gift, as Part III attempts to configure. From this perspective the gospel narratives themselves present an ontological crisis of epochal proportions, which introduced a *katargēsis*[51] of Hebrew and Greek thought and conceived an experimental counterpolitical servant community. The sensitive progress of this innovative way of life was diverted by a miscegenation with empire embodied in the writings of Eusebius of Caesarea.

The ongoing consolidation of this partnership can be traced in, and characterized as, an over-realization of eschatology accompanied by an under-realization, which together amounted to a de-eschatologization that left the *ecclesia* effectively powerless to critique its own reconfiguration. After the collapse of the Western Roman Empire the same genealogy of church and imperial power can be traced through the Frankish and Saxon conflicts that culminated in the triumph of Carolingian Christendom. The synchronic case studies that are the subject of the first and second conduits explore the theological consequences of this epochal choice in terms of ontology and Christology and the resultant soteriological impact. The third and fourth conduits then trace its genealogy on into the modern and postmodern worlds. At the climax of medievality theological formulations were developed that overlaid christological innovations upon the ontological assumptions configured by Eusebius. This culminated in the assignment of supreme authority to both pope and emperor at different times, as is considered in detail with reference to Pope Innocent III and Emperor Frederick II. In time this led to a consummation of medievality that stretched the political compatibility of the structures of church and empire to breaking point and issued in the reconfigured expressions of sovereignty that substantiated the modern world.

---

51. This is the Greek word used by Paul to indicate the nullification or abolition of the Old Covenant, which Agamben and others have indicated carried the sense of a fulfillment as well as an end. See Agamben, *The Time That Remains*, 108.

(B) From medievality to modernity

The culmination of medievality can first be seen in papal schism and then in the division of the Reformation and ultimately in the carnage of the Thirty Years War. As has been described, nominalist thinkers such as William of Ockham had already challenged the boundaries of universal power, and Copernicus and later Renaissance figures like him confronted the hegemony of the institutional parameters of certainty in the final centuries of the medieval period. But, despite the increasingly untenable struggle for sovereignty within and between the structures of church and empire, it will be argued that the transition to modernity was not characterized by radical discontinuity as if there were a sudden revolution against absolutist ecclesiastical or monarchic rule. Instead modernity was marked by the development of a multiplied form of imperial power which, although precipitating violent upheaval, remained consistent with the supposed fourth-century choice of sovereignty in pursuit of peace. It is this multiplication of sovereignty discussed in the previous section that distinguishes modernity from medievality. However, the persistence of the role of imperial sovereignty throughout medieval Christendom including the early centuries of the Reformation is strong evidence of the partnership of church and empire as the parents of the modern world. It is for this reason that the closing decades of the seventeenth century emerge so obviously as the seminal case study for the inception of modernity as narrated in the third conduit. The convergence of Latitudinarianism, the Dutch-English collaboration in the war against French Catholic absolutism, and the founding of the Bank of England enabled the acquisition and multiplication of sovereignty in an innovative configuration that extended to a whole new clientele who together conceived a new world order.

(C) An uneven progress

It is acknowledged that Eusebius's work is being used here as a symbolic dividing line between initial gospel testimony and medievality in a partly artificial way. In point of fact investigation of the pre-Eusebian sources reveals an uneven progress in the transition from the early testimony to the medieval world. Attitudes to property, war, and government are uncertainly stated, often qualified, and at times confused in the writings of the Christian fathers, but they are certainly less than legitimative of the imperial order. The earliest post New Testament writings such as the late second-century *Epistle to Diognetus* clearly emphasize the counter-imperial nature of divine being. The writer describes the One who sent "the very artificer and creator of the universe himself . . . not as a man might suppose, in sovereignty (*tyrannis*) and fear and terror . . . but in gentleness and meekness . . . not compelling, for compulsion is not an attribute of God."[52] Tertullian states unequivocally that "Nothing is more foreign to us than the state (*republica*). One state we know, of which all are citizens—the universe."[53] Lactantius emphasizes that there are no hierarchical categories in his understanding of the creator's intention. "With him there is no slave or master. Since we all have the same father, so we are all alike his freeborn children. No one is poor in his eyes, except for want of justice; no one is rich, except in moral qualities."[54] He continues to make a direct contrast between divine and imperial power and asserts: "neither the Romans nor the Greeks could sustain justice, since they had so many levels of disparity in their societies, separating . . . powerless from powerful." As is indicated in the final section of the first conduit, Eusebius himself acknowledges that Irenaeus and Dionysius had a very participatory attitude to authority. All of this is indicative of an early Christianity significantly free from obligation to juridico-political control, manifesting in a theological freedom of thought that Oliver O'Donovan and Joan Lockwood O'Donovan describe as "the elusive logic of the pre-Nicene church."[55]

While the overall purpose of this project is to investigate the subsumptive relationship of church and empire, the existence of other ecclesial expressions both within and without the imperial formation is recognized. However, these alternative ecclesial forms are difficult to establish and describe with accuracy because of their vulnerability to being categorized as heresy due to their opposition to both the institutional church and the government. It seems relatively certain that many groups, such as the Paulicians, persisted throughout the early centuries of Christendom and others, like the Bogomils, were influential in Eastern Europe from the tenth century onwards. There have been several attempts to chart the genealogy of these alternative expressions of church, such as that by E.H. Broadbent,[56] which suggest an impor-

52. Lake, *The Epistle to Diognetus*, 365.
53. O'Donovan and O'Donovan, *From Irenaeus to Grotius*, 26.
54. Ibid., 52.
55. Ibid., 40.
56. Broadbent, *The Pilgrim Church*.

tant and potentially fruitful field of historical theology. The emergence of the monastic rules, as noted in the examples of Benedict, Joachim of Fiore and Francis of Assisi in the second conduit, initially pushed at the boundaries of institutional power. Other radical streams both preceded and continued alongside the Reformation including the various Anabaptist groupings, as Leonard Verduin and Donald F. Durnbaugh have delineated.[57] The seventeenth century saw the emergence of some of the most well-documented, radically alternative movements such as the Diggers and Levellers about whom Christopher Hill has written extensively.[58] The third conduit takes note of the revolutionary figure of Gerrard Winstanley who paved the way for the Quakers, and the subsequent radical political experiments of William Penn. The eighteenth- and nineteenth-century evangelicals included a stream of radical social reformers, as Donald Dayton has detailed.[59]

While it is not the primary thrust of this book, the attempt has been made to offset each conduit with the signs of progress of alternative ecclesial expression and thought. This opens up the way for the deliberations toward a creative theopolitical theology that are intimated in Part III. Nevertheless, notwithstanding the persistence of radical expressions of gospel and *ecclesia* to the present day, it is the considered impression of this research project that the supposed fourth-century lapsis had such a profound effect on the proceeding phases of Christendom that even the most radical alternatives have tended to default to the machinations of sovereign power. It is the ongoing and contemporary vulnerability of ecclesial form to distortion, and practical theological reflection to dislocation, that makes the genesis of the alignment of faith and imperial power a matter of such urgent and ongoing interest. With this in view the next chapter now investigates the supposed subsumption of church and gospel in the writings of Eusebius of Caesarea.

---

57. Verduin, *The Reformers and Their Stepchildren*; Durnbaugh, *The Believers' Church*.

58. Hill, *The World Turned Upside Down*.

59. Dayton, *Discovering an Evangelical Heritage*.

2

Conduits of Christendom

Eusebius of Caesarea

THIS FIRST CONDUIT OF Christendom explores the work of Eusebius of Caesarea in the hope of casting new light on the relationship of the church and empire. Beginning with the distinctive understanding of the church found in his *Commentary on Isaiah*,[1] it moves to an investigation of the theology of the cross in his panegyrics, before tracing the importance of imperial sovereignty in the *History of the Church*.[2] In so doing alternative paths through the familiar territory of his more popular writings are disclosed. The significance of this perspective for his depiction of the christological controversy of Nicaea is then considered. Finally, early impulses of Christendom are identified that disclose that, despite Eusebius's insights into the task of the church in the world, his embrace of imperial sovereignty embodies a profound fall in the *ecclesia*'s perception and practice of the presence of God.

It is likely that Eusebius was born around 260 CE. Shortly after Constantine's edict of toleration in 313 he became Bishop of Caesarea, where he had lived and worked, probably as a presbyter of the church, for many years previously. It is known that he was taught by Pamphilius, a presbyter of the church there who was a teacher in the theological school founded by Origen. Eusebius collaborated with Pamphilius in the latter's *Apology for Origen* and probably studied in his famous library, which would have provided the likely resources for Eusebius's prodigious body of writing.[3]

---

1. Hollerich, *Eusebius of Caesarea's Commentary on Isaiah*.
2. Eusebius, *The History of the Church*.
3. For a comprehensive list see McGiffert, *The Church History of Eusebius*, 28–44.

By the time Constantine was proclaimed emperor in York in 306, in place of his father Constantinius, the Roman Empire had already lasted for five hundred years and the city of Rome for more than a thousand. The empire would continue as a political power in the West for another one hundred and seventy years and in the East for another eleven hundred and fifty. The so-called "golden age" of Rome had come to an end by the beginning of the Severan dynasty at the end of the second century and it was now in a slow decline. This is the period that historians describe as the Late Empire. For the fifty years from 235 to 284 there had been military anarchy and nearly twenty emperors.[4] However, this period had been brought to an end by the reforms of the emperor Diocletian who established the Tetrarchy, which had united the Empire for twenty years under the leadership of four emperors, known as Augusti. This was also a time of persecution and martyrdom of Christians, which Eusebius lived through, and which included Pamphilius, and during which he was himself briefly imprisoned in Alexandria.[5]

When Constantine was proclaimed emperor in 306, it was only as emperor of the West, one of the four Roman emperors, the others being Galerius, Severus, and Maximian. His situation was highly volatile because Galerius appointed Licinius as emperor to replace Constantine's father, and although Constantine had been proclaimed to be the emperor by his own army, the Praetorian Guards had proclaimed Maxentius as emperor in Constantinius's place. On top of this, Constantine was one of two Caesars waiting in hope of the emperor's crown, the other being Maximinus. Soon after this Severus was deserted by his men and captured and slain by Maxentius, the result being that there were now six emperors or claimants.[6] It was not until his defeat of Licinius in 324 that Constantine became the undisputed single monarch of the Roman Empire. It was against this backdrop that Eusebius wrote his *History*, which he appears to have begun well before 290, but the final chapters of which were not completed until a generation later.[7] This coincided with Constantine's ascendancy and culminated in the same period that he was writing his famous panegyrics of Constantine and the *Commentary on Isaiah* that, together with the *History*, form the focus of this conduit.

4. Boardman, *The Oxford History of the Roman World*, 505.

5. Eusebius, *The Church History*, 11.

6. Macmullen, *Constantine*, 19, 63; Grant, *The Emperor Constantine*, 21–27.

7. Grant, *Eusebius as Church Historian*, 14; Barnes, *Constantine and Eusebius*, 128, 346.

It has long been a matter of debate as to whether Eusebius is more eulogist than historian. This particularly applies to material such as his *Oration in Praise of Constantine,*[8] given on the occasion of the thirtieth anniversary of the emperor's reign, but is generally true of the *Life of Constantine*[9] and the final three chapters of the *History*. Eusebius's role as the first and most comprehensive historian of the Christian era and Constantine's position as the first apparently Christian emperor ensure that this debate has ongoing political and theological import. The central question is whether Eusebius's presentation of Constantine as the consummation of contemporary eschatological progress is to be regarded more as a culturally determined panegyric than a serious theopolitical assessment. The recent work of M.J. Hollerich on Eusebius's lesser-known *Commentary on Isaiah*[10] has now made it possible to read these other primary works of Eusebius in a more carefully nuanced manner. While they survive comparison as serious works, it is no longer easy to regard them as making a simple identification of empire and eschaton. Instead Eusebius's focus is seen much more specifically to be the church, albeit in the context of a Christian empire. Without this readjusted focus, his famous suggestion that the sanctuary built on the site of the Holy Sepulcher represented a prophetic fulfillment of the New Jerusalem tends to highlight empire and emperor as the consummation of eschatological development. When the insights and expository leanings of the *Commentary on Isaiah* are brought to bear, it is not the political construct of Constantine's empire that is the primary carrier of eschatological significance, but the church itself. Seen through the lens of his *Commentary,* the empire was neither the agent nor fulfillment of eschatological progress but rather this was the destiny of the church, and the establishment of the Roman peace was the evidence of its growing success. From this perspective the particular impact of his writings is to present the church as the embodiment and instrument of eschatological progress.

---

8. Eusebius, "The Oration in Praise of the Emperor Constantine," 581–610.

9. Eusebius, "The Life of Constantine," 471–559.

10. Hollerich, *Eusebius's Commentary on Isaiah.*

A. THE CHURCH AS INSTRUMENT
OF ESCHATOLOGICAL PROGRESS

Viewed through his *Commentary on Isaiah*, this ecclesiological perspective on Eusebius's work is indicated in his writings in three ways. Firstly, the church is seen as the godly polity influencing the society of the day, and embodying the New Jerusalem in fulfillment of prophecy. Secondly, the continuing strength of the church and the developing *pax Romana* are seen as the evidence of progress towards the fullness of prophetic history. Thirdly, it is shown that the death and resurrection of the Christ is the critical factor in the consummation of the destiny of the Jews and its transition to the agency of the church. Although this operation is spiritual in nature, it is shown to be political in its transformative effects, which affirm and strengthen the development of imperial sovereignty. These themes will now be considered in turn.

1. Church as Godly Polity

Eusebius's exegesis of the messianic peace prophesied in Isaiah 2:2–4 locates its fulfillment in the conjunction of the *pax Romana* and the birth of Christ.[11] This is borne out in his eulogy in the *Oration in Praise of Constantine*, where he states, "by the express appointment of the same God, two roots of blessing, the Roman empire, and the doctrine of Christian piety, sprang up together for the benefit of men."[12] But whereas in his panegyric the two roots appear to be afforded equal weight, the terms of this conjunction are elucidated and qualified by the *Commentary*, in particular by Eusebius's deployment of the phrase "godly polity," and his exposition of Jerusalem as a description of the church. Hollerich has given careful attention to the choice of the term "godly polity" (*to theosebes politeuma*), noting that, as a means to Eusebius's exegesis of Isaiah, it affirms the notion of an ecclesial prehistory that was already central to Eusebius's understanding of the relation of the church both to Israel and to the Gentile world. Hollerich explores the use of the family of words derived from *polis* in the centuries leading up to Eusebius's time, from which his phrase "godly polity" derives, demonstrating that, despite a broadening out of meaning from an exclusively political sense in the classical Greek period to include general lifestyle and personal com-

11. Ibid., 23.
12. Eusebius, "The Oration," 606.

portment, the distinctly political component remains.[13] Church viewed as "godly polity" is thereby located as a religious community (always a *godly* polity) but with specifically political characteristics and effects. In Eusebius's thinking, the history of this community related to the moment of eschatological culmination in a way that the history of empire did not. In his *Commentary* Eusebius does not suggest that the empire is a godly polity, or that the church is a polity without the qualifying adjective "godly." Rather, "the godly polity described in the *Commentary on Isaiah* is a community organized under the leadership not of an emperor but of the bishops."[14] With the political and liturgical demise of Israel as the identifiable people of God, the church is presented as the inheritor of the priestly theocratic community. But this theocracy is not now in the context of a specific land but in relation to the empire's universal peace.

Eusebius's exposition of the bejewelled eschatological New Jerusalem in Isaiah 54:11–12 is to similar effect, with the sapphire seen as the "prophets and apostles who are the foundations," and the jasper "those in the church who strengthen the faith with intellectual means, being like battlements of the godly polity."[15] The *Commentary* is replete with similar exegeses of eschatological content applied to the institution of the church of Eusebius's day. Interpreting the five cities that Isaiah says the Lord will one day establish in the land of Egypt,[16] Eusebius states that "the five cities of God in the church would be the various states divided into the five ranks."[17] The five ranks he enumerates are first bishops, then priests, deacons, the baptized laity, and finally those still under catechetical instruction. In this way the whole church is positioned as the fulfillment of Israel's influence among the nations.

2. Burgeoning Church and Empire

The growing ecclesial strength and the increasing imperial peace are seen to be the attestation of the church's stewardship of God's prophetic intent. This is borne out by the introductory setting to Eusebius's *History*

---

13. *Politeuestai* had meant to live and act as a citizen; *politeia* had meant life in a civic order, forms of political activity, and the state constitution. *Politeuma* meant political acts and dealings. See Hollerich, *Eusebius's Commentary on Isaiah*, 105–16.

14. Ibid., 31.

15. Ibid., 128.

16. Isaiah 19:18.

17. Hollerich, *Eusebius's Commentary on Isaiah*, 170–1.

where the beneficial influence of the people of God is seen as preparing the way both for the church of the incarnate Word and for the Roman Empire. *Book I* presents the Jews as the initiators of a growing world peace. "Their Law became famous and like a fragrant breeze penetrated to every corner of the world. From the Jews the movement spread, and soon the characters of most heathen races began to grow gentler, thanks to the lawgivers and thinkers in every land. Savage and cruel brutality changed to mildness, so that profound peace, friendship, and easy intercourse were enjoyed."[18] Proceeding to describe the resultant advent of "the heavenly Word of God . . . in the early years of the Roman Empire," he locates the process firmly in the eschatological context of the coming of the kingdom of God. Quoting the vision of the Ancient of Days in the prophecy of Daniel, where "One like a Son of Man" is presented with everlasting authority and an indestructible kingdom,[19] he then introduces the church as the new but "numerous . . . indestructible and invincible" inheritors of Israel,[20] no longer, as we have seen, in relation to the land of Israel but in relation to the empire of Rome. In this way Eusebius lays the foundation for his consistent theme of the strength of the church and the development of the universal Roman peace, despite the exigencies of heresy and persecution that characterize parts of his *History*. This parallel development of church and empire is seen in his choice of an annalistic arrangement for his material following the passage of the Roman emperors from Tiberias to Constantine, and his selection and introduction of his sources by bringing together leading churchmen with influential Roman cities.[21] His detailed work in establishing episcopal succession focuses on centers of both ecclesial and imperial significance,[22] and his record of persecution and martyrdom locates courage and heroism in terms of both ecclesial and imperial honor.[23] Finally Constantine is introduced in terms that bring together piety and militancy: "a religious man and son of a most religious man . . . was roused by the King of kings, God of the universe, and Saviour against the two most irreligious tyrants and declared war on them."[24]

18. Eusebius, *The History of the Church*, 39.

19. Ibid., 40.

20. Ibid., 46.

21. Ibid., 32.

22. Ibid., 124.

23. Ibid., 298.

24. Ibid., 368.

3. The Spiritual Nature of Eschatological Progress

Eusebius presents Israel as the agent of progress for world peace in pre-Christian history and sees their law and liturgy producing a civilizing effect on the peoples of the earth. But this took place, as he puts it, "without actual, open initiation." Instead, the testimony of the godly polity of Jews and proselytes was accompanied by the supernatural help of the heavenly Word of God who had given the Jews their laws and symbols in the beginning. Once the whole of mankind was prepared, and with the Roman Empire as a sign of its readiness, the incarnation took place.[25] It is important to note that in Eusebius's view neither the benign Jewish influence nor the political powers of empire were adequate to bring about the consummation of the prophesied peace. Only "when that instrument of our redemption, the thrice holy body of Christ . . . was raised" could the "delusion of polytheistic error" energized by "powers of darkness" and "evil spirits" be overthrown.[26]

Eusebius saw an inseparable link between Jewish monotheism and imperial monarchy.[27] He describes Constantine's rule as a "semblance of heavenly sovereignty" and "according to the pattern of that Divine original . . . in its conformity to the monarchy of God," and declares that "He only is the author of sovereign power, who decrees that all should be subject to the rule of one."[28] In the same way as he recognized this inevitable synergy between monotheism and Roman imperial authority, Eusebius saw an inextricable connection between polytheism and the plurality of governments and leaders. He regarded this pluralism as demonically induced and directly responsible for the "war and strife, depopulation and captivity which raged in country and city with unceasing fury."[29] Only the death and resurrection of Christ could separate the spiritual union that held this pluralism of gods and nations together to the detriment of the prophesied eschatological advance. Even once this obstacle to world peace was removed, the ongoing role of the church as the bearer of victory was still required. When, after three centuries of further political and religious development, Constantine emerged and the empire fully embraced monotheism, Eusebius regarded it as the result of the ongo-

---

25. Ibid., 39.

26. Eusebius, "The Oration," 606.

27. Fowden, *Empire to Commonwealth*, 3; Petersen, *Theologische Traktate*, 38.

28. Eusebius, "The Oration," 584.

29. Ibid., 606.

ing work of the Word of God through his people and not the institutional development of imperial politics. As Oliver O'Donovan and Joan Lockwood O'Donovan point out, in Eusebius's view Constantine grew up like Moses in Pharaoh's court and "the legitimation of Constantine owed nothing to the institutional succession of the imperial throne, but was given directly by the activity of God's Word."[30]

It is clear that for Eusebius these crucial developments of eschatological progress were obtained by the Word of God at work in the death and resurrection of the Christ, in fulfillment of the task of the pre-ecclesial godly polity and by its ongoing expression in the institution of the church. The theological and practical impact of this work of the Word was therefore extremely important for him. This makes sense of the amount of space devoted to the subject in the *Oration* and the strong emphasis that he places on Constantine's vision of the cross and its powerful role in securing military victory in the *Life*. For Eusebius it was the cross of Christ and the resurrection that followed that destroyed the evil spirits and opened the way for the church and empire to thrive, seemingly unhindered, for the good of mankind. The next section of this chapter exposes this unique role for the cross and its ongoing mediation through the life of the church in more detail.

B. THE STRATEGIC FUNCTION OF THE CROSS

There is a tendency for Eusebius to be criticized for emphasizing the didactic function of the incarnation at the expense of the atonement.[31] It is easy to form this impression from the early chapters of the *History* where the only theological reference to the incarnation, death, and resurrection is brief in the extreme.[32] The obvious place for an exposition of the cross and resurrection is occupied instead by evidence of the practical impact of the incarnation on the surrounding Gentile world in the story of Jesus' correspondence with the Prince of Odessa.[33] However, Hollerich points out from the *Commentary* that, while Eusebius does often interpret Christ's incarnation didactically,[34] he also expounds the

30. O'Donovan and O'Donovan, *Irenaeus to Grotius*, 57.

31. See Wallace-Hadrill, *Eusebius of Caesarea*, 100ff.

32. Eusebius, *The History of the Church*, 39–40.

33. Ibid., 65.

34. Hollerich cites Eusebius's exegesis of Isaiah 43:8–11 in Eusebius, *Commentary on Isaiah*, 279.4–9.

atonement strategically as expiatory sacrifice and redemption from the power of Satan.[35] Hollerich concludes, "Where the *Commentary on Isaiah* is concerned, there is scant evidence for an imbalance between a didactic-revelatory theology of the Incarnation and a redemptive, atoning theology of the Cross."[36]

Nevertheless, even if the strategic implications of the atonement were not an important theme in Eusebius's *Commentary,* it is arguable that the impact of the ecclesiological perspective on eschatological progress that is found there leads the reader to look elsewhere for further insight into Eusebius's theology of the cross. For if the pre-ecclesial godly polity had contributed to the growing imperial peace in a way that the didactic influence it shared with the institutional forms of empire had not, what was the critical component of its influence? What was it that the church proceeded from and carried, of which the *pax Romana* was the evidence and result, but could not itself provide? These questions lead us naturally to what might otherwise be regarded as Eusebius's unexpectedly strong emphasis on the work of the cross in the *Oration,* and on its peculiarly powerful role in deciding the outcome of the imperial battles that he describes in the *Life.*

1. The Word and the Cross in the Oration and the Life of Constantine

In the first six chapters of the *Oration,* the "only begotten Word of God"[37] is variously described as "Preserver of the universe,"[38] the Sovereign whose "Word and royal Law is One,"[39] and the "interpreter of legitimate sovereignty and imperial power to man."[40] While this latter power is seen to motivate the military action with which Constantine subdues the physical adversaries of the empire, Eusebius makes clear that it is the Word himself that overcomes Constantine's spiritual enemies and "drives far away . . . those apostate spirits."[41] The chapters culminate with

35. Hollerich cites Eusebius's comments on Isaiah 43:1; 50:4–7; 52:13–53:12; 63:5–6.

36. Hollerich, *Eusebius's Commentary on Isaiah,* 65.

37. Eusebius, "The Oration," 583.

38. Ibid., 583.

39. Ibid., 584.

40. Ibid., 585.

41. Ibid., 583, 591.

the Word's role as the source of Constantine's heavenly vision of the cross.[42] The following four chapters are mainly taken up with an explanation of these human and spiritual forces arrayed against the progress of the Word, showing the cross to be the means to victory.

Eusebius explains that human beings have two distinct natures, body and spirit, a division mirrored corporately in the material and spiritual world. The "barbarous and savage enemies" of the Word are therefore both humans and demons.[43] The barbarians were enslaved to polytheism and persecuted their fellow countrymen under the influence of "unseen foes, more cruel far than barbarians . . . soul destroying demons whose course is through the regions of the air."[44] The "salutary and life-giving Sign" of the cross is repeatedly identified as the means by which the Word defeats these spiritual foes.[45] The *Life of Constantine* retains the association of the cross with spiritual power, but whereas the *Oration* expounds the theopolitical context, the *Life* focuses more on the historical account of Constantine's battles. As a result, the emphasis is less on the material and spiritual nature of his enemies and more on the link between the *labarum*[46] and the supernatural victories obtained through it.[47] These range from its appearance to allay Constantine's original concern about the wicked and magical enchantments being used against him by Maxentius,[48] to the supernatural interventions at Milvian Bridge,[49] and Licinius's divinations before his battle with Constantine and the supernatural manifestations that overcame them.[50] Nevertheless, the stories convey vividly the spiritual dynamics of Constantine's political victories.

The second part of the *Oration* marks a distinct transposition from the first section with its culmination in the power and impact of the

42. Ibid., 589.

43. Ibid., 589–90.

44. Ibid., 590.

45. Ibid., 593.

46. The military title for the standard bearing the sign of the cross.

47. Some commentators have struggled with the supernatural content of the story behind the *labarum* despite Eusebius's account and Constantine's alleged testimony on oath, cf. Barnes, *Constantine and Eusebius*, 43. In any event the *labarum* and the vision behind it are clearly of central importance for Eusebius.

48. Eusebius, "The Life," 489.

49. Ibid., 493.

50. Ibid., 501–2.

"salutary Sign," and the theme returns to a more theological analysis of the initiating role of the Word. The change is so noticeable that it is generally accepted that there are two orations, the first of which finishes at this point and a second sermon follows.[51] If this is the case, they have clearly been joined together to the effect that they provide two complementary expositions of the cross. The first introduces it in pragmatic terms, as salutary sign, and the second in theological manner as both didactic source and strategic victory.[52] The first six chapters of the second section set the incarnation of the Word and the ensuing death and resurrection as "the reasons and motives" for the emperor's "pious works."[53] Eusebius explains the nature and necessity of the Word in creation and communication and then introduces the incarnation as a "fitting means of communication with mankind"[54] in terms of the Word of God's desire to save humanity from idolatry and human sacrifice. In common shape with the first section these chapters culminate in the cross: "the crowning facts of all; . . . his death, the manner of his passion, and the mighty miracle of his resurrection after death."[55]

Eusebius first describes the necessity of the resurrection of the Christ in terms of the impossibility of an incarnate mighty sovereign employing mortality but subsequently fleeing death. This would result in his being regarded as a phantom, or devaluing his humanity.[56] Eusebius presents the Word with two alternatives, to consign his body to corruption and bring the incarnation to dishonor, or prove victorious over death and render mortality immortal by divine power. He then expounds three overall approaches to the atonement, two didactic and one strategic. Firstly, it supplied ocular proof to his disciples of the promised resurrection as a motive for rising above fear of death in pursuit of a

---

51. Barnes, *Constantine and Eusebius*, 271.

52. Averil Cameron highlights Eusebius's use of the sign of the cross in the *Life* as an example of the way that the traditions of imperial rhetoric and those of Christian writing are combined as a means to the progress of Christian thought in a previously pagan context. This makes the complementarity of sign and theology in these two sections of the *Oration* the more striking. Cameron, *Christianity and the Rhetoric of Empire*, 50–54.

53. Eusebius, "The Oration," 596.

54. Ibid., 603.

55. Ibid., 604.

56. Ibid., 604.

godly life and encouraging others to do the same.[57] Secondly, it proved to humanity that the incarnate Word was worthy of greater honor even than an imperator, for he did not only die in the cause of victory but rose again.[58] Thirdly, he was the "salutary victim" taken from among "the common race of men," in having a mortal body like theirs and offered up for the whole human race.[59]

It is this third explanation of the atonement that sheds light on Eusebius's understanding of the unique intervention of the Word that no amount of didactic could achieve, either through the godly polity or the *pax Romana* engendered by it. It is this strategic component of the atonement that coincides with the particular emphasis that he gives to the salutary sign. The point being made here is not that Constantine's use of the cross had no didactic or inspirational effects. These must have been considerable. But it was the peculiarly supernatural character that Eusebius ascribed to the cross that gave to the church its distinctive eschatological power. This aspect of the cross centers on the Christ as a victim "offered to the Supreme Sovereign of the universe for the whole human race." Eusebius describes this offering as having two purposes, the need of the human race and the overthrow of the errors of demon worship. The need is developed as the guilt of all nations for "impious superstition." Eusebius consistently uses this and similar phrases to refer to polytheism and the consequential plurality of governments and national identities with their offence against the sovereignty of God and the possibility of universal peace for humanity.[60]

The second purpose, the overthrow of demon worship, conflates the gods of polytheism and the deluding spirits generally identified by Eusebius. He states that as soon as "the one holy and mighty sacrifice, the sacred body of our Saviour, had been slain for man," the power of "the impure and unholy spirits" was utterly abolished. This means, taking his previous usage of the terms and his current identification of them with the gods themselves, that the demons and the ongoing power of polytheism were destroyed by the sacrifice of the Christ. Eusebius identifies this sacrifice as the removal of the sins of the world by the Lamb of God in John 1:29 and the wounding of the suffering servant of Isaiah 53:4–7. It

57. Ibid., 605.
58. Ibid., 605.
59. Ibid., 605–6.
60. Ibid., 606.

seems that for Eusebius this sacrifice is the defining distinction that the "Saviour Word"[61] has given the church, in fulfillment of the destiny of Israel, and as the means to the culmination of eschatological progress. It remains to consider how Eusebius saw the church as embodying and applying the ongoing power of this sacrifice.

2. The Church as Bearer of the Ongoing Power of the Cross

In the final conclusion of the *Oration*, immediately following his exposition of the atonement, Eusebius proceeds to demonstrate its success by describing the universal impact of the Roman Empire and the Christian Religion. He distinguishes the weight of responsibility carried by each. The Word dealt with the spiritual powers by the cross, and then, "the causes of multiplied governments being thus removed," the Roman Empire "effected an easy conquest of those which yet remained."[62] Eusebius shows how, in his understanding, these two responsibilities, the one primary and the other secondary, continued to be exercised. He describes how God and the church are the parents of world peace in fulfillment of numerous biblical prophecies.[63] He explains how the Savior, who had driven away the evil spirits from human society with an "invisible and yet potent hand," has given his people power to banish "the remnant of those wicked spirits" by the invocation of his name, unfeigned prayer, and the offering "of those bloodless sacrifices which are performed by prayer and the secret worship of God."[64]

Eusebius uses the word "secret" in this passage in two ways, once to refer to the church's worship and then to refer to the "secret" power by which the Word abolished the animal and human sacrifice systems, thus linking worship, the atonement, and the ongoing establishment of the Christian empire. He then refers to the many altars and churches now dedicated to "these spiritual and rational sacrifices." This positioning of the church is essential for the health and progress of the imperial peace. However, there is a further and more fundamental way that Eusebius's recognition of the church as the primary instrument of eschatological progress, and his strategic exposition of the atonement, shed light on

61. Ibid., 595.
62. Ibid., 606.
63. He cites in particular Psalm 72:7–8 and Isaiah 2:4.
64. Eusebius, "The Oration," 607.

his understanding of necessary ecclesial form. For if the purpose of the atonement is to appease the "Supreme Sovereign" for replacing his rule with polytheism and polyarchy, then the need for the church to embody and pursue sovereignty in its ecclesial formation and influence is seen to be paramount. It is to a deeper investigation into Eusebius's understanding of this importance of sovereignty that the next section now turns.

C. THE NECESSITY OF SOVEREIGNTY

It is now clear that by the time of his mature works in the years of Constantine's consolidated empire, Eusebius understands the atonement in terms of the appeasement of sin against divine sovereignty. He regards polytheism and the political pluralism that accompanies it as the cause of the wars, barbarities, and troubles of humanity, and he sees these in turn as the responsibility of demonic powers. The appeasement of divine sovereignty restores humanity to a proper relationship with God, which destroys the power of the demons and opens up the way for the eschatological vision of imperial peace to be fulfilled. In this way Eusebius presents the pre-existent Word wielding the godly polity of Israel as his instrument to prepare the world for salvation and shows how the task of fulfilling this passed to the church after the incarnation. From this perspective the work of the church in the aftermath of the death and resurrection of Christ becomes the embodiment and exercise of sovereignty.

1. *The Godly Polity and Hierarchical Shape*

Eusebius's introduction to the *Oration* sets the subject of sovereignty at the heart of the "divine mysteries" that the scriptures uncover and the "sacred rites" that engage the worship of true disciples.[65] The "Sovereign Lord of all" is the "Mighty Sovereign" to whom alone Eusebius and his colleagues of church and empire "owe that imperial power" under which they live. The only begotten and pre-existent Word is seen as providing the emperor with "as it were, a transcript of the Divine sovereignty" for the administration of human affairs.[66] The supreme heavenly monarch "decrees that all should be subject to the rule of one" and is the "author of empire itself" and has in his grace given rational human beings the

65. Ibid., 581.
66. Ibid., 582.

mental ability to see this by forming them in his own image.[67] These introductory descriptions of God, his Word, and their relationship to the politics of empire place the ongoing eschatological task of the church firmly in the context of sovereignty.

With this in view the emphasis on the hierarchical shape of the godly polity in the *Commentary* is completely appropriate. Eusebius declares that the old community of the Jews has been replaced "throughout the whole world by the Church of Christ" and that its leaders have "received rule from the apostles and disciples of our saviour and even now from this succession . . . the presidents of the church of God bring forth fruit."[68] The segregation of the church along hierarchical lines is a major theme of his *Commentary*, and texts with keywords that refer positively to dominant roles such as *archontes, presbyteroi, leitourgoi,* and *hēgemones* are invariably applied to the leaders of the church.[69] Eusebius uses narrative passages, such as the story of the removal of the unworthy steward and his replacement by Eliakim, to symbolize the passing away of the old priesthood after the passion and the establishment of the new priesthood in the church through the resurrection.[70] It is the task of this new priesthood to embody and promote the sovereignty of God through the church, where the bishop inherits the place of Christ himself,[71] to the world, where emperors are entrusted to bring the universal political peace.

2. Sovereignty in the History of the Church

The introductory pages of the *History* give us insight into the exegetical basis of the youthful Eusebius's ontology of the divine, written a lifetime before the *Oration* and many years before the advent of a Christian emperor.[72] They give us good cause to conclude that, despite the development of Eusebius's thinking over the years, his view of the sovereignty

---

67. Ibid., 583.

68. Hollerich, *Eusebius's Commentary on Isaiah*, 165.

69. Ibid., 169.

70. Ibid., 184.

71. Ibid., 180.

72. The first seven chapters of Eusebius's *History of the Church* and his *Chronicles* on which they were based were likely to have been written by 290 CE, some thirty years before the mature works such as the *Commentary on Isaiah* and the final chapters of the *History* and forty years before the *Oration*. See Grant, *Eusebius as Church Historian*, 14; Barnes, *Constantine and Eusebius*, 128, 346.

of God was a central and unchanging facet of his theology from the beginning.[73] In his summary of the teaching of Moses in the Pentateuch on the nature of the Father and the pre-existent Christ, he states, "The Father and Maker he introduces as giving commands like a supreme ruler by imperial fiat; the divine word, who holds the second place to Him—none other than the One whom we proclaim—as subserving His Father's behests."[74] He develops a Christology of the Son whose priesthood, theocratic leadership, and kingship are all understood from an Old Testament perspective unqualified by an incarnational theology. Once more with recourse to Moses, he describes the Christ's names in imperial terms. He notes that the first person to which the title Christ applied was the Jewish High Priest, the most powerful office in the leadership of Israel.[75]

Eusebius then suggests that by distinguishing the name "Joshua,"[76] from "Hoshea," for the name of his successor, Moses was enabled by the Holy Spirit to foresee the name "Jesus" as a title imbued with special privilege and fit to be given to Joshua, the one "he knew would after his own death succeed to the supreme authority."[77] He then argues from the practice of anointing (*chrisma*) the Israelite kings that there is a direct connection between "the patterns of the kingly, sovereign authority" and "the one true Christ, the divine Word who reigns over all."[78] Although Eusebius drew on Old Testament Hebrew imagery, Donald Cupitt points out that what he was doing was effectively Christianizing the Hellenistic view of kingship where the king was a kind of incarnate god. Christ was now configured as the universal cosmic emperor and the earthly emperor was his servant and vicar. "The entire imperial cult and ideology was refocused on Christ, while in turn Christ crowned his earthly deputy and validated his rule."[79]

Eusebius's understanding of the centrality of sovereignty to the form and purpose of the church is apparent throughout his *History* and

73. Grant, *Eusebius as Church Historian*, 15.

74. Eusebius, *The History of the Church*, 35.

75. Ibid., 41.

76. Joshua is transliterated in Greco-Latin as Jesus.

77. Eusebius, *The History of the Church*, 41.

78. Ibid., 42–43.

79. Cupitt cites Baynes, *Byzantine Studies*, IX. See Cupitt, "The Christ of Christendom," 139.

can be traced through all six of its central themes: great men and their writings, apostolic succession and episcopacy, the emergence of the New Testament Canon, heresy, retribution, and persecution. His introduction to the outstanding leaders and heroes presents a church segregated along lines of relative power based on influence within the imperial world.[80] The quantity of work involved in recording the apostolic succession in the foremost sees of the church is extraordinary; Eusebius lists nearly one hundred apostolic successors in the four most significant bishoprics alone.[81] Establishing these imperial structural forms by substantiating the apostolic authority of the monarchical bishops back to the time of Christ and the apostles was clearly extremely important for him.

His work on the New Testament Canon can be demonstrated to be dependent on the authoritative opinion of those in the line of succession more than by the excellent textual expertise of which he showed himself capable in his other work. His incisive overview and rejection of the heretics was primarily in defense of the episcopacy at the heart of whose authority their peculiar views were aimed. If Christ was not equal with God, such as the Ebionites,[82] Marcion,[83] and Paul of Samosata[84] claimed, then he did not carry supreme power and neither did his chosen successors. If true authority lay with special secret knowledge only accessible to a chosen few outside the recognized line of succession such as the Gnostics suggested,[85] then their power was once again undermined. If an imminent and immanent expression of an alternative rule to the leadership of church and empire was to be expected such as Cerinthus[86] and Nepos[87] advocated, then the status quo could be under serious threat. As far as his treatment of retribution is concerned, it is difficult to account for the frequency and sometimes shocking tone of his judgmental

80. Crossan and Reed enumerate ten characteristics that tend to support and uphold empire, including hierarchy, patrony, assemblies and groupings formed for the purpose of influence and patronage, and language that accepts and reinforces this as normal. Eusebius's introduction to his sources displays traits of all of these. Crossan and Reed, *In Search of* Paul, chs. 5 & 6.

81. Williamson in his introduction to Eusebius, *The History of the Church*, 22.

82. Ibid., 136–7.

83. Ibid., 164–5.

84. Ibid., 235.

85. Ibid., 158–9.

86. Ibid., 138.

87. Ibid., 307–9.

reveries without suggesting that they reveal a necessary and ultimate deterrent undergirding his view of God's sovereignty. Finally, Eusebius's work on persecution and martyrdom, while acknowledging that they occurred as a result of refusal to accept Caesar as Lord or offer sacrifice within the imperial cult, presents the accounts in both a literary form and an historical context that sets them positively within the Roman imperial culture.

3. *The Convergence of Sovereignty, Passion, and the Church*

We have already taken note of the comparative weakness of the early books of the *History* in terms of the lack of weight they give to the passion. However, this is not the case with the final chapters added in Eusebius's latter years. The lengthy *Festival Oration* at Tyre in *Book 10*, for example, is introduced in the context of the atonement,[88] and its subject matter focuses on the death and resurrection of the Christ and its function in restoring the sovereignty of God both at the incarnation and in the advent of Constantine. Eusebius connects the sovereignty of God not with the emperor, as the traditional view of his perspective on Constantine might have expected, but with the Bishop of Tyre. As he puts it, "What indeed could withstand the sovereign Lord and Ruler, the Word of God Himself?" He then responds with reference to the young prelate that there is another, who "it is possible could take second place . . . made like the Son of God" and "having the whole Christ, the Word . . . impressed upon his soul."[89] He continues to press home the hierarchical authority of God and the bishop with reference to the architectural form and furnishings of the building, with the "thrones high up, to accord with the dignity of the prelates" and "in the middle the Holy of Holies—the altar." It is interesting to note how often he uses the book of Isaiah[90] to give weight and direction to his sermon, and the complementarity of the *Festival Oration* and the *Commentary* should not be overlooked. The practical occasion serves to illustrate the theoretical emphasis of the *Commentary*. Nevertheless, the question remains as to what extent the ecclesial perspective provided by Eusebius's *Commentary on Isaiah*, and his mature recognition of the

88. Ibid., 383.
89. Ibid., 388–9.
90. Ibid., 398–9.

importance of the cross in restoring sovereignty, was really the result of his considered biblical and historical research. It is possible that the presence of sovereignty as an overriding theme from the early days of his *History*, without an accompanying emphasis on the cross, suggests that his lifelong commitment to sovereignty as a foundational principle came from elsewhere, a question that, among others, the final sections of this chapter will attempt to explore.

4. Hints of Another Way to Rule

As has already been indicated in the previous chapter and will be taken up again in Part III, the connection between transcendence and sovereignty is not a necessary one. However, Eusebius clearly regarded it as such. This is not to say that a more kenotic approach to power never emerges in his work but that it tends to be quickly submerged by the overarching operation of sovereignty. That this aspect of power existed in the church as Eusebius depicted it is clear in parts of the *History*, particularly in the examples of Irenaeus and Dionysius, bishops whom Eusebius draws on heavily and honors greatly. It is particularly Irenaeus's affirmation of apostolic succession and rule and his work as a defender of the faith against heresy that are for Eusebius the evidence of this orthodoxy and devotion. So Irenaeus's recognition of the importance of sovereignty is not in doubt.[91] Eusebius's narrative of two instances of the two bishops' exercise of leadership provides us with evidence of a non-imperial use of sovereignty. In the case of Irenaeus it was the dispute over the celebration and date of Easter. As Eusebius describes, in the late second century, Victor, "the head of the Roman church," was excommunicating whole dioceses on the grounds of heterodoxy because they did not keep Easter in the same way as he recommended. Irenaeus's response is very significant, for he was not legalistic about it at all, being of the opinion that "the divergency in the fast emphasizes the unanimity of our faith."[92]

In the case of Dionysius, his gracious but firm diplomacy in the face of theological controversy and heresy was utilized by Eusebius as an example of the protection of the church's reputation for order and unity. But he is also a clear example of a different direction in leadership.[93] The issue that stands out was the rebaptism of repentant heretics, which

91. Ibid., 180–1.
92. Ibid., 232.
93. Ibid., 287–90.

was a long-term custom in some dioceses but opposed in others, a disagreement with the potential to cause a serious rift within the church. Dionysius shows himself to be reticent at the notion of rebaptism but, similarly to Irenaeus on Easter, was eager to maintain a flexible and nondogmatic approach to those who held an alternative view. Of those in Africa who had long practiced rebaptism he said, "I would not think of upsetting their arrangements and involving them in strife or contention. 'You shall not move your neighbour's boundaries, which were fixed by your ancestors.'"[94] These examples advance an exercise of sovereignty that could challenge the solidity of imperial political structures and provide hints of possible directions for an alternative. By encouraging unity in diversity and flexibility on matters of fundamental church practice, they point the way to a possible kenosis of sovereignty. However, it is not a departure that Eusebius appears to recommend as, in the case of Easter, the Nicaean deliberations demonstrate.

D. THE CHRISTOLOGICAL CONTROVERSY OF THE COUNCIL OF NICAEA

Eusebius maintains an inseparable link between the monarchy of God and empire. He condemns pluralism as the demonic cause of political disorder and disruption. As the above exposition demonstrates, the work of the Word and the propitiatory sacrifice of the cross consummated a victory over every pluralistic challenge to monarchy and secured the desired eschatological peace. The ongoing role of the church was to consolidate this achievement through offering up the sacrifices of prayer and the eucharist, and in providing a continual embodiment and legitimation of sovereignty. The advent of the Christian *pax Romana* was the sign of increasing ecclesial success. Seen in this light it is not surprising that the Christology controversy that surfaced in the years of Eusebius's maturity and came to a head at the Council of Nicaea centered round the sovereignty of the Father and the nature of the Son's relationship to it. The authority of the ecclesiastical hierarchy as the agents of peace through sovereignty resided in the bishops' apostolic succession from the Son, who necessarily had to be one in status with God for their monarchic role to be legitimated. But any suggestion of a plurality of divinity was potentially corrosive of monarchy. It follows that a christological

94. Ibid., 290.

formulation was needed that could both substantiate monarchy and resist plurality. The four seminal issues that follow assist in understanding the eventual choice of the word *homoousios* as the official Nicaean formula for the incarnational relationship between Father and Son, and the phrase *mia hypostasis* to which it gave way at the succeeding Council of Sardica.

1. Eusebius's Initial Acceptance of Arius's Position

It is clear that to begin with, Eusebius, together with his namesake Eusebius of Nicomedia, tended towards the Arian position in the controversy. This affirmed the priority of the Father and asserted that the Son originated from the Father at a moment (not in time), by an act of will that had no association with division or change.[95] Eusebius wrote extensively on the subject in the *Proof of the Gospel* before it became seriously controversial, stating both that "the Word who we love to call Christ was not the Omnipotent God, but a secondary Being,"[96] and "The One, perfect in Himself and first in order as Father, and the cause of the Son's existence, receives nothing towards the completeness of His Godhead from the Son: the Other, as a Son begotten of Him that caused His being, came second to Him, Whose Son He is, receiving from the Father both His Being, and the character of His Being."[97]

As George Huntston Williams points out, the Arian view was well suited to the new political circumstance in which church leaders increasingly found themselves working as partners within a framework of imperial authority.[98] Arius's claim affirmed the sovereign initiative of the Father and the consequent subordination of the Son, as Eusebius elucidates in the early Christology of his *History*. It legitimated the emerging temporal monarchy and accorded with Eusebius's theology of the Word and the cross, preparing the way for the *pax Romana*. But it catered less for the view clarified by his *Commentary on Isaiah* where the church and not the emperor was the primary agent of God's sovereignty. This needed a more substantially shared sovereignty of the Father and the Son to legitimate the monarchical authority structure of the church and

---

95. Stead, "'Eusebius' and the Council of Nicaea," 86–87.

96. Eusebius, *Demonstratio evangelica*, 26.

97. Ibid., 167.

98. Williams, "Christology and Church-State Relations in the Fourth Century," 7.

its bishops. But pragmatically the Arian view could be seen to provide a means by which the church might fulfill its role as agent of the peace to affirm imperial sovereignty and embrace the now apparent eschatological hope. However, the Arian position was resisted and outlawed by the majority of the bishops at the council at Antioch prior to Nicaea, resulting in both Eusebius of Caesarea and Eusebius of Nicomedia being temporarily excommunicated from the fellowship of the bishops represented there.[99]

2. The Significance of the Specific Historical Circumstances

It is important to emphasize the specific historical moment in which the christological controversy erupted, for both Arius and Eusebius of Nicomedia were operating under the rule of Licinius who, according to the *Life* and the *Oration,* represented the last bastion of demonic pluralism. The Council of Antioch in which they and Eusebius of Caesarea were temporarily outlawed began in the December of 324. Just a few months earlier in July of that year, according to Eusebius's description, Constantine had overthrown Licinius with the aid of the salutary sign of the *labarum*. In the September, Eusebius of Nicomedia was interceding for Licinius together with Licinius's wife Constantia, Constantine's own half-sister, at the gates of the city.[100] It is surely implausible to evaluate the christological crisis without reference to this shift from plurality to monarchy, which was taking place at exactly the same time. The argument over whether the Son and the Father consisted in a seeming plurality of shared substance or a monarchical hierarchy was no theoretical matter in the context of the literal battle for temporal monarchic exclusivity. This tends to suggest that both the two namesakes were attempting to play their part in shaping an incarnational theology that allowed the *ecclesia* to operate as the agent of the hoped for peace in the midst of a struggle to the death. But it did not mean that their doctrinal position was complete or final, and in the case of Eusebius of Caesarea it clearly was not.

---

99. Grant, "Religion and Politics at the Council of Nicaea," 4.

100. Ibid., 2.

3. The Apparent Uninterest of Eusebius in the Minutiae of the Debate

It is likely that the vulnerable position in which the partial excommunication at Antioch placed Eusebius was one reason for the noticeably
circumspect approach of his account of the controversy in the *Life*. He
was apparently stretched between his leadership role within the church
as agent of the eschaton and the volatile contractions of its temporal
emergence under Constantine's leadership. Nevertheless, his narrative is
replete with evidence of his conviction that the precise details of the controversy were insignificant compared to the primary responsibility of the
church to support the emperor's position as the embodiment of divine
monarchy on earth, without which there could be no true eschatological
peace. The concluding chapters of Book II of the *Life* introduce the controversy into a context in which a flourishing church is encompassed on
every side "by a bright and most profound peace through the favour of
God."[101] Constantine's interventions are couched in terms of his motivation to bring the diverse judgments concerning the Deity to a condition
of settled uniformity and "to restore to health the system of the world,"
the one by the "secret eye of thought and the other . . . by the power
of military authority."[102] Eusebius repeatedly records Constantine's frus-
trated insistence that the controversy was over trivial matters compared
with the underlying fundamental unity of the quarrelling ecclesiastics in
their commitment to one body, be it expressed in terms of communion,
fellowship, religion, or faith.[103]

Such is the insignificance of the detail of these theoretical matters
in comparison to the cosmological significance of the hour that nowhere
in the *Life* does Eusebius enumerate them. He regarded the real problem
in this context as demonic and associated with the idolatrous rule of
Licinius, required to be overcome by orderly philosophical debate and
military victory. Once the military victory was secured, the war against
"the secret adversary who was disturbing the peace of the church" could
begin at the Council of Nicaea, which as Eusebius describes was aptly
named from "Victory."[104]

---

101. Eusebius, "The Life," 515.
102. Ibid., 516.
103. Ibid., 517.
104. Ibid., 521.

4. The Likely Early Rooting of Homoousios
in Greek and Egyptian Imperial Theology

The one substance position favored by bishops such as Athanasius and Eustathius was more affirming of the shared substantial monarchy of the Father and Son and the derived authority of the bishops. From this perspective it was less supportive of the direct correlation between God and the emperor that the *Life* and the *Oration* maintain. However, patristic research has shed important light on the pagan roots of the term *homoousios* accepted at Nicaea, which, according to Eusebius, was specifically Constantine's own choice of words. Although G.C. Stead brackets *homoousios* with *ousias* in his discussion of the role of the two Eusebii at Nicaea, it is *ousias* and the phrase *ek tēs ousias* that he cites from a letter from Eusebius of Nicomedia to Paulinus that is the subject of his discussion.[105] It is this latter phrase that eventually found its way into the Nicene Creed. But the term *homoousios*, as Pier Franco Beatrice has recently argued, is actually much rarer and may well have been embarking on an original Christian usage when Constantine proffered it to break the impasse at Nicaea. Beatrice points out the real difficulty of explaining the seemingly paradoxical fact that this word, along with the explanation given by Constantine, was accepted by the "Arian" Eusebius, whereas it left no traces at all in the work of his opponents. It cannot be found in the writings of the leaders of the anti-Arian party such as Alexander of Alexandria, Ossius of Cordova, Marcellus of Ancyra, or Eustathius of Antioch, who are usually considered as Constantine's advisors and the strongest supporters of the council. "Neither before nor during Constantine's time is there any evidence of a normal, well-established Christian use of the term *homoousios* in its strictly Trinitarian meaning."[106]

Beatrice presents a convincing and original argument that establishes a pagan etymology to the word. Drawing on the *Poimandres* and the *Theosophia*, he demonstrates that in the theological language of Egyptian paganism, the word *homoousios* meant that the Nous-Father and the Logos-Son, who are two distinct beings, share the same perfection of the divine nature.[107] Beatrice maintains that Eusebius understood

---

105. Stead, "'Eusebius' and the Council of Nicaea," 85.

106. Beatrice, "The Word 'Homoousios' from Hellenism to Christianity," 243.

107. Ibid., 257–8, 260–1.

and welcomed Constantine's explanation of the word *homoousios* at Nicaea because the mild subordinationism implied in his own distinction of the two divine hypostases had significant, objective affinities with Constantine's Hermetic philosophy of the consubstantiality of the two gods.[108] This sheds important light on the legitimative potential of a theology of hierarchy within the concept of shared divine substance for affirming imperial absolutism rooting back into the Greek and Egyptian empires and now manifesting in the Roman. It is likely that this Hermetic genealogy of *homoousios* made it possible for Constantine to maintain the identity of substance between the Father and Son yet retain the overall monarchy of God.

In the concluding section that follows, the implications of these issues for the ensuing development of theology will be underlined. Suffice it to say now that from this overview of Eusebius's perspective, the Nicene formula was less anti-Arian than has been generally understood. It can also be stated with some conviction that both the Arian position and the Nicene formulation of the incarnational relationship of the Father and the Son establish both as sovereign powers although in the former case hierarchically and in the latter more corporately. But at no time during the controversy does it appear that the flow of the gospel narratives towards arguing *from* Jesus of Nazareth *to* the nature of God, which Part III will explore, was considered at all. In the Arian controversy all was in the opposite direction, *from* God *to* the Son. The sovereignty of the divine transcendent was apparently accepted without discussion.

E. IMPULSES OF CHRISTENDOM

The preceding overview of Eusebius's work reveals a political thinker who well understood the location of the church within the *saeculum*. His acknowledgment of its role in a spiritual battle for the material world and the centrality of the cross in that conflict brings a timely metaphysical perspective from an earlier age. In sum his presentation of the church as the agent and embodiment of eschatological progress provides a serious vantage point for the development of a contemporary theology of the kingdom of God. However, it is impossible to avoid the central issue of his understanding and legitimation of imperial sovereignty as the means to eschatological fulfillment. So while recognizing his contribution to

108. Ibid., 267.

ecclesial and political theology, it is submitted that Eusebius's preoccupation with sovereignty resulted in a foundational misalignment of the eschatological peace and the Roman Empire with devastating effect for the subsequent history of the church. As a result, the theology and praxis of sovereignty that Eusebius's writings embody became the determining character of the church, the accompanying soteriology of the cross defined its temporal agency, and its authority depended on an imperial Christology that made little recourse to the gospel testimony.

1. The Theology and Praxis of Sovereignty

For Eusebius, to be divine is to be sovereign. The problem with this characterization of transcendence is that it makes imperial power paramount. In so doing it fails to provide substantial grounds for a moral distinction between the divine and human apart from absolute force. This is very clear with regard to Eusebius's differentiation between monotheism and polytheism. Despite his condemnation of the evils and brutalities of polytheism and the accompanying polyarchy, his primary argument against them is made on the ground that their adherents fail to recognize the sovereign authority of the One. This reduces the main argument for the superiority of monotheism to power alone. The One God has more power than the demonic polygods and so ought to be worshiped. His sovereignty may issue in acts of apparent love and justice, but these are subordinate to the exercise of power. The demons may cause brutal acts of war and bloodshed but what makes them evil is their opposition to the higher power. But it is difficult to see how a righteous judgment against plurality can be made on this basis. If sovereignty is the "good," then the only difference between monarchy and polyarchy, the divine and the demonic, is a difference of degree. The plurality of gods can be declared "vile" by Eusebius,[109] but their inadequacy lies in their lack of ultimate authority not in their actual behavior. This is borne out by his exposition of the incarnation and the development of his Christology, which concentrate on the supreme authority of the pre-existent Word and the sovereign rule of the Christ. As a result there is no essential moral content to Eusebius's gospel of sovereignty. The Sovereign God's right to rule lies in his ultimate authority and the degree of power he wields, not in his character or the way in which his power operates.

109. Eusebius, "The Oration," 588.

By presenting the church as the agent of the Word in the continuing work of exactly this kind of sovereign peace, Eusebius choreographed what was to become the practice of power for the medieval church. This consisted in the maintenance of sovereignty through the hierarchical structure of the apostolic succession expressed by the deliberations of monarchical bishops in their local administrative role and at church councils. It was promulgated by the task of carrying the victory of the Word as consummated in the cross through the "secret worship" manifest in the sacrifices of prayer and the eucharist, as the ensuing section develops. Consequently the mediation of monarchical power became the primary *telos* of the church. Its success was determined in terms of the territorial, military, and economic strength of the empire and the parallel growth and stability of the godly polity. The importance of this conjunction of monotheism and the church in imperial progress is affirmed by commentators such as Garth Fowden and Erik Petersen. Fowden posits that the defining characteristic of late antiquity "was its conviction that knowledge of the One God both justifies the use of imperial power and makes it more effective"[110] and that it was the emergence of monotheism via Christianity and Islam that brought about the potential of fully universal empire.[111] He is of the opinion that this did not happen as suddenly or as completely under Constantine as the *History* and the *Life* suggest, but recognizes the influence of what he regards as Eusebius's monotheistic political configuration of church and empire.[112] He suggests that Islam was more successful than Christianity in this regard because the Western empire gave way more rapidly to a form of commonwealth.[113] The ensuing conduits trace this transition, and attempt to demonstrate that if empire is defined as the rule by the few over the many for the benefit of the few, commonwealth as described by Fowden remains an imperial formation. Petersen takes up the specific connection between monotheism and monarchy[114] and argues that it presents a theological-political paradigm problematic for its tendency to render trinitarian theology impossible,[115] an assertion also taken up below.

110. Fowden, *Empire to Commonwealth*, 3.

111. Ibid., 9.

112. Ibid., 86.

113. Ibid., 108.

114. Monotheism only emerged as a separate term to monarchy in the ontology of God in the seventeenth century.

115. Petersen, *Theologische Traktate*, 38.

This alignment of imperial sovereignty and the divine will brought Eusebius to a point of effective de-eschatologization and lost the counterpolitical potential of the anticipated peace. It is now possible to state with some certainty that the primary function of the depictions of an imminently anticipated temporal peace in the Hebrew prophetic genre from the rise of Assyria onwards was the provision of a counterpolitical critique of empire. The role and nature of the Hebrew prophetic movement from the seventh century BCE is the subject of much contemporary research and will be explored in some depth in Part III. It is now clear that the milieu of the gospel articulation of the kingdom of God was the immanent critique of empire. From this perspective the excision of such an important aspect of eschatology at a time when the church as agent of the kingdom was embarking on a whole new relationship with empire was an omission of epic proportions. It was, however, the inevitable result of the de-eschatologization that was the consequence of Eusebius's potent combination of both over- and under-realized eschatology. In orthodox eschatology, the kingdom of heaven is here in the incarnation and in those ways that the incarnation is still immanent, and exists also in heaven and in the heavenly kingdom to come. A future time is expected when the kingdoms of this world will become the kingdom of God and his Christ, a total conflation finally effected by the return of Christ. Over-realized eschatology tends to de-eschatologization by replacing the hope of the future eschaton and eliding the immanent aspects of the kingdom of God, by the substitution of a supposed eschaton that is merely the contemporary political form. Eusebius's affirmation of a partnership in sovereignty between the church and Constantine's empire conflated his experience of mundane life with the eschaton and thereby exemplifies over-realized eschatology. However, in leaving a reified under-realized heaven in place, as described in the *Commentary on Isaiah* in which leaders are the lords of heaven as they are monarchical bishops on the earth,[116] he closed the eschatological circle of sovereignty. De-eschatologization was the inevitable result. As a consequence the church he presents is both the legitimator and carrier of empire.

116. Hollerich, *Eusebius's Commentary on Isaiah*, 186.

2. The Distinctive Soteriology of the Cross

The soteriology of the cross lies at the heart of Eusebius's vision. It embodies the spiritual work of the Word in resolution of the legal guilt and political pluralism consequent on the violation of God's monarchical rule. At the cross God's offended sovereignty is appeased, the demons of idolatry are exorcized, and the resurrection is the evidence. He sees the church's responsibility as the continuation of this work in prayer and the celebration of the eucharist akin to the military mopping-up process after a decisive battle has already won the war. It has been suggested that Eusebius's view is representative of the Arian position that emphasized the cosmological and corporate aspects of salvation, in contrast to the Nicaeans who recognized the specific historical character of the sacrifice of the Christ. George Huntston Williams argues in this way, concluding that "the Arian was attentive to the Sermon on the Mount, the Catholic emphasized Bethlehem and Calvary." Citing Eusebius as his example, he states that the Arians were "confined to the more modest role of proclaiming afresh the oneness of God and of reminding men of their natural mortality."[117] However, as has already been demonstrated, this seriously underrates Eusebius's application of the historical role of the cross. His theology did emphasize the didactic role of the cross but it was emphatically also about dealing with the human guilt in rejecting the divine law, God's anger at humankind's disobedience, and resolving the cosmological effects of abrogating the sovereign rule of the One. The strategic application of the divine Word in the atonement dealt with the consequences of infringing sovereignty by fulfilling the righteous penalty of death, assuaging God's righteous anger towards the world, and by overcoming the demonic and material results of pluralism. The celebration of the mass embodied the success of this resolution.

This view of the function of the atonement as resolving offended sovereignty is vulnerable to the same kind of overall criticism as that already associated with asserting power as the paramount aspect of God's being. It presents a morally weak but imperially strong atonement that makes the sacrifice of the Christ effective in comparison to the rejected pagan sacrifices by degree and not in kind. For if the sin addressed by the death and resurrection of the Christ is humanity's failure to honor the ultimate sovereignty in heaven and earth, then the strategic impact

---

117. Williams, "Christology and Church-State Relations in the Fourth Century," 12–14.

of the atonement is its ability to satisfy this highest power. The difference between the sacrifice of the Christ and the human or animal sacrifices given to the gods appears to be one of quantity. The sacrifice of Jesus works because he is a greater offering than animals or humans. The blood of Christ placates the highest Spirit and displaces the lesser "evil" spirits that oppose the rule of the higher power. This implies that there is no essential difference between animal sacrifices, human sacrifices, and the passion of the Christ. Offended sovereignty requires appeasement and the greater the sovereignty the greater the blood-sacrifice needed to assuage it. The chief offence is not then one of specific personal or social sin but a failure to submit to the ultimate authority. This has the effect of making the primary task of the church the enforcement of the divinely sanctified sovereign ecclesiastical and political structures by the exercise of the soteriological instruments embodied in the cross. The moral, pastoral, and experiential aspects of faith are subordinated to the overarching demands of achieving and preserving the eschatological peace. It is this that hints at the contrivance that underlies sovereignty as the means to peace, and that configures the soteriology of the cross in resolution of its offence. While it is recognized that there were those such as Anselm who may have interpreted the cross differently,[118] as the second conduit will consider, it was Eusebius's view and its impact and transformations that became the driving motivation of the future church. In the ongoing investigation and analysis pursued in the ensuing conduits, it is the trajectory of these primary soteriological operations and its tendency to displace both the gospel Jesus and the multitude on whom he had compassion that impels the genealogy of church and empire.

3. An Imperial Christology

It is unlikely that the christological controversy of Nicaea would have emerged as the defining theological debate of the period except for the church's identification of the *pax Romana* as evidence of the eschatological peace. The coalescence of the ecclesial means to the peace with the exercise of sovereignty exemplified in Eusebius's writings, discloses the accompanying importance of aligning the Christ and the sovereign God. The seminal point here is once again the impact of ontological sovereignty. Simply put, this presented a problem for Christology because of

---

118. See Milbank, "Forgiveness and Incarnation," 92–128.

the difficulty of maintaining the sovereignty of both the Father and the Son. This applies to both Arian and Nicaean positions in three ways. The first two are philosophical and the third is anthropological. They can be expressed as three questions: Firstly, how can there be two supremely divine beings who share the same substance without one having precedence? Secondly, and importantly, even if it were explicable, how can it possibly affirm monarchy? Thirdly, how can the human, kenotic figure of Jesus of Nazareth share in substance with an imperially sovereign God? It is this last question that the ontological element of the controversy of Nicaea masked. Any harmonizing approaches to the gospel narratives, whether oral or written, from a perspective supportive of incarnation, tend to affirm a human and kenotic Christ. This human Jesus confronts the ontology of sovereignty. The first philosophical question of course remains even for a non-imperial perspective on Jesus. But both the Arian and Nicaean sides of the Christology argument and the *homoousios* formula that Eusebius describes, aimed to resolve the second question. In order to do so it necessarily tended to subdue the human kenotic Jesus and ascribe sovereignty to both the Father and the Son.

This is the outcome that consolidated the "theological-political paradigm problematic for its tendency to render trinitarian theology impossible" described by Petersen above. For while it is recognized that the trinitarian being of the Father and the Son presents a theological challenge, the impossibility referred to by Petersen is vested in the paradigm that requires the conjunction of the human Jesus and the sovereign God. If Nicaea in fact choreographed the conjunction of imperially subsumed divinity and the Christ into a doctrine of incarnation foundational to Christendom, then this has profound implications for the definitive paradox of Western Christianity. This has been characterized as two ends of a spectrum, the sovereign and the kenotic, or, as Linda Woodhead describes, a Christianity of a higher power and one of an inner power. "For a Christianity of higher power, he [God] is a transcendent being who must be obeyed; whereas for a Christianity of inner power, he is a spiritual being who can inspire, in-Spirit and divinize human life."[119] But as this book attempts to demonstrate, the pole of higher power continually wins out. The thesis presented here seeks out the ontological genealogy behind the apparent prevalence of the sovereignly transcendent higher power, suggesting that the Nicaean formula

119. Woodhead, *Christianity: A Very Short Introduction*, 2.

was successful precisely because it held together a paradox that was less a spiritual mystery and more a political device to combine two irreconcilable perceptions of the divine in which the sovereign one generally subdued the other. Part III will attempt to reconfigure the incarnation without this supposed subsumption.

As a result of the continued masking of the human kenotic Jesus consequent on the assumption of the imperial nature of divine sovereignty, the originally counterpolitical impact of the gospel was gradually displaced from the developing Christendom. In the explorations of the synchronic historical studies that now follow, the continuing impulses of this ontologically configured sovereignty and its implementation via the soteriological instruments of its enforcement, form the primary template for discerning the ensuing stages of the genealogy of an increasingly normative partnership between the church and empire.

PART II

A Genealogy of Subsumption

3

Conduits of Christendom

Innocent III and His Seminal Contemporaries,
Frederick II the Hohenstaufen, Joachim of Fiore,
and Francis of Assisi

THE EARLY YEARS OF the thirteenth century were momentous ones for the Western church. The young pope, Innocent III, having come to power in 1198, was already stamping his authority on the papal lands and seeking out an emperor through whom to recover Christendom. In the autumn of 1201 his ward, the seven-year-old Hohenstaufen heir, Frederick II, was tearing clothes and flesh in furious resentment at the illegal regency of Markward of Anweiler in his court in Palermo.[1] The following year Joachim, the theological innovator credited with declaring the end of clerisy and prophesying Frederick as Antichrist, lay dying in his Sicilian abbey. Francis of Assisi was in prison in Perugia prior to "taking the cross" and joining the army of Walter of Brienne to rescue the young emperor-in-waiting.[2] The coincidences of time and place in these ways connected four seminal protagonists in the developing interface of church and empire. In so doing they provide the ingredients for an illuminating second conduit of Christendom.

As seen from the previous conduit, the work of Eusebius presented the church as the instrument of eschatological progress. His "godly polity" was a theocratic community in the tradition of the Old Testament Jews, no longer in relation to the territory of Israel, but as consolida-

1. Masson, *Frederick II of Hohenstaufen*, 31.
2. Smith, *Francis of Assisi*, 37–38.

tor and guardian of the Roman Empire's universal peace. The church fulfilled its strategic role by the orderly maintenance of its sovereignty, the history and efficacy of which were embodied in the soteriological components of the cross and replicated in the faithful enactment of its liturgy. In the ongoing strength and legitimacy of these foundations the imperial government continued its military and economic success. Such were the foundations of Christendom. Nine centuries later under the leadership of Innocent III, the church's role in relation to the eschatological peace had developed considerably from this starting point. Four major changes had taken place, the first with respect to the church, and the remainder with regard to the hoped for peace. To begin with, the pursuit of sovereignty by the church had settled into a strong ecclesiastical hierarchy around the bishop of Rome. Secondly, the collapse of the Roman Empire in the West in the mid fifth century had left the Eastern empire, with its capital at Constantinople, continuing in waning strength. Thirdly, in the lands of the former Western empire, the princes of Europe were vying for power, and finally, in the Middle East, Islam had emerged under Mohammed's leadership from 630 CE and begun its spectacular territorial expansion.[3]

These developments posed serious challenges to the anticipated eschatological progress. Tensions over the increasing claims of the Roman church to universal authority led to schisms between Alexandria and Rome in the sixth century, Constantinople and Rome in the ninth century, and the separation of the Eastern churches by mutual excommunication in the eleventh century.[4] By the year 800 CE Charlemagne, king of the Franks, had consolidated power across Europe from France to Italy and been crowned Holy Roman Emperor by Pope Leo III.[5] The ensuing years saw a variety of uneven attempts by the Frankish king's successors to maintain their rule. Meanwhile Islam's alternative eschatological empire encompassed much of the eastern and southern lands of what had once been the evidence of the expected universality of Rome's reign of peace.

This second conduit of Christendom traces the transitions through which these changes distributed the theological impulses of

3. See Johns, "Christianity and Islam," 172ff.

4. Southern, *Western Society and the Church in the Middle Ages*, 52ff.; Ware, "Eastern Christendom," 151ff.

5. Stephenson, *Mediaeval History*, 151.

Christendom by means of four complementary narratives. These exemplify the way in which the ecclesial agency for peace through sovereignty bifurcated, and became conflictual in the attempt to regain territory and meet the ongoing need for monarchy. Firstly, the story of Innocent III's recourse to law and violence in his defense of papal lands and search for an imperial partner illustrates the transformation of the soteriological components of the cross that constituted the foundations of the peace. Under these conditions, the vicarious violence of the cross was expanded in the *negotium crucis* to include the sufferings involved in recovering and defending lost ecclesiastical and imperial territory. The second narrative then describes the rise of Frederick the Hohenstaufen and his attempt to configure an autonomous model of kingship. This provides the parallel secular expression of Innocent's reaffirmation of temporal power through law and war and the deliberate application of Christology to earthly kingship. Thirdly, there follows an account of how the immanent propitiatory power of the eucharist was strengthened to reflect these soteriological developments. It is suggested that the inversion of the *corpus verum* of the Christ away from the human Jesus and the historical church to the sacramental elements at each celebration of the eucharist, a transference generally placed towards the end of the twelfth century, came to its culmination in this need of greater and more immediate authority for both sacerdotal and state power. The location of the characters and events of this conduit at the turn of the twelfth and beginning of the thirteenth century provides a window on this critical inversion. Fourthly, the conduit presents the work of Joachim of Fiore and Francis of Assisi as examples of alternative routes to peace that were emerging outside the existing sovereign structures at this time.

The following narratives deliberately aim to engage the reader in the legal and military struggles in which the pursuit of peace through sovereignty enveloped the church. They therefore go into some detail, while attempting to point out the soteriological implications as they unfold. The concluding section of the conduit then reviews the theological developments arising from these evocatively embodied currents of medievality, focusing in particular on the core elements of ontology and soteriology, indicating their potential as impulses of modernity.

A. THE PAPACY OF INNOCENT III

Bifurcation and conflict were the inevitable consequences of adherence to sovereignty as both the definition and means of peace. This is borne out by the single-minded determination of Innocent's fight for the Papal States and the tenacity of his search for an emperor with whom to partner. The ecclesial pretensions for peace were predicated on an adequate and potentially universal temporal government that shared its vision. Constantinople, however, was ruled by an emperor and patriarch who refused to acknowledge the primacy of the pope and the Roman Catholic Church, the Holy Roman Empire in the West sought sovereignty over Rome to give integrity to its title, and the Holy Land itself was in Muslim hands. In this situation the impulse of ontological sovereignty predisposed the church to take the role of final law-maker with *plenitudo potestatis* in the absence of a suitable partner, not in order to dispense with such a collaborator, but to enable it to hold the remaining ground and facilitate the quest. This was seemingly unavoidable given its dual role as both agent and embodiment of sovereignty. The writings of Innocent suggest that he recognized this. The three short treatises he wrote as a young cardinal expose the temptation to vice among senior ecclesiastics, the quality of justice required from secular and ecclesiastical rulers, and his view of the primacy of the bishop of Rome over the entire church, three themes displayed in his ensuing papacy.[6] Even before he was fully instituted as pope, he wrote to the bishops of the papal province of Ravenna, "ecclesiastical liberty is nowhere better served than where the Roman church holds full power both in temporalities and in spiritualities."[7] Within days of his investiture he made clear to them how he proposed to apply his assumed legal authority. He described the papal and imperial authorities as two great dignities instituted by God, the former compared to the sun and the imperial authority as the lesser, dependent light of the moon.[8] This was the role of secular power that

---

6. The three treatises are *De miseria condicionis humane* (On the Misery of the Human Condition), *De missarum mysteriis* (On the Mysteries of the Mass), and *De quadripartita specie nuptiarum* (On Four Types of Marriage), cited in Moore, *Pope Innocent III*. Other original sources are the papal letters found in the Vatican archive *Register of Innocent III*, and a chronicle, *Gesta Innocentii III*, written about 1208 by an anonymous member of the curia who apparently knew Innocent well.

7. *The Register of Innocent III*, 1:27.

8. Abulafia, *Frederick II*, 94.

Innocent, building on the Gregorian reforms of the eleventh century, looked for a leader to fulfill.

The Gregorian movement, based on the theopolitical thinking of Pope Gregory VII, represented a crucial expansion of the sovereign law, upheld in the atonement, into canon laws that aimed to develop the papacy as the supreme court of Europe. His twenty-seven *Dictatus Papae* included "That the Roman Pontiff alone is rightly to be called universal," "That the Pope is the only one whose feet are to be kissed by Princes," and "That he may depose Emperors."[9] The majority of the clergy were trained in schools that taught this view. It is not hard to see why the relationship of emperor to pope had come to be regarded in this way. The ongoing pursuit of the eschatological reign of peace by the church required an emperor with the competency to help deliver it. But such an institution had to be submitted to ecclesial authority for several important reasons. Firstly, the church needed to maintain its position as primary instrument of eschatological progress both in the absence of a suitable partner and in the face of corrupt contenders for power.[10] Secondly, it had to be able to correct the immoral behavior of Christian princes and their officials, which, as Innocent believed, was a cause of the loss of territory and the spread of heresy.[11] Finally, and most urgently, it had to be able to call on the secular authorities for military support in regaining lost territory. For the eschatological role of the church in its responsibility for the universal peace this was the most pressing need, and in particular the defense of the papal lands. For if it was to fulfill its obligation to regain the lost empire, ongoing power struggles over the papal homelands could not be allowed to undermine ecclesiastical authority. These developments led to territory becoming once again, as for Israel before them, central for the godly polity.

1. In Defense of the Papal States

Innocent's espousal of papal temporal power was by no means theoretical. He was prepared to consolidate it with full diplomatic and military force. By the time he became pope, Ravenna had been in the hands of the German Markward of Anweiler for several years, as part of Emperor

9. O'Donovan and O'Donovan, *Ignatius to Grotius*, 242.

10. Smith, *Innocent III Church Defender*, 3–9.

11. Abulafia, *Frederick II*, 42.

Henry VI's attempts to subdue Rome as his capital at the expense of papal authority in the region. Only the year before Innocent assumed the papacy, the imperial Hohenstaufen house who had been striving for a generation to establish their authority over the city of Rome, seemed increasingly successful. His predecessor, the ageing Pope Celestine, could do little to stop them. Henry VI was Holy Roman Emperor, his brother Philip was Duke of Tuscany, Conrad of Urslingen, Henry's representative in Sicily, was Duke of Spoleto, Diepold of Schweinspeunt was Count of Acerra, and Markward of Anweiler ruled Ravenna, Ancona, and Abruzzi. As a result "German dominance settled like a net over Italy."[12] Henry VI's sudden death, barely six months before Innocent's accession, created an opportunity to reclaim sovereignty that Innocent was determined not to miss.

The history of the papal lands begins with the sixth-century attempt to reconquer Italy by the remaining Eastern Roman Empire. This was eventually opposed by the Lombards who entered the peninsula from the north and conquered much of the countryside. By the seventh century, Byzantine authority was mainly limited to a diagonal band running roughly from Ravenna to Rome and south to Naples. The bishop of Rome, as the largest landowner and most influential figure in Italy, began by default to take on much of the ruling authority that the Byzantines were unable to maintain. This enabled the development of the papacy and the protection of the church's sovereignty from the uncertain impact of the competing powers. The Lombard ruler, Liutprand, eventually recognized the pope's authority in the Donation of Sutri in 728, ratified again by the Donation of Pippin after the Frankish emperor conquered Northern Italy in 756, and extended by Charlemagne and the Holy Roman Empire after 800.[13] However, in real terms, the Carolingian Empire lasted only a century, and the years before Innocent's day saw the rise and fall of several elected dynasties with many fluctuations in their influence and claim to authority of which the Hohenstaufens had been the latest.

The emperor's death revealed how tenuous the German hold really was. Angry Italians rose up against them immediately, forcing Philip to

---

12. Moore, *Pope Innocent III*, 13.

13. Duchesne, *The Beginnings of the Temporal Sovereignty of the Popes*; Partner, *The Lands of St Peter*.

withdraw to Swabia and Conrad of Urslingen to return to Germany.[14] Markward of Anweiler, however, tried hard to hold on to his principalities. Innocent saw the opportunity to regain hold of the Papal States as a buffer between Sicily the island and Apulian Sicily to the south and east, in the hope of preventing the linking of the German and Sicilian interests. But despite the impact of Innocent's advice to the bishops of Ravenna, Markward did not return to Germany but moved southward to Sicily, seeking to maintain the Hohenstaufen imperial cause there.[15] This was not something that Innocent was prepared to tolerate. Markward, having first of all attempted to get Innocent's support for his role in southern Italy, found help in Diepold who had also moved south. In October 1199 Markward crossed over into the island of Sicily, raising a considerable army and falsely claiming that Innocent had appointed him regent of his young ward Frederick, the heir to the Hohenstaufen cause. Excommunicating and damning Markward as a perjurer in no uncertain terms,[16] Innocent sent a military force under the command of his own cousin, James the Marshall, to assist Frederick's supporters and decisively defeated the German.[17] However, Frederick's supporters failed to pay Innocent's army and they withdrew, leaving Markward to regroup, attack Palermo, and capture Frederick in November 1201.

It was at this point that Walter of Brienne, a relation by marriage to Tancred, the deposed claimant to the Sicilian throne, was persuaded to enter the fray.[18] He was already a crusader who had "taken the cross" and saw the defense of the papacy and its lands as an extension of his vows in the way that the coming section on Innocent's theology of the *negotium crucis* will explicate. Walter was strikingly successful on Innocent's behalf, defeating Diepold and Walter of Palear, the Sicilian chancellor, and quelling local disturbances in the papal lands together with the papal army. The setback of Markward's victory in Palermo and capture of Frederick was for Innocent fortuitously resolved by Markward's death through sudden illness. Capparone, the German who took Markward's place in Palermo, was soon removed. By the time Walter of Brienne was himself assassinated by Diepold in June 1205, Innocent's tenacity was

14. Waley, *The Papal State in the Thirteenth Century*, 30, 33.

15. Moore, *Pope Innocent III*, 33–34.

16. Van Cleve, *The Emperor Frederick II of Hohenstaufen*, 40–42.

17. Binns, *Innocent III*, 36.

18. Ibid., 40.

recognized by both Palear and Diepold, who agreed to rescue Frederick and return him to Innocent's influence. He declared Frederick of age the following year. While historians vary in their assessments of these efforts by Innocent to consolidate his grip on the Papal States and to maintain a positive influence on Sicily,[19] his determination is clear.

Innocent was not only a highly politicized military and diplomatic strategist. Brenda Bolton's important work on his life has even suggested that "he was above all a pastoral pope."[20] In the food shortages in Rome in early February 1202 he fed more than eight thousand people personally.[21] Three times a week he sat with cardinals and clerks to hear the problems of those who came to seek his advice and help. Nevertheless, his concern for the spiritual condition of the church appears to have been particularly because of its impact on its temporal power, which, in his view, made it responsible for the loss of empire and the Muslim threat to the Holy Lands and Spain. As a result Joseph Canning concludes that Innocent's spiritual concerns were conditioned by the need to recover and maintain temporal sovereignty.[22] To this end Innocent told the Cistercians that the monastic life, although meritorious, was not as useful as the active life.[23] In the end "Lordship was the stronger model than that of servant in Innocent's actions."[24]

2. Finding an Adequate Emperor

The first apparent contender for the imperial throne was the hated Markward. But it is more likely that he was guarding the Hohenstaufen interests, and faithful in this to Frederick and his uncle, Philip of Swabia. The young Frederick had been placed in Innocent's charge by his mother, the dying widow of Henry VI, Queen Constance of Sicily. As heir to the Norman monarchy of Sicily, she was herself no supporter of the Hohenstaufen cause. Her desire was for her son to become king only of Sicily and not Holy Roman Emperor. This suited Innocent very well, hence his battles to keep Frederick from Markward. If Markward was

---

19. Moore, *Pope Innocent III*, 68.

20. Bolton, *Studies in Church History*, 165.

21. Moore, *Pope Innocent III*, 86.

22. Canning, "Power and the Pastor," 246.

23. *The Register of Innocent III*, 7:210.

24. Moore, *Pope Innocent III*, 267.

not a direct contender for the imperial throne, Henry's brother Philip Hohenstaufen of Swabia clearly was, and a definite threat to Innocent's determination to keep Sicily separate from the rest of the imperial territories until he could be sure of his or any other potential emperor's pretensions. For there were other contenders; two imperial dynasties competed for power among the German princes, the Welfs and the Hohenstaufen, who drew on the English and the French respectively for their support. Within months of Henry's death, Philip had been elected as king and future emperor in Mühlhausen, and the Welf Otto of Brunswick had been similarly elected in Cologne.[25] Innocent's pragmatic approach was to require a promise not to attempt to regain Italy and an acknowledgment of the pope's right to temporal rulership of the papal lands before crowning either candidate. He was probably not surprised when Otto agreed to the promise and Philip declined.

At the end of 1200 the curia reviewed the issues surrounding Philip's, Otto's, and the young Frederick's suitability, and instructed their legate to require the German princes to put forward an alternative worthy person or accept Innocent's preference for Otto.[26] Innocent subsequently named him as emperor elect in March 1201. A stalemate ensued in which Innocent refused to approve or crown Philip but could do little to further promote Otto while his potential ally Philip Augustus of France refused to support him. Eventually Otto's main allies, the English, lost their influence and a large part of their French possessions in 1204. The following January Philip of Swabia was crowned king of the Germans in Aachen, the seat of Charlemagne. Not surprisingly he proceeded to send his agent, Bishop Lupold of Worms, to regain control of the provinces of Central Italy and to reestablish his role as guardian of the interests of Frederick.[27] Innocent's forces crushed Lupold, who was recalled to Germany. A rapprochement ensued between Philip and Innocent in the knowledge that the latter's promotion of Otto of Brunswick's claim to the emperorship was now unlikely to succeed.[28] Innocent's position was again suddenly and fortuitously enhanced at this time by the apparently unrelated murder of Philip of Swabia. For the time being it looked as if there would be no threat to unite Sicily with the empire and threaten

25. Van Cleve, *The Emperor Frederick II*, 31.
26. Moore, *Pope Innocent III*, 69.
27. Ibid., 51–52.
28. Ibid., 52.

the autonomy of the Papal States. This seemed to Innocent a real sign of God's favor at a time in which he was consolidating his position as legislator for all Christendom by commissioning a formal collection of his decretals.[29] Innocent moved to confirm Otto as emperor when he in effect promised to place his imperial power at the papacy's disposal. He crowned him in 1209, but Otto's elevation seriously misfired.[30] Hardly had he taken office when he broke his promises and enforced a plan to remove the threat of Frederick, unite Sicily and the empire, and reappoint Diepold as "Grand Captain of Apulia."[31]

Innocent secured the support of Otto's enemy, Philip of France, and some German princes that Otto had alienated, and intervened for Otto's removal. Together they began to advance the young Frederick towards the post of Holy Roman Emperor.[32] Innocent must have known this to be a risk, but Frederick was just seventeen years old and his ward after all. The group of anti-Welf princes influenced by Philip declared the by now excommunicated emperor deposed, and elected Frederick emperor in his stead, dispatching messengers to the pope and Frederick for approval.[33] Frederick was in fact in dire straits and had a ship at the ready to flee into exile. The resultant eleventh-hour escape in the spring of 1212 made the year one of the best of Innocent's papacy, in which events appeared to demonstrate the divine favor.[34] July saw the united Spanish princes' victory over the Muslims and Frederick beat Otto to Constance, where he was feted by the German princes and bishops. In the strength of this, the following year Innocent wrote to all the princes of Europe, asking for their prayers and summoning them to the Fourth Lateran Council to be held in November 1215.[35] Here the vital role of the *negotium crucis* in securing the victories of the church was strongly affirmed and the doctrine of transubstantiation was introduced. The interrelationship of these two important theological innovations will be developed in the ensuing sections.

29. Ibid., 186.

30. Ibid., 187–9.

31. Ibid., 188.

32. Van Cleve, *The Emperor Frederick II*, 29.

33. Ibid., 76–79.

34. Moore, *Pope Innocent III*, 203.

35. Ibid., 206–7.

1. Frederick as Innocent's Glorious Crusader

Frederick was in many ways the embodiment of Innocent's concept of crusader glory. This is apparent in his seemingly miraculous scramble to Constance, his coronation in Aachen, and his eventual entry into Jerusalem. Ernst Kantorowicz describes the romantic journey of the "Apulian lad" with a tiny entourage setting out for Germany via the pope's court in Rome, and their extraordinary appearance at Constance just three hours before Otto was due to arrive.[51] When presented with the pope's excommunication of Otto by the legate traveling with them, the bishop of the city gave way to the surprising entrance of the boy king. Otto arrived only hours later with inadequate forces and withdrew without daring even to risk a battle. Kantorowicz asserts that Frederick always quoted this as his first clear call from God, a sign from heaven "against all the probabilities and hopes of men."[52] Then there was his enthronement in Charlemagne's original capital Aachen in July 1215 and his "taking the cross" there.[53] Although already crowned at Mainz, Aachen was highly significant for Frederick as the seat of Charlemagne. The task of converting the heathen was part of the imperial office. He picked up the cross and made an immediate emotional appeal to the knights and princes present to follow his lead to a new crusade. As David Abulafia states, "The very act of taking the cross, it must be emphasized, had tremendous symbolic importance: the cross of the crusader represented the cross of redemption, raised at Golgotha outside Jerusalem, found again by Constantine's mother near the future Church of the Holy Sepulchre, seized by Saladin, along with Jerusalem itself in 1187, and, like Jerusalem, in urgent need of recovery."[54] Then there was his eventual victorious entrance into Jerusalem accompanied by Hermann of Salza, the grand master of the Teutonic knights. Kantorowicz points out that Frederick had realized the Davidic kingship of the Carolingian at last.[55]

Abulafia views the study of Frederick as many layered "like an archaeological site."[56] At the top level "lies the reputation the emperor has acquired in modern public consciousness." Here he places the work

51. Kantorowicz, *Frederick the Second*, 61; Masson, *Frederick II*, 50.

52. Ibid., 53.

53. Van Cleve, *The Emperor Frederick II*, 96–97.

54. Abulafia, *Frederick II*, 121.

55. Kantorowicz, *Frederick the Second*, 201.

56. Abulafia, *Frederick II*, xix–xxiii.

of Kantorowicz and his predecessors Eberhard Gothein and Jacob Burckhardt. This level saw Frederick as a Nietzschean new man, part Renaissance Prince, part Oriental despot, and a man before his time. At the second level is the thirteenth-century view of Matthew Paris and Salimbene before him, where Frederick is a "wonder of the world . . . the valiant warrior fighting against papal pretensions." Below this is the substratum that needs handling with the most care because it consists of the propaganda campaign unleashed against him "that in its intensity exceeded anything that had gone before." Finally there comes the hardest layer to penetrate, the "real Frederick" that Abulafia believes reveals the emperor as much more normal and generally medieval than the other views have purported.

Through all these levels there still emerges Frederick the crusader king. It is this image, of the emperor fulfilling his destiny in imitation of his Lord, which fulfills Innocent's vision of the *negotium crucis*, but at the same time reveals the increasingly conflictual sovereignty of church and empire, pope and emperor indicated above. This was consummated when, as an excommunicate contravening the will of the papal legate of Jerusalem, Frederick crowned himself, invoking the direct relationship of emperor to God without the mediation of the church. In so doing he set the direction for his own developing self-understanding of Caesar-like authority. Innocent's expansion of the legal authority of papal temporal power, building on Hildebrand's work, and his expansion of the sufferings of the cross into knightly crusading glory, had issued in the direct empowerment of imperial supremacy. As Frederick described in his letter to King Henry III of England, "we wore the crown which God the Omnipotent, through his special grace, provided for us to wear."[57]

2. Frederick as Roman Caesar

From his coming of age at fourteen, Frederick worked to establish power in Sicily, first by military strength[58] and, after his return from his investitures in Germany, by the introduction of an innovatory administration based on Roman law. According to Van Cleve there could be but one form of success in statesmanship for Frederick, "the attainment of Caesarism, comparable to that of Roman antiquity."[59] Frederick drew

---

57. Roger of Wendover, *Chronica, sive Flores historiarum*, 192–3.

58. Van Cleve, *The Emperor Frederick II*, 66–67.

59. Ibid., 167.

on the work of the emperor Justinian, the codifier of Roman law, and published his own famous *Liber Augustalis* at Melfi in August 1231. Although he also had recourse to Lombard and Norman influences, he did not view his laws merely as precedents, but saw himself as a kingly Christ figure, believing that "God subjected the laws to the Emperor and gave him as a living law to men."[60] His preamble to the *Constitutions* sets out the monarchical sovereignty of rulers as God's gift of justice for fallen humanity and protection for the church and mother of mankind, in order that the people might enjoy the blessings of peace and justice. It concludes that he himself is a special gift of God elevated above all other rulers to the supreme office of Roman Emperor.[61]

On the basis of these *Constitutions*, Frederick was able to establish a pyramidal bureaucratic structure over his Sicilian domains where legislation, administration, and justice were all in the hands of the emperor.[62] At this time he minted gold currency known as *Augustales,* depicting himself as Caesar Augustus.[63] Kantorowicz states that "this renewal of the antique was for Frederick, as also for the Renaissance, the practical expression of a sincere conviction: namely, that the age of Christ, and with it the age of Augustus, had come again."[64] As will be discussed in the next section, this Christ figure was unashamedly imperial. However, while it might seem that Frederick was exactly the partner in the universal peace that Innocent and his successors were looking for, there were several problems. Firstly, the papal requirements for a suitable emperor were, as has been made clear, freedom from interference in the appointing of officials, openness to correction on matters of personal behavior, and readiness to initiate the recovery of territory and the removal of the rebellious and heretical. While Frederick was more or less happy with the latter as crusading knight, as ultimate Caesar he wanted to retain the right to appoint his own church officials and resented the pope's interference in his peculiarly Eastern marital arrangements.[65] Secondly, Innocent's original condition of support for the imperial candidates was

---

60. John of Viterbo, *De Regimine Civitatum*, ed. Salvemini, 128, cited in ibid., 243.

61. Van Cleve paraphrases "Frederick II, Constitutiones," in Huillard-Bréholles, *Historia diplomatica Frederici II*, 3–5. Ibid., 258.

62. Ibid., 256.

63. Andrewes, *Frederick II of Hohenstaufen*, 27.

64. Kantorowicz, *Frederick the Second*, 225.

65. Andrewes, *Frederick II*, 8.

their promise not to attempt to regain Italy or challenge his temporal authority over the Papal States. But Frederick, like his forbears, was eager to maintain the unity of the north and south of his dominions and the imperial integrity of direct rule over Rome.[66]

All of this put him on a collision course with the papacy. But more importantly than all of these, as far as the future of the peace was concerned, Frederick, like Innocent, while claiming fullness of power, was disinclined to use it beyond what suited him. Innocent, despite his theoretical power, looked first to God and then to the emperor to reestablish the eschatological peace. But notwithstanding Frederick's own universal claim to sovereignty, it seems that he had no pretensions to be a Constantinian co-partner to the church's vision of universal sovereignty. While he desired full sway over his Sicilian domain and peace in his wider empire, it was in order to devote himself to the life of chivalric knight and huntsman facilitated by a Caesar-like statesmanship within the secure bounds of his own territories. He never seriously attempted to establish military domination and Roman law within wider Europe, where he relied on diplomacy and a more federal model to maintain power. In return for the support of the German princes for the installation of his infant son Henry as king of the Romans, Frederick granted them generous privileges.[67] When his son Henry lost his status at the Diet of Worms, Frederick made no attempt to regain it and Germany became a princely oligarchy.

Some historians, assuming in Frederick the desire for universal power, have wondered at his failure to take the opportunities open to him for centralizing sovereignty in Germany.[68] However, it seems that his approach was much more pragmatic. Rather than Sicilianize the whole empire, Frederick strengthened the princes and thus gained their support.[69] When the challenge of recovering the Holy Land vied with the need to consolidate his own territories, the more domestic pressures generally won.[70] But even the needs of his own kingdom were subjected to his personal concerns. His bureaucratic administration allowed the

---

66. Ibid., 32.

67. *Privilegium in Favorem Principum Ecclesiaticorum* 1220.

68. Van Cleve, *The Emperor Frederick II*, 120.

69. Kantorowicz, *Frederick the Second*, 379.

70. Ibid., 141ff.

leadership class no real freedom[71] and the entire governmental organization of the Sicilian state was designed to provide the royal treasury with
the maximum income.[72] From this perspective, his *Justitia*, while issuing
in an impressive and successful government machine functioning out of
an extraordinary network of palaces with an artistic and creative court at
its heart,[73] was a means to the maintenance of Frederick's own personal
vanity and his consuming commitment to hunting with falcons.[74] All
this served to fuel the growing papal conclusion that he stood in the
way of the church's vision and purpose and was not the kind of emperor the Roman church was looking to partner with after all. Joachim
of Fiore allegedly prophesied Frederick to be the Antichrist.[75] If he was,
it was more through an independent self-aggrandisement than a desire
to compete with the papacy as supreme ruler of the world. In this he
pointed towards the coming modern elevation of the self indicated with
reference to Paul Fletcher in chapter 1, where monarchs, in the desire to
preserve their own personal position, were willing to limit their, and the
church's, sovereignty to the emerging rule of the nation state.

C. THE INVERSION OF THE BODY OF CHRIST

The developments since the days of Eusebius and Constantine that led
to the resurgence of the significance of territory for the church have
already been described. They had vital implications for the extension
and consolidation of sovereignty. In the foundations of Christendom the
theocratic authority of Israel was seen to have ceased with their dispos-
session from the land and passed to the church in relation to the Roman
eschatological reign of peace. In the days of ecclesial and imperial success, the analogies of high priestly office and Davidic kingship were applied to substantiate existing ecclesiastical and liturgical authority rather
than to legitimate the control of territory. Although both anointings had
been used by Eusebius to legitimate the authority of both emperor and
bishop, they were seen as fulfilled and secured by the incarnation and
atonement, and wielded from heaven by the glorified Christ. While applied to the emperor as well as the monarchical bishops, this had not

71. Van Cleve, *The Emperor Frederick II*, 249.

72. Ibid., 271.

73. Masson, *Frederick II*, 185–7.

74. Andrewes, *Frederick II*, 51.

75. Van Cleve, *The Emperor Frederick II*, 274.

been conflictual in its effect. However, with the return of the direct ecclesiological significance of territory, in the circumstances of the apparent weakening of the manifest authority of both church and empire, the theology of Christ's divinely anointed kingship was reapplied to the legitimation of both ecclesiastical and imperial authority over land. As both pope and emperor appealed to the same authority, this became a serious source of controversy.

1. Christological and Divine Foundations of Rulership

With the pressing need to regain and maintain territory, a highly developed discussion of the christological and divine foundations of rulership engendered and reinforced the bifurcation of power. As already intimated, the Gregorian reforms that Innocent built on claimed the fullness of power for the pope. Innocent made frequent use of the phrase *plenitudo potestatis*,[76] and introduced the increasingly exclusive papal use of *vicarius Christi*, not simply in common language but in the precepts of canon law.[77] While he did not always use the fullness of power that he believed was his, it was there for him when he needed to recover papal lands or excommunicate his princely enemies, as is clear from the preceding narratives. It was there too for his successors, Honorius III, Gregory IX, and Innocent IV, when they wanted to oppose, excommunicate, and depose Frederick.[78] The main theological basis for this plenitude of power was a juristic development of three concepts: St Peter's vicariate, the structure and unity of the *corpus Christianum*, and, in increasingly explicit detail, Christ's earthly kingship, "which was the foundation of the edifice."[79] While the elaboration drew heavily on three sources, the Vulgate Bible, Roman legal theory, and earlier canonical collections, and was largely the work of canon lawyers, guided by canonist popes, it also represented a continuation of Eusebius's Old Testament orientated monarchical Christology.

As already indicated, Christ's earthly kingship was also cited in justification of the conflictual claims to direct sovereignty made by secular rulers such as Frederick when they wished to advance their position

76. Moore, *Innocent III*, 257.

77. Kantorowicz, *The King's Two Bodies*, 91.

78. Frederick's relationship with the papacy deteriorated with Honorius III and culminated in his being excommunicated three times; cf. Kantorowicz, *Frederick the Second*, 171; Van Cleve, *The Emperor Frederick II*, 428 and 484–6.

79. O'Donovan and O'Donovan, *Ignatius to Grotius*, 232.

despite the opposition of the curia. This precipitated a significant development in the bifurcation of sovereignty that Kantorowicz exposes. For, as can be seen in the argument of the *Liber Augustalis*, Frederick combined Christ's earthly kingship with the Roman concept of the divine Caesar. Arguing for the conjunction of the origin and exercise of justice within the Roman Prince he states, "The Caesar, therefore, must be at once the Father and Son of Justice."[80] In this way, Kantorowicz supposes that Roman law and Christian theology overlap to reveal Frederick as a transitional monarch fusing both Christ's territorial kingship as "the Son on the Altar, seen in the imitation of Christ in taking the cross, and on divine right modelled on the Father in Heaven and focusing on a philosophy of the Law rather than the physiology of the two natured mediator."[81] However, if, as has been suggested, the concept of the two-natured mediator already hid within it both the affirmation of sovereign law in Christ's death to fulfill its legal requirements, and the vicarious sufferings that propitiated offended sovereignty, then what was happening was transformative rather than innovative.

The recourse to a Roman view of law was nothing new, but simply the fuller disclosure of the imperial sovereignty that the Council of Nicaea had already attempted to unite in substance with the incarnational Jesus. Now it emerged more overtly in the sovereign Caesar Christ. Probably the fullest articulation of this is to be found in the influential work of the early twelfth-century theologian and nameless cleric known as Norman Anonymous,[82] "one of the staunchest defenders of the spiritual essence of Christ-like kingship."[83] His tract *De consecratione pontificum et regum*[84] makes various attempts to evince a christological basis for imperial sovereignty from the incarnation without recourse to papal authority. Appealing firstly to the supposedly pre-ecclesial authority of the apostles and then applying it to secular rulers,[85] the argument proceeds by positing a Christ-like *geminal* (twin) character or *persona mixta* for bishops and kings. By analogy with Christ's two natures, divine and human, it argues that there are two natures in man, a higher and a lower, represented by king and priest. The divine is the

80. Kantorowicz, *The King's Two Bodies*, 99.

81. Ibid., 93.

82. Writing in opposition to the Gregorian reforms in around 1100 CE.

83. Kantorowicz, *The King's Two Bodies*, 45.

84. Cited and expounded at length in ibid., 46–61.

85. O'Donovan and O'Donovan, *Ignatius to Grotius*, 258.

kingly, whereas the natural and fallen for which Christ died is represented by the priest.[86] Having ascribed Christ's kingly quality to both bishops and kings, Anonymous develops this in particular regard to kings, invoking, as Innocent did for his crusader knight, the imitation of Christ. Anonymous describes how "the Spirit 'leaped' into the terrestrial king at the moment of his consecration to make him 'another man' (*alius vir*) and transfigure him within Time . . . The king *becomes* 'deified' for a brief span by virtue of grace, whereas the celestial King *is* God by nature eternally."[87] However, looking in vain for a territorial manifestation of this supposedly celestial sovereignty in the Christ of the incarnation, Anonymous reaches the conclusion that Jesus of Nazareth's contemporary, the Emperor Tiberius, is more divine than the lowly Christ.[88] While it was easier for him to reach this revealing conclusion in the context of applying his argument to the divine supremacy of kings, the same argument would apply in looking for the divine predecessor of the *plenitudo potestatis* of the pope. This conclusion marks a watershed in political theology. From the point of view of the proposal of a fourth-century lapsis in which Roman sovereignty overwhelmed the counterpolitical opposition to the Caesar cult represented by the gospel Jesus, it effectively completes the circle of subsumption.

2. The Ratification of the Doctrine of Transubstantiation

This loss of the humble, human Jesus of Nazareth in the search for Christ the territorial king, with whom to legitimate sovereign power in pope and emperor, was the corollary of the theology of the cross by which the enactment of sovereign power had been substantiated. It is hardly surprising therefore to discover that this loss of a body was also expressed liturgically. As Henri de Lubac makes clear, up until the middle of the eleventh century the church and the incarnational body of Christ were regarded as the true body of Christ, and the sacrament as the mystical body.[89] In the years that paralleled this struggle for temporal sovereignty between pope and emperor, a gradual but marked change of use weakened the connection between the sacraments of the eucharist and the incarnational body of Christ. Instead of the traditional view, which had

---

86. Kantorowicz, *The King's Two Bodies*, 254.

87. Ibid., 47.

88. Ibid., 53.

89. de Lubac, *Corpus Mysticum*, 80.

regarded the true body of Christ as the incarnational body in unity with the ecclesial body, and had described the eucharistic elements of bread and wine as the mystical body, an inversion of the *corpus verum* and the *corpus mysticum* took place. Now that the practical soteriological content and import of the cross were demonstrated in the sovereign power of the divinely ratified monarchs of *sacerdotum* and *regnum*, the soteriological function of the eucharistic elements in the transaction of sovereignty came to be recognized as the *corpus verum*, while the description *corpus mysticum* was applied to the church and the increasingly displaced Jesus of Nazareth.[90] The role of the elements in appeasing offended sovereignty and keeping at bay the demonic and political opponents who gained power in consequence became vital to the ecclesiastical and imperial leaders' ongoing success. In the end the question of who was really the supreme power would rest with whoever held the authority to mediate the transaction of the sacrament, thereby affirming the law and establishing sovereign power and the anticipated peace on earth.

While recent theological argument has suggested that the medieval configuration of the atonement, famously represented by Anselm, may be understood otherwise than as this kind of propitiation, the appeasement arguments appear to have been the dominant ones.[91] It seems clear that when the Protestant reformers took exception to the doctrine of transubstantiation it was not because it configured appeasement but because it portrayed it as happening repeatedly rather than once for all. John Scott Lidgett's respected comprehensive coverage of the theology of the atonement concludes that the prevailing answer of the Protestant writers for the reason for the sufferings and death of Christ "strikes a deeper note" than Anselm in its conception of the way that it "bears the full weight" of the punishment that the majesty and honor of God require.[92] For Western Catholic and Protestant alike appeasement appears to have remained the controlling theme.

The inversion of the incarnational body and the eucharistic body was confirmed by Innocent in the ratification of the doctrine of tran-

---

90. Ibid., 89–92.

91. David Bentley Hart, "A Gift Exceeding Every Debt," 339–49, and Hans Urs von Balthasar, *The Glory of the Lord,* vol. II, cited in Bell, "A Theopolitical Ontology of Judgement," 211.

92. Lidgett, *The Biblical Doctrine of the Atonement,* 142.

substantiation as the first canon of the Fourth Lateran Council, the very council at which he crowned Frederick as Holy Roman Emperor.[93]

> There is one Universal Church of the faithful, outside of which there is absolutely no salvation. In which there is the same priest and sacrifice, Jesus Christ, whose body and blood are truly contained in the sacrament of the altar under the forms of bread and wine; the bread being changed (transsubstantiatio) by divine power into the body, and the wine into the blood, so that to realize the mystery of unity we may receive of Him what He has received of us. And this sacrament no one can effect except the priest who has been duly ordained in accordance with the keys of the Church, which Jesus Christ Himself gave to the Apostles and their successors.[94]

It is important to note the contrast here between Innocent's emphasis on Christ's true body and blood in the sacrament on the altar and the mystery of unity with which he now describes the church. It is also important to note that this transubstantial restatement of the eucharist was prefaced by a strong reaffirmation of the one substance. As Innocent's council stated, "We firmly believe and openly confess that there is only one true God, eternal and immense, omnipotent, unchangeable, incomprehensible, and ineffable, Father, Son, and Holy Ghost; three Persons indeed but one essence, substance, or nature absolutely simple; the Father (proceeding) from no one, but the Son from the Father only, and the Holy Ghost equally from both, always without beginning and end." By prefacing the transposition of the substance of the incarnational Christ to the sacramental elements, with the reaffirmation of the one substance of the Father and Son, the essential link between the elements of the eucharist and the supposed ontological sovereignty of the Godhead is, quite literally, substantiated. This link remained so fundamental that it proved almost impossible to overcome. As the coming section makes clear, despite radical hermeneutical and practical attempts to reconfigure the church away from the traditional administrative structure of the ecclesiastical order, papal authority and propitiatory sacrifice remained central. The result was that although both Joachim of Fiore and Francis of Assisi made bold and radical attempts to re-access the now mystified and displaced body of Christ and reconfigure truly innovatory ecclesial

93. Kantorowicz, *The King's Two Bodies*, 196–7.
94. Halsall, *Lateran Council 4*, constitution 1.

expressions, they ultimately remained in thrall to the sovereign power, as the ensuing narratives show.

D. THE INNOVATIONS OF JOACHIM OF FIORE AND FRANCIS OF ASSISI

1. Joachim's Prophetic Ecclesiology

Neither Innocent nor Frederick had will or sovereignty enough to restore universal empire. This questioned the ecclesiastical and imperial vision of Eusebius's historical perspective. Joachim, as if in anticipation, while drawing on Eusebius, introduced a hermeneutic with the eschatological capacity to reinterpret history.[95] Born around 1135, he had several formative spiritual encounters during a visit to the Holy Land.[96] After a diplomatic career he joined the Benedictines but later separated from them to found the order of St Giovanni in Fiore in 1196. He died in 1202.

(A) AN APOCALYPTIC HERMENEUTIC

Joachim was a prophetic scholar of enduring influence whose chief work, *The Eternal Gospel*, consists of an exposition of symbols viewed as keys to the scripture, and an allegorical portrayal of the trinity in relation to history. He also wrote a *Life of Benedict* and a *Book of Figures* depicting the future shape of the *ecclesia*,[97] which is regarded as essential to the interpretation of the whole.[98] While twelfth-century exegetes had used apocalyptic to identify the significance of historical events, Joachim "formulated this tendency into a coherent new theory."[99] Exposing principles of concord and allegory, he discovered a dynamic intentional progress in the history of humanity's interaction with God.[100] Whereas Eusebius had highlighted divine characteristics, Joachim suggested a parallel between the nature of God's being and the structure of time. From a trinitarian ontology he developed a three-phased theory of history through which

---

95. West and Zimdars-Swartz, *Joachim of Fiore*, 37.

96. Bett, *Joachim of Flora*, 6–7.

97. For a useful overview of Joachim's works see West and Zimdars-Swartz, *Joachim of Fiore*, 4–9.

98. See Wessley, *Joachim of Fiore and Monastic Reform*.

99. McGinn, *Apocalyptic Spirituality*, 101.

100. Reeves, *Joachim of Fiore and the Prophetic Future*, 2.

he located the contemporary situation. This had enormous implications for the conception of time, suggesting that the age of the Father and the age of the Son flowed into an age of the Spirit that would arrive in the immediate future culminating in the third age of humanity. Some saw these periods as chronological eras implying that the clerical system was about to be superseded by the monastic orders. However, his choice of the Latin *status* to refer to each period and his careful exposition of them suggests the overlay of each in the progressive revelation of history, not the replacement of one by another.[101]

(B) An alternative ecclesiology

Contemporary research demonstrates that Joachim saw himself in fulfillment of Benedict's mission, establishing his new order in preparation for the age of the Spirit.[102] This adds weight to his proposed monastic reforms[103] and positions them as alternatives to Innocent's and Frederick's achievements. The Florensian order, depicted in the "Arrangement of the New People of God" in the *Book of Figures,* provides an innovatory template for the church and *saeculum.* The model consists of five oratories dedicated to contemplatives, arranged in four houses surrounding a fifth that is described as "a house of prayer" and "the seat of God," and inhabited by those men to whom God "has given the gift of counsel." The entire community is governed from this oratory by a spiritual father. The other four houses are for contemplation, the spiritual disciplines, learning, and those with old age, ill health, and handicap. Below them and at a distance are two more oratories that house the secular clergy and the religious laymen.[104]

Relating this structure to the trinitarian pattern of history, Joachim asserted that the new shape of the people of God carries the era of the Father (the married) and the era of the Son (the clerics) into the era of the Spirit (the monastic contemplatives). He relegated the secular imperial government to the imminently anticipated Antichrist, and claimed that the pope would emerge alongside the newly ordered community within

---

101. Ibid., 6.

102. Wessley, *Joachim of Fiore and Monastic Reform,* 8–14.

103. See McGinn, "Apocalyptic Traditions and Spiritual Identity in Thirteenth-Century Religious Life," 5.

104. For a helpful overview of the *novus ordo* see West and Zimdars-Swartz, *Joachim of Fiore,* 26–29.

the new time frame.[105] However, despite the radicalism of Joachim's practical interpretation of the age of the Spirit, the fundamental motif of imperial sovereignty remained unchanged. The monastery is still ruled by a monarchical father and Joachim consistently resorts to papal support for his reconfiguration of the godly polity.

(C) THE RESILIENCE OF HIERARCHY

E.C. Ronquist offers an illuminating comparison of both Joachim's and Innocent's practice of structuring items into a hierarchy, as evidence of the way sovereignty was submerged in medieval thought.[106] Pointing to Joachim's stratified arrangement of the people of God, he contrasts it with Innocent's treatment of the women in his sermon The Resurrection of the Lord.[107] "These three women signify the three lives: lay, regular, and clerical. The life of laymen is active and secular; the life of the religious is contemplative and spiritual; the life of clergymen is rather mixed and shared, partly secular inasmuch as they possess worldly things and partly spiritual inasmuch as they administer divine things."[108] Ronquist notes that while the two come to different conclusions about the relative importance of the modes of life, the same method of differentiation is used by both.[109] He concludes, "the allegorical construction of hierarchies, stacking subordinate and overriding concepts, does give evident support to what is theocratic, feudal, aristocratic and paternalistic."[110] In this way it was possible to exegete matters counter to hierarchical sovereignty without challenging its underlining power. This is borne out by the way contemplation is placed above the active life of empire in the New Order, yet a monarchical father still rules over the community.

The persistence of sovereignty is further illustrated by the qualified place Joachim gives to poverty in his innovations. Rejecting the active life as detrimental to the life of contemplation, and drawing on two key

---

105. McGinn, *The Calabrian Abbot*, 122–3.

106. Ronquist, "Learning and Teaching in the Curia."

107. Based on Mark 16:1.

108. Ronquist cites Innocent III: Sermon 27.

109. Ronquist, "Learning and Teaching in the Curia," 93.

110. Joachim of Fiore, "*Liber de concordia Noui ac Veceris Testamenti*," 3.1.3, 203–12, in *Transactions of the American Philosophical Society* 73/8, ed. E. Randolph Daniel (1983), cited in ibid., 247.

scripture passages, the story of the rich young ruler[111] and the communal sharing of the primitive Jerusalem church,[112] he commends poverty as a way of life suitable for the contemplatives at the heart of the community. However, "while to sell all and give to the poor and then follow Christ is the injunction for monks; it is not meant for the *conjugati* who have sons and family."[113] In this way he commends aestheticism for the order while the deeper underlying foundation of imperial sovereignty for the politics of the church and the economics of the *saeculum* is uncontested. It remains for us to consider whether Francis of Assisi's embrace of poverty provides a more comprehensive alternative to empire in the functioning of the church as the instrument of eschatological peace.

2. Francis of Assisi

Since his conversion at twenty-five in 1206, his early death at forty-five, and his canonization two years later, Francis has attracted an interest arguably greater than any other Christian since apostolic times. Within a century of his death thirteen biographies were already in circulation.[114] The level of attention continued into the modern and postmodern world with another fifty biographies compiled during this last century.[115] While recognizing the breadth of opinion, this brief account emphasizes three aspects of his life and work. His embrace of poverty is presented in contradistinction from sovereignty, the Rule is viewed as an alternative configuration of the church's agency, and finally the incongruence is exposed between his incarnational apprehension of apostolic life and his relationship with the curia's institutional power.

(A) The path to poverty

While Joachim commended poverty as an aid to contemplation, Francis espoused it as a means to social engagement. His progress to absolute poverty centered around three divine visitations: the dream of military

---

111. Matthew 19:21.

112. Acts 4:32–35.

113. Wessley, *Joachim of Fiore and Monastic Reform*, 66.

114. For the thirteen works see Raphael Brown, "A Francis of Assisi Research Bibliography."

115. Habig, *St. Francis of Assisi Omnibus of Resources*, 1699–1702; Robson, *St Francis of Assisi The Legend and the Life*, 281–9.

weaponry[116] that deterred him from the *negotium crucis*; the vision of poverty as his bride[117] by which he became "absorbed with the question of Poverty;"[118] and the third at the decaying church of St Damian when he heard the words "Francis, go, repair my house."[119] His response was to take the cloth from his father's shop and sell it to provide building materials for the ruined church.[120] His rejection of the *negotium crucis* led inexorably to the repudiation of the business of the market. This is demonstrated by Francis' response to the authorities when they insisted that he must return his father's property as it was "not right that the church benefit from money to which it was not entitled."[121] Stripping himself naked publicly he returned the money for the cloth together with his own clothes stating, "from now on I will say 'Our Father who art in heaven,' and not Father Peter Bernadone."[122] By this powerful act he opposed nakedness to the contemporary political and economic norms, and poverty to Christ's territorial sovereignty. Allegiance to the heavenly Father is interpreted as the rejection of the city fathers, together with the military chivalry and economic practices on which they depended.[123]

(B) FRANCIS AS INNOVATOR

Francis was a radical innovator. Not only did he reject the contemporary military and economic mores, but in response to Christ's call to follow without money, food, shoes, or extra clothes,[124] he declared, "this is what I want to do with all my heart."[125] His Rule rejects any indolence in the dependency on alms, requiring the deployment of practical skills and manual labor.[126] The resultant order offered a profound engagement with

116. Moorman, *St Francis of* Assisi, 12–25.

117. Celano, *Sacrum Commercium, Vita prima*, 3:7; *Trium Sociorum*, 3:7. This is the same Lady Poverty whom Francis sought so eagerly on the mountains "faint with love," in *Sacrum Commercium*, 1:8–13.

118. Moorman, *St Francis of Assisi*, 15–16.

119. Celano, *Vita secunda*, 6:10.

120. Bonaventure, *Legenda Major*, 2:1.

121. *The Legend of the Three Companions*, 6:19.

122. It is recorded by all the main sources: Celano, *Vita prima*, 6:15; Celano, *Vita secunda*, 7:12; Bonaventure, *Legenda Major*, 2:4; *Trium Sociorum*, 6:20.

123. Robson, *St Francis of Assisi*, 11.

124. Matthew 10:10.

125. Celano, *Vita prima*, 9:22.

126. "The Earlier Rule," 7:3, 115.

society, spreading rapidly and involving many lay people. As Sabatier claims, "it was a social revolution."[127] This is confirmed by the alignment of rich and poor achieved when Francis intervened in the political affairs of Assisi. The agreed *pace civile* stated: "Without common consent there shall never be any sort of alliance either with the pope and his nuncios or legates, or with the emperor, or with the king . . . or with any city or town, or with any important person."[128]

This new egalitarianism marked Francis' relationships with his fellow friars. He declared that God "delights to be with the outcasts of the world and with the simple."[129] His non-hierarchical approach was evidenced in giving others the lead on his journeys[130] and relinquishing it altogether long before his death. However, these innovations supplemented rather than replaced sovereignty in his underlying perception. As assumed hierarchies impinge on Innocent's and Joachim's writings, so neo-Manichean thought forms are present in Francis' work. This manifests in his famous "Canticle to Brother Sun" where there is no praise for Brother or Sister Man, instead only the statements "no man is worthy to mention your name" and "praise Sister Bodily Death from whom no living man can escape."[131] From this perspective his embrace of poverty included a partial rejection of the human.[132] For all its revolutionary socio-political implications it seems that his perception of poverty was primarily spiritual. This is borne out by his tendency to idealize poverty, identifying it with the Lord, the Virgin, and most typically as our Lady Poverty,[133] the true bridal queen of knightly chivalry. Michael Robson concludes, "this perception of Lady Poverty was inspired by the

---

127. Sabatier, *Life of St Francis of Assisi*, 156.

128. Sabatier cites Cristofani, *Storia d'Assisi*, 123–9. Sabatier, *Life of Francis*, 118.

129. Celano, *Vita prima*, 12:31.

130. *The Legend of the Three Companions*, 12:46.

131. Armstrong and Brady, *Francis and Clare*, 38–39.

132. Francis appears to make no distinction between sinful flesh and mortal flesh. Cf. "The flesh is always opposed to every good," in *Admonitions*, I:12, and "A person who is truly poor in spirit hates himself," *Admonitions* I:14, and "All those who love the Lord with their whole heart, with their soul and mind, with their whole strength and love their neighbours as themselves and hate their bodies with their vices," in *The First Version of the Letter to the Faithful*, I:1.

133. *Sacrum Commercium*, I:12; *Salutation of the Virtues*, 2; *The Testament Written in Siena*, 4.

gospels, but was supplemented by the world of romantic literature and chivalry."[134]

(c) Francis and ecclesiastical authority

Despite his focus on the Jesus of the gospels, a strong emphasis on the inverted Christ of the eucharist is prevalent in Francis' theology. The following statements from his *Admonitions* are typical: "those who see the sacrament of the Body of Christ . . . upon the altar at the hands of the priest in the form of bread and wine, and who do not see and believe according to the Spirit and the Godhead that it is truly the most holy Body and Blood of our Lord Jesus, are condemned."[135] It is this that helps explain his commitment to the ecclesiastical hierarchy despite his personal imitation of Jesus' lifestyle. "Inasmuch as their ministry is greater in that it concerns the most holy Body and Blood of our Lord Jesus Christ, which they receive and which they alone minister to others . . . those who sin against them commit a greater sin than if they sinned against all the other people of this world."[136] The two senior clerics with whom Francis built the closest relationships were Bishop Guido, the richest landowner in Assisi and a fierce defender of his power and riches against the civil authorities,[137] and Cardinal Ugolino of Ostia, later Pope Gregory IX,[138] who became protector of the fraternity and did not hesitate to use the friars to hunt down heretics supportive of Frederick II.[139]

Paul Sabatier's controversial view that these ecclesiastical connections were part of a deliberate struggle to defend the fraternity from the contrary values of the institutional church has some weight but cannot fully explain Francis' determination to secure papal approval of his *Rule*. Robson's disclosure of the medieval elevation of the heroic leadership of St Peter and the saints of Assisi from beyond the grave[140] contributes a more convincing interpretation of Francis' veneration of ecclesiasti-

---

134. Robson, *St Francis of Assisi*, 117.

135. *Admonitions*, 1:8–9; see also *A Letter to the Clergy*, 1–11; *A Letter to the Entire Order*, 12–21; and the second version of *The Letter to the Faithful*, 22–24; and *The Testament*, 6–11.

136. *Admonitions*, 26:1, 3–4.

137. Robson, *St Francis of Assisi*, 117, 31, 42.

138. Ibid., 126.

139. Van Cleve, *The Emperor Frederick II*, 190–1.

140. Robson, *St Francis of Assisi*, 1–4, 63–64.

cal authority and is borne out by the stories of Francis' visit to Peter's shrine in Rome.[141] It seems that the acceptance of apostolic sovereignty undergirded by heroic martyrdom remained, for Francis, the essential structural ontology of the medieval church.

E. CURRENTS OF MEDIEVALITY; IMPULSES OF MODERNITY

This conduit has attempted to show how, despite the decomposition of Rome in the West and the tenuous attempts to secure the peace, the on-going de-eschatologizing effects of the fourth-century lapsis predisposed the church to continue to seek for an immanent temporal peace through imperial sovereignty. The resultant pressure towards the maintenance and recovery of territory led to the bifurcation of sovereign power and growing conflict between pope and emperor. It became more and more obvious that the consequent division and competition was a hindrance to the church's agency for the peace and this provided the impulse for it to seek alternative ways for its procurement. In the end this led to schism and division within the church and the pragmatic redefinition of the relationship between the Holy Roman Empire and the other kings of Europe, both those who acknowledged their status within it and those who resisted it.[142] After the Protestant Reformation this increasingly moved the church and the competing monarchies towards the forma-tion of the nation state as a sovereign instrument that could contain and limit multiple sovereignties, as the third conduit explores.

In the course of this second conduit, specific trajectories have been exposed to show how the consolidation of the temporal power of the church was enacted by the transformation of the initial soteriological instruments of the anticipated peace identified in conduit one. Through the expansion of the understanding of divine law that the cross was seen to have affirmed in the fourth-century fall, the pope emerged as God's vicarious law-maker and the Christian monarch was defined as the geminally immanent celestial ruler. Through the *negotium crucis*, the violent sufferings of the atonement were extended to secure the defense and recovery of territory, which, in the increasingly normative

141. Robson explains that for the reforming popes the body of St Peter was "the most significant fact in Christendom . . . It was pre-eminently through his continuous physical presence that St Peter continued to bless and to curse, to cure and to guaran-tee." Ibid., 63.

142. Ullmann, "The Development of the Medieval Idea of Sovereignty," 3.

circumstances of bifurcation and conflict, meant that the willing sacrifice of soldiers in war became the accepted foundation of the future nation state. The transformation of the mystical role of the celebration of the eucharist by the reconfiguration of the liturgical, propitiatory role of the cross as transubstantiation transformed it into the immanent recompense of offended divine sovereignty and the present destruction of demonic powers. This eventually provided the currents of a further transformative impulse towards the legitimation of an exchange-based economy. In these ways the developing soteriological instruments of the imperially defined eschaton began to be manipulated under the pressure of the division and competition of sovereign power into the exercise of law, war, and money in the acquisition of the peace through multiplied sovereignty, as exposed in the coming conduit.

These developments were undergirded by a distinctly Old Testament configuration of Christology and had a huge impact on contemporary conceptions of the Christ. They not surprisingly tended to embody the sovereign view of transcendence and continued to displace the counterpolitical gospel Jesus. The inversion of the *corpus verum* furthered his replacement by the sacrificial exchange Christ, the military crusader Christ, and the territorial Christ of Davidic or Caesarean hue. These all combined to provide an impulse towards a legal, military, and economic Jesus. Such was the extent of sovereignty's penetration of medieval thought forms that innovative eschatological initiatives such as those of Joachim and Francis could still only make prophetic, transient moves towards an alternative Jesus and *ecclesia* that pointed to a radically different realization of the eschaton. As the subplot provided by their story has described, despite their creativity and courage, they remained supporters of the sovereign hierarchy at a fundamental level. At best their impact can be seen to have furthered the impulse towards the multiplication and limitation of sovereignty that was to be the eventual consequence of the bifurcation and conflict. Despite their intervention, the procurement of ultimate authority remained an intensely pressurized component of medieval politics, which led to ever stronger articulations of certainty imposed through violent conflict and theological argument. It led inexorably to the defining religious wars and decisive philosophical debates of the sixteenth and seventeenth centuries. The resultant reconfiguration of the relationship of church and empire is the subject of the next conduit.

4

Conduits of Christendom

Church, Sovereignty, and Money in the Genesis of the Modern World

THE SELECTION OF A suitable period to follow the late medieval vantage point of the previous conduit and provide a bearing on the genealogy of the church-empire relationship on into the modern and postmodern worlds was obviously a crucial task. The exigencies of enlightenment, reformation, and the advent of capitalism had to be somehow acknowledged and included. To this end, recent historical research into the seventeenth-century latitudinarian cleric Gilbert Burnet drew attention to the critical role played by his partnership with William of Orange in the transition of the agency of church and empire to the nation state. The recognition of the extent to which this strategic transitional partnership was dependent on the foundation of the Bank of England and its innovatory money supply, presented this as par excellence the opportune time period for investigating the shift from the medieval to the modern world. As a result, this conduit sets out the proposal that the multiplication of sovereignty and the passage of the agency for peace from the church to the nation state are substantial theological processes central to the genesis of modernity. It claims that they can be traced in the evolution of latitudinarian churchmanship, the interaction of monarch and people in the formation of the Dutch States, and the founding of the Bank of England.

Gilbert Burnet has, until recently, been a relatively little-known historical figure. However, current research is increasingly making clear that William of Orange's successful invasion of England, assumption of its crown, and deployment of its resources against Louis XIV's pretensions to universal power, would have been almost impossible without him. An underestimation of the role of William III has compounded the neglect of Burnet. The coincidence of the timing and partnership of them both, however, as two influential players at the heart of the genealogy of church and empire as it shifts from universal to multiplied sovereignty propels them to the historical foreground.

The events of 1681 and 1682 encapsulate the heart of this third conduit. With the passage of the Exclusion Bill in 1681 Burnet must have realized that, despite the interdiction of the Catholic James, Charles II's ambivalence towards imperial power still left the cleric searching for a partner with whom to reconfigure the operation of sovereignty. The suitability of William of Orange was perhaps not yet clear to him. But it was increasingly obvious to William himself, whose passionate opposition to domination by a single power was the purpose of the Association League ratified that same year to oppose Louis XIV.[1] Aware that the league might fail, William was as usual ready to defend it by force. But such passionate promotion of multiplied sovereignty needed money, lots of money. So in 1682 Sir William Petty's prescient answer to the question "What Remedy is there if we have too little Money?" pointed the way to the fulfillment of both Burnet's and William's hopes. In so doing it identified the ascending tide of modernity. "We must erect a Bank, which well computed, doth almost double the Effect of our coined money: and we have in England Materials for a Bank which shall furnish Stock enough to drive the Trade of the whole Commercial World."[2]

In order to identify the genealogy of the partnership in sovereignty of church and empire to this critical point, it is necessary to provide the broad brush strokes of some critical developments in the intervening centuries. Since the fourth century, the Western church had taken increasing responsibility for the social, educational, and administrative needs of society. The care of the poor, the university system, and the maintenance of written records were mainly in ecclesiastical hands. As a result the intensifying conflict between competing powers described in the previous conduit was widely disseminated. By the end of the thir-

---

1. Bevan, *King William III*, 75.

2. Petty, "Quantulumcunque concerning Money," cited by Clapham, *The Bank of England*, 4.

teenth and beginning of the fourteenth centuries, there were two and even three popes simultaneously as the church and the various proponents of empire vied for power. The attempt to resolve these disputes led to a resurgence of the conciliar movement.[3] However, while this secured a return to unity from the confusions of the papal schisms, the papacy soon reasserted its sovereign claims.[4] This issued in a plethora of centralized papal offices, bureaucracy, and expense that bred widespread discontent. The perception of an abuse of power associated with these social and political activities attracted much criticism. When Luther described the officials of the Roman church as "a swarm of parasites," he was only expressing the same sentiments as many orthodox clerics and secular leaders.[5] It is hardly surprising therefore that, when the Reformation broke out, it struck at the heart of doctrinal issues and religious practices that lay behind the corruption and exploitation.

Four defining facets of the Reformation countered the struggle for universal power. Firstly, the understanding of justification by faith that issued from Luther's struggle for assurance of salvation was a reform of the means rather than the nature of salvation. The proposal that justification was not dependent on exercises or ceremonies mediated by priests but was the result of God's merciful gift to be received by faith, effectively disempowered the ecclesiastical hierarchy.[6] Salvation implied, in Luther's words, that "a Christian is a perfectly free lord of all, subject to none."[7] Secondly, Protestantism effectively reversed the Fourth Lateran Council's affirmation of the transubstantiation of the eucharistic Christ. Liturgical enactment was rendered subsidiary to personal faith. Once justification was by faith alone, the offering of the mass was no longer necessary for salvation. The certainty of Roman Catholic authority that had been rooted in the exclusive priestly function of offering up Christ's true body was directly challenged. Thirdly, Luther used New Testament texts to affirm the priesthood of all believers and set aside the papal and ecclesiastical claims that asserted the hierarchical separation of spiritual

---

3. The most significant councils were those of Pisa (1409) and Constance (1414). See Heinze, *Reform and Conflict*, 49–52.

4. Pope Pius II's papal bull *Execrabilis* (1460) prohibited appeals to councils. Ibid., 51.

5. Cameron, *The European Reformation*, 30.

6. Skinner, *The Foundations of Modern Political Thought*, vol. II, 11.

7. In Janz, *A Reformation Reader*, 100, cited by Heinze, *Reform and Conflict*, 93.

and temporal estates and the superiority of the clergy. He regarded the medieval division of society into two estates as a deception.[8] This effectively made the apostolic succession and the whole Catholic ecclesiastical system irrelevant as no one now needed a bishop to ordain them. Fourthly, while the setting aside of papal authority implied neither the rejection of episcopal nor imperial monarchy per se, the rejection of the papal succession, the sacrifice of the mass, and the mediatory priesthood suggested that sovereignty was available on a far wider spectrum than before.

It was becoming clear that universal power in church or *regnum* was at the expense of the emerging ecclesial and political formations and their protagonists. Not surprisingly these looked for partners with whom they could create new agencies for the pursuit and embodiment of the desired peace. These political forms were required to guarantee the multiplication of sovereignty to the new contenders for power, while preserving the position of those existing authorities willing to make room for them. The endurance of sovereignty as the accepted means to peace propelled the church to rediscover its eschatological responsibility in new over-realized political forms identified, in the terms of chapter 1, as multiplied limited sovereignty. In order to engender these forms, the church needed to redefine its partnership with sovereign rule and create a new body that could encompass the emerging rights to power. This issued in theopolitical forms that expanded the already delineated shift from the passive theocracy of the church in relation to the *pax Romana* and the active theocracy of the church in relation to the recovery of territory.

This, as the last conduit has already shown, led to the expansion of the essential instruments of soteriology into the canon and Justinian law used to legitimate the temporal power of pope or monarch, the attempted military defeat of the enemies of the universal peace in the *negotium crucis*, and the inversion of the true body of Christ into the elements of the eucharist. Now, in the emergence of multiplied sovereignty, the first two of these expanded into the law-based latitudinarianism of Burnet and the warrior kingship of William, and were applied against the operation of universal power. The two trends came together in a soteriological combination of salvific law and sacrificial war that required a further soteriological transformation to complete their potential. It was

8. Ibid., 91.

this that the new currency of the Bank of England supplied. This third conduit traces these developments via three narratives. The first choreographs the theological and legal development of sovereignty through the political initiation of Gilbert Burnet. The second depicts the progress of military salvation through the career of William of Orange, and then the third narrative recounts the founding of the Bank of England in terms of the inverted Christ of propitiatory exchange reconfigured as the new money. Finally, the contemporary parallel biographies of Gerard Winstanley and William Penn are seen as counterpolitical challenges to this developing process but which again proved vulnerable to the ongoing imperial paradigm.

A. GILBERT BURNET AND THE DEVELOPMENT OF A LATITUDINARIAN APPROACH

The ensuing narrative attempts to show how Burnet's latitudinarianism contributed to a new phase of Christendom, in which the primary agency for the peace passed from the church to the nation state, for the maintenance and protection of limited sovereignty for both church and monarch. It did so by elevating the unity of the church and state above matters of theological certainty and by qualifying ecclesial and monarchical pretensions to power. As the means to achieve this continued in the cause of the eschatological peace, they continued to be soteriological in character. While the attempt to create an inclusive, comprehensive *ecclesia* within the bounds of multiplied sovereignty greatly reduced its future role, the outcome remained consistent with the genealogy of church and empire. From its theocratic role in relation to the *pax Romana*, through to the renewed focus on land that occurred in the aftermath of the dissolution of Rome in the West, the church's theocratic destiny and its concern for territory now combined together to configure the nation state. This account of Burnet's role in this crucial phase in the genealogy of church and empire draws extensively on T.E.S. Clarke and H.C. Foxcroft's early-twentieth-century biography.[9] From it we discover a man of prodigious literary output[10] who had an extraordinary impact

---

9. Clarke and Foxcroft, *A Life of Bishop Burnet.*

10. Clarke and Foxcroft list 154 published items consisting of sermons, reflections, histories, biographies, letters, and theological works. Another 164 unpublished letters are extant. See ibid., appendices II and III.

on the politics of his time.[11] Recent research has produced a new body of work, which significantly supplements the biography.[12]

Using these resources and Burnet's own writings, three particular factors can be highlighted in the transference of the church's agency for the peace. Firstly, a form of churchmanship unfolded in which, although the details of liturgy, doctrine, and ecclesial form remained within the church's provenance, they were subordinated to the multiplied sovereignty of which the state was now the guardian. Secondly, while a monarch could be the recognized head of church and state, he or she was also required to submit the final responsibility for the peace to the new construct. Thirdly, an approach to power gradually developed in which the emerging political structure could be secured and maintained militarily. The three sections that follow trace these trajectories: firstly in the development of Burnet's churchmanship; then in his search to find an adequate political partner in first the Scottish Secretary Lord Lauderdale, then Charles II, James II, and William and Mary; and finally in his gradually changing position on the necessity of force for obtaining and securing the desired structural change.

1. Burnet's Churchmanship

Born in 1643 to the Scottish lairds of Banchory-Ternan, Burnet was precipitated into the struggle for power between imperial sovereignty and the emerging new ecclesial and political forms. His mother, Rachel, was a prominent Presbyterian and his father Robert an ardent Episcopalian. Both played leading roles in the controversies of the time.[13] In Scottish Presbyterianism, church government and discipline originated from the congregation, following the Geneva model, and there were no hierarchical bishops.[14] However, sovereignty was multiplied not removed, and Presbyterians were supportive of the monarchy. Nonetheless, they

---

11. His *History of the Reformation of the Church of England* (1679) was the primary source for understanding the Reformation in England for at least a century and his *Reflections on the Thirty-Nine articles of the Church of England* had lasting influence on Anglicanism. The six-volume *History of His Own Time* remains a comprehensive historical resource.

12. In particular the work of Tony Claydon, Martin Greig, Andrew Starkie, Martha C. Franks, and Jennifer Farooq.

13. Clarke and Foxcroft, *A Life of Bishop Burnet*, 6–10.

14. Heinze, *Reform and Conflict*, 235–7.

opposed royal intervention in the doctrine or leadership of the church. When Charles I insisted on Archbishop Laud's liturgy, there was open revolt resulting in a move to abolish episcopacy, the leader of which was Rachel's brother, Archibald Johnston. Burnet's father, Robert, refused to support this, and twice fled the country.[15] With the advent of the Civil War, Scotland sided with parliament and, exactly one week after Burnet's birth, the English and Scots signed the Solemn League and Covenant abolishing episcopacy in Scotland in return for their military support in the parliamentary cause. Burnet's father refused to sign and left for exile a third time. Throughout this period his mother continued as an ardent supporter of the Presbyterian party.

Growing up in the midst of this was certainly a tumultuous experience. Burnet wrote of his mother, "She was a good, religious woman, but most violently engaged in the Presbyterian way," whereas of his father he wrote, "He treated those who differed from him with great earnestness and often with many tears."[16] Influenced by his life-long friend and mentor Bishop Leighton, it was the demeanor of peacemaker that Burnet chose. Although a much more retiring character than Burnet, Leighton can be regarded as the embodiment of the latitudinarian principles that the young cleric determined to build on. In summary of the impact of the bishop's views he wrote, "He quite emancipated me from the servility I was in to systems and received opinions, and spoke always of religion as a thing above opinions and parties."[17]

Burnet's precocity provided rapid opportunities for influence. Master of Arts before he was fourteen, he became Professor of Divinity at Edinburgh when still only twenty-six years old. It seems he never questioned the familiar equation of sovereignty and the work of the church. Securing the attention of Lord Lauderdale, Secretary of State for Scotland, he was soon on personal terms with Charles II and his brother, the Duke of York, later to become James II. Despite association with royalty, Burnet's zeal for the wellbeing of ordinary people is well documented. From his initial living at Saltoun where he visited the sick daily, to his untiring work as bishop of Salisbury a generation later, his concern for his parishioners reveals a clergyman whose pastoral commitment remained integral to his ecclesiastical and political leadership.

15. Clarke and Foxcroft, *A Life of Bishop Burnet*, 9–14.

16. Ibid., 17.

17. Burnet, *History of His Own Time*, vol. I, 243.

Notwithstanding William III's alleged castigation of him as "*Ein rechte Tartuffe*,"[18] Burnet was no hypocrite. From his early years in Scotland onwards, he endeavored to bring about a structural unity of church and *regnum* that would protect them from the impact of extremes of power. This can be seen when, despite the belligerence of Lauderdale and the increasingly autocratic rule of Charles II, he and Leighton attempted to maintain an inclusive church through the Act of Accommodation, in which both Presbyterians and Episcopalians would continue to work together.

The developments taking place throughout Europe provided the wider context for Burnet's theopolitical vision. He made two fact-finding tours of the continent where he acquainted himself with the progress of the Reformation, and observed the practical and political innovations of the Dutch Republic. He was impressed by their care for the poor and the high level of freedom in conscience and thought.[19] During his second journey he obtained Catholic insights on current affairs at Rome and used them to explain the horrors of Huguenot persecution consequent to Louis XIV's revocation of the Treaty of Nantes seen on his return journey. He recognized that the Catholic Church's absolutism required it to "extirpate heretics," and remarked that Swiss Calvinism displayed a similar tendency in requiring every minister to sign the *Consensus Helvetius*.[20] This balancing of Catholic and Protestant coercion typified Burnet's response to extremes of power and drew on the views of contemporary thinkers such as Leighton, Richard Hooker, and the Cambridge Platonists.[21] It consisted of a distinctively inclusive understanding of the church in which comprehension rather than toleration was proposed as the answer to the problem of dissent. This required a compromise in which conflicting powers could be limited yet satisfied. He determined that the Anglican Church could be broad enough to achieve this and that the Thirty-nine Articles provided sufficient flexibility to encompass his position theologically. As a result he took a stronger stand against

18. Bevan, *King William III*, 22.

19. Clarke and Foxcroft, *A Life of Bishop Burnet*, 48–50.

20. Ibid., 214.

21. Burnet was particularly attracted to Hooker's concept of *adiaphora*, the distinction that he made between those beliefs absolutely essential to salvation and those indifferent that are neither helpful nor hurtful in obtaining eternal life. Martin Greig, "Gilbert Burnet and the Problem of Nonconformity in Restoration Scotland and England," 3–4.

dissent than even Tillotson and Stillingfleet, his other latitudinarian friends. This was made clear in his tract in opposition to the *Naked Truth*, a pamphlet that they supported and that strongly opposed the Test Act of 1673. This Act aimed at the exclusion of Roman Catholics from public office, including the heir to the throne, James, who, although not yet publicly a Roman Catholic, had ceased taking the Anglican sacrament. Burnet's anti-Catholicism was confirmed when he preached before the Commons in 1680 and stated, "If any sect of Religion continues to breed frequent and almost uninterrupted disturbances in any government and it is evident, as it certainly is in this case, that their doctrine sets them on, . . . then such sect should be summarily banished from the realm." [22]

Burnet's anti-Catholicism and European orientation are central to his latitudinarianism and distinguish it from the traditional view that regards it as merely an Anglican initiative of moderation. Taking note of studies that question its existence as a distinct movement because of its stridency against dissent,[23] Tony Claydon suggests that the underlying sources of Burnet's thinking can be explained as products of his apocalyptic two-church model, as displayed in his pamphlet *The Mystery of Iniquity*.[24] He points to the way that Burnet identifies the Antichrist church as specifically coercive and persecuting while the true church provides peace and protection for the people. Claydon uses this to explain why Burnet sets the Anglican Church on the European Protestant stage, and why his anti-Catholicism is consistent with a commitment to spiritual diversity. As Claydon puts it, "It was religious coercion that was evil. Spiritual diversity was merely a necessary price."[25] Viewed from this perspective, latitudinarianism was not primarily about tolerance, but a strategic means of protecting limited sovereignty without giving way to universal power.

2. Burnet's Quest for Political Partnership

While Burnet and Leighton were working to secure their policy of accommodation for the Scottish church, Burnet published his *Vindication of the*

---

22. Clarke and Foxcroft, *A Life of Bishop Burnet*, 169.

23. Claydon, "Latitudinarianism and Apocalyptic History in the Worldview of Gilbert Burnet," 577–97.

24. Clarke and Foxcroft, *A Life of Gilbert Burnet*, 320–1, 523.

25. Claydon, "Latitudinarianism and Apocalyptic History in the Worldview of Gilbert Burnet," 577–97.

Authority, Constitution and Laws of the Church and State of Scotland.[26] Dedicated to Lauderdale, it outlines the view that royal authority is not inherited but is a contract between monarch and people, which cannot be broken except by mutual consent. His particular reading of kingly magistracy is that once established, "the sword is only in the magistrate's hands, and the people have no claim to it."[27] He asserts that if, in the extreme circumstances of anger or madness, the king exposes his kingdom to invasion, then "the laws and sense of all nations agree" that parliament should assume power "till he recover himself." But Burnet will not yet allow that this included the defense of religion, in which "the duty of the people is passive obedience." In this he accords with Luther who similarly holds two conflicting viewpoints in tension, stating on the one hand that no one should obey a monarch's exhortation to evil and, on the other, that if the ruler seizes your property and punishes your disobedience, you must passively submit because tyranny is not to be resisted but endured.[28] While these two positions were typically justified from Paul and Acts, they represented a fundamental shift from the traditional argument that the earthly power of emperor or pope proceeded directly from the sovereignty of God and Christ's earthly kingship. Now the pretensions to absolute sovereignty were set aside and the monarch's power qualified. No longer total, it depends in part on the sovereignty of the people. However, the people's power is not absolute either, because it is given away in submission to the monarch except in the rare case of madness or malevolence. In Luther and Burnet the authority of the church is no longer the means to the universal peace manifest through the imperial rule of the monarch, but the responsibility is assigned instead to a partnership of multiplied and limited sovereignty that their doctrine of kingly magistracy legitimates. This is a transformation of Eusebius's position where the church is primary agent of the peace and its soteriological activity in sovereignty and liturgy produces the universal power of the emperor; it is also a shift from the increasing polarity of *sacerdotum* and *regnum* in the second conduit, where the poles of sovereignty struggle for supremacy. This conflict now resolves and the agency of the future peace shifts decisively from church and empire to a new institution altogether. The church transfers its responsibility to

26. Clarke and Foxcroft, *A Life of Bishop Burnet*, 109–11.
27. Ibid., 110.
28. See Skinner, *The Foundations of Political Thought*, 14–15.

a partnership of people and monarch that together form an agency in which neither people nor monarch nor church have absolute power, but where the limited sovereignty of all existing powers prevails.

Burnet's *Vindication* indicates that from the beginning of his career he had a clear conception of the politics he was pursuing and the kind of monarchical partner he was looking for to achieve it. However, its dedication to Lauderdale was an immediate embarrassment. When Charles II's relationship with Louis XIV put him under pressure to include Catholics in public office, it caused such strain between king and parliament that Lauderdale looked to Scotland for support. Lauderdale blamed the ensuing opposition on Burnet and, as it involved a public demonstration in which two of his female cousins and his now aged mother played a leading part, it is likely that this hastened his decision to move to London. Lauderdale was by this time not only Scottish Secretary but part of the Cabal, the inner circle of intimates around Charles. Now out of favor with Lauderdale, whose charges against him he had not hesitated to refute publicly, Burnet arrived in London as an outsider. But he was still in pursuit of political partnership. Probably with the helpful influence of his wife, Lady Margaret Kennedy, Lauderdale's cousin, Burnet found the opportunity to preach and publish a number of influential sermons. In one of these, *Subjection for Conscience Sake Asserted*,[29] he emphasized the view that people should submit to "the supreme power God hath put in our Sovereign's hands,"[30] apparently in hope of restoring his favor with the king and Lauderdale. While it failed in that respect, it temporarily won an open door to the heir presumptive, James, Duke of York, Charles's brother, with whom he was invited to frequent audiences in 1675. That year the opposition party broke the Cabal and turned to Burnet for evidence of Lauderdale's wrongdoing. He gained considerable influence among them as a result.

During the next four years Burnet consolidated his relationship with his fellow latitudinarians, Tillotson, Stillingfleet, and Lloyd. At the end of the period he became involved with the affair of Titus Oates and the supposed papist plot against the king. His intervention for Charles's protection restored him to his confidence.[31] However, his support of the

29. Preached on King Charles Day 1674.

30. Clarke and Foxcroft, *A Life of Bishop Burnet*, 134.

31. Such was Burnet's reinstatement in the king's esteem that his *History of the English Reformation* was published with royal warrant and support in 1679.

Exclusion Bill sealed his fate as far as the eventual succession of James was concerned. When the duke eventually became king in 1685, Burnet knew that his own days of influence in England were numbered and he left for the continent where the request came for him to attend the court of William and Mary at The Hague. There Burnet conducted himself in his typically bold manner, subjecting the prince to a thorough cross-examination of his political and ecclesiastical opinions. He was taken so fully into their confidence as to find the opportunity to raise the question of Mary's submission to William in the event of her succession to the English throne and to gain their agreement that this would be the basis of any future reign.[32] Despite the fact that James II remonstrated with his daughter for fraternizing with Burnet, far from desisting, she shared her father's letters on the subject with him for advice on how she should reply. It seemed to Burnet that at last he had found the partners with whom he could pursue the desired new configuration of power.

3. Military Intervention

The *Vindication* had argued that once a monarch had been formally accepted by the people, then the sword was his and the people had no claim to it. The exceptions Burnet delineated did not include the defense of religion. However, by the time of his speech to the Commons on the occasion of the Exclusion Bill, he had made a major step forward towards the use of compulsion. In making the case that the adherents of any sect of religion whose doctrines encouraged them to cause serious disturbance to the government should be expelled from the country, he was clearly placing such persons outside government protection, albeit professedly for the sake of the peace. The progress of Burnet's thinking towards this position was accelerated when, in 1683, his friend Lord Russell was caught up in the Rye House plot, together with a group of supposed conspirators that included Burnet's staunchly Presbyterian brother and cousin.[33] The outcome was Russell's execution, which caused Burnet to reexamine his position on armed resistance. For whether or not Russell was guilty of conspiracy, his refusal to recant his public commitment to armed resistance in defense of religion made his death almost unavoidable. Qualifying the position of the *Vindication,* Burnet

32. Burnet, *History of His Own Time,* vol. III, 129–31.

33. The plot aimed to assassinate the king in favor of greater scope for Presbyterianism. Ibid., 186.

remarks that "but for the force of reason and conscience" his emotions might have tended towards "a bias rather in favour of resistance than against it."[34] These sentiments clearly gained ground in the last years of Charles's reign. With the succession of James, it became increasingly clear that there could be no way ahead without either a change of heart in the British crown or a shift in Burnet's position on the use of force. This became obvious once his partnership with William and Mary was forged and he was committed in his attempt to secure his desired new political configuration in Britain together with them. In the *Declaration of Reasons for appearing in arms in the Kingdom of England*, which was translated and in part shaped by Burnet,[35] William's threat of force was justified not in the cause of monarchical power, but in protection of parliamentary freedom. It was "a quite remarkable milestone in relations between crown and legislature,"[36] making the unequivocal point that the king could not act legally without the rest of parliament. It presented William's expedition as "a necessary preservative of English right and freedoms, which all honest and law-abiding subjects must support."[37] It is to the career of this apparent champion of latitudinarians and parliamentarians that we now turn.

B. WILLIAM III AND THE MULTIPLICATION OF SOVEREIGNTY THROUGH DIPLOMACY AND WAR

Spanning the half century from 1650 to 1702 and growing up at the height of the Dutch Golden Age, William III represents the role of limited monarchy in the multiplication of sovereignty in what was probably the first truly successful modern nation state. As heir to the House of Orange, and potential contender for the English throne as grandson of Charles I, he was the beneficiary of imperial sovereignty but also its victim. For the burgeoning imperial power of the French monarchy threatened his lands in Orange and his tenuous relationship with the English crown, while the increasing independence of the States-General was eroding the influence of his House in the Dutch States. In the face of this, William pursued the peace through compromise with republicanism

34. Ibid., 198.

35. Written by Gaspar Fagel, Burnet also edited and supplemented it. Ibid., 286–8.

36. Claydon, *William III*, 64.

37. Claydon, *William III and the Godly Revolution*, 26.

and resistance towards all pretensions to universal power. In so doing, he embodied the instrumental shift from monarchy to nation state and its developing structures. Whether or not he understood the soteriological significance of the strategy that was evolving through his displacement, reinstatement, and eventual advance on England, cannot be stated with certainty. That Burnet deliberately presented him as "the glorious instrument of the great deliverance of the kingdom from popery and arbitrary power" is without question.[38] What is clear is that the effect of William's policies of war and diplomacy was both the limitation and the multiplication of sovereignty. The narrative that follows positions William's role in the line of erstwhile Caesar-Christ monarchs like Frederick II, yet now distinct from them, and, in common with the Reformation kings, ostensibly delivering the people from the oppressions of universal pretensions to power. It thus recognizes his ongoing warrior status as fulfilling the ramifications of the soteriology of the *negotium crucis*. It investigates his career in the light of these considerations, firstly by setting his life in the context of the Dutch Golden Age, then in expounding the progress of multiplied limited sovereignty in the history of the House of Orange, and finally in exploring his defense of the emerging constructs of the nation state through war and diplomacy.

1. The Dutch Golden Age

The progress of the Dutch Golden Age in the two centuries that provided the background to William III's career can be viewed in four stages from inception to decline. During the first stage, the understanding of human freedom, inseminated in the Netherlands in the late fourteenth and fifteenth centuries by the spiritual movement *devotio moderna* and related forms of Christian humanism, led to an unprecedented prosperity that made them the richest region of the Holy Roman Empire.[39] As a result, the developing Dutch provinces were both utilized and opposed by the Emperor Charles V and his son Philip II in their competition for power with France. The emperors attempted three simultaneous moves against the emerging Dutch, employing their prosperity through taxation and loans for war,[40] opposing their burgeoning independence by cooperating

---

38. Ibid., 28, 31.
39. Israel, *The Dutch Republic*, 41, 241.
40. De Vries and Van Der Woude, *The First Modern Economy*, 93–94.

with the Roman Catholic Church to restrict reformed thinking through the Inquisition,[41] and working with the church to restructure the Dutch episcopacy in order to preserve Catholic Hapsburg control.

By the second stage in and around the 1560s, these three strategies of the Hapsburgs had pushed the emerging plural sovereignty within the Dutch provinces to breaking point, especially in Holland. The consequent revolt, motivated by the desire for multiplied sovereignty and the hope of peace, opposed the ongoing exercise of Hapsburg domination with a threefold response. They resisted imperial control by a self-funded military offensive against Hapsburg-dominated towns and provinces; secondly, they developed a sense of their own autonomy with recourse to reformed theology and Calvinist teachers, thereby turning the tables on Roman Catholic dogma and practice; and, thirdly, they replaced the new episcopal structure with a fluid and largely spontaneous priesthood of all believers, much of which consolidated over time into an institutional Presbyterianism. In stage three the eventual success of civil war against the strongholds of the Holy Roman Empire and its Spanish counterpart within, and eventually on, the provincial borders, led with astonishing rapidity to a Dutch Golden Age of worldwide economic dominance.

This seems to have come about in consequence of three main developments. Firstly, their military success opened up trade and economic prosperity both internally and externally, resourced by the easy availability of public and private loans.[42] Secondly, their theological and rational humanist thinking undergirded the multiplication of sovereign right while marginalizing the Roman Catholic Church, and, thirdly, the priesthood of all believers and the institutionalizing of Presbyterianism legitimated both the increasing prosperity and the ongoing multiplication of sovereignty. There followed a final stage in which a downturn in Dutch fortunes began, whereby their international dominance passed to other developing nation states and particularly to England. This decline appears to have been the result of a further three factors: there was a shift of the initiative for universal monarchical sovereignty from the Hapsburgs to the French Sun King, Louis XIV, whose ever-pressing territorial aspirations threatened Dutch survival and depleted their economy in an enduring defensive war; an over-dependence on a limited monarchical sovereignty for leadership and military expertise rendered them

41. Israel, *The Dutch Republic*, 78–83, 99–101.

42. De Vries and Van Der Woude, *The First Modern Economy*, 115.

in need of a greater measure of monarchy to defend themselves; and, finally, their consequent reliance on William III of Orange eventually led to dependence on the economic and military resources of England. As a result the Dutch States waned and Britain grew in power.

2. *The Progress of Multiplied Sovereignty in the History of the House of Orange*

It is possible to delineate four distinct phases in the progress from single to multiplied sovereignty marked by the career of William III and his immediate predecessors. These consist in a shift of allegiance from the delegated power of the Holy Roman Empire to the representative authority of the Dutch Republic, the faltering attempts to establish a monarchy, the testing of the boundaries of republican and monarchic power, and the assumption of military leadership. In the first phase, while the Dutch provinces were ruled by the Hapsburgs, the House of Orange was aligned with the Holy Roman Empire in its domination of the emerging states. Before the Dutch Revolt each province had a governor known as a *stadtholder* who was the emperor's deputy. Under the rule of Charles V and Philip, this position was held in the provinces of Holland, Zeeland, and Utrecht by William I of Orange, William III's great-grandfather. After the revolt of 1588 the role became redundant and the States-General of the Seven United Netherlands ruled sovereignly without an overall monarch. With the break from Spain, the Dutch parliament felt the need for a figurehead in their relations with other sovereign powers and appointed William I to this position. His leadership now shifted to the support of the emerging Dutch Republic against the Hapsburg Empire. This inserted a strand of monarchy into the emerging republicanism.

By the second phase, the Oranges were exercising power on behalf of the Dutch States against the imperialism of the Hapsburgs while attempting to preserve their own monarchy. With William I's death, his son Maurice was given the role of *stadtholder* and captain-general of five provinces and admiral-general of the whole Republic although the overall authority was retained by the States-General. He steered a middle course between monarch and parliament, which was supported by the political theorist Hugo Grotius and the Dutch Reformed Church.[43] However, after Maurice's death, his brother Frederick added captain-general to

---

43. Troost, *William III, the Stadtholder King*, 2–3.

his powers, thereby gaining full military control. His son William II continued to press for one-man rule and came into open conflict with the States-General. He only survived Frederick by five years, but in that time violently opposed any peace with Spain or France. He died suddenly of smallpox at only twenty-four years of age. In consequence his son William III was born posthumously into a situation fraught with controversy over the location of sovereignty within the Dutch Republic. Contradictory pamphlets were everywhere arguing either for the separate sovereignty of the individual provinces or for the supreme power of the States-General in concert with the House of Orange.[44]

The third phase tested the boundaries of monarchy and republic at the same time as the parliamentary forces in England were executing Charles I. In the Dutch States the proponents of the *True Freedom* theory, under the leadership of Johan de Witt, advocated the full power of the States of Holland without the rulership of a *stadtholder*. They held a Great Assembly at The Hague to decide "matters of union, religion and militia."[45] The conclusions asserted that overall sovereignty did not lie with the States-General, but with each separate province, and the States of Holland at the heart. The army, while under the control of the States-General, was to be directed by officers appointed provincially. But de Witt's approach, while focused on the limitation of monarchy, never moved to extinguish it altogether. Although he consolidated power to the detriment of William's position by the Act of Seclusion of 1654, he recognized the importance of the House of Orange and took personal responsibility for the prince's education, tutoring him in republican politics from the age of fifteen.[46] When William later observed to Gilbert Burnet that "he understood the good of a commonwealth,"[47] he knew what he was talking about.

In the fourth and military phase, the multiplication of sovereignty increased as both States-General and the House of Orange resisted the advance of universal power. By the time of William III this was focused in the meteoric rise of Louis XIV, who attacked the Dutch merchant fleet and declared war in 1670. De Witt had been an irenic leader, so when Louis led the French army of 120,000 troops across the Spanish

44. Ibid., 15–16.
45. Troost, *William III*, 19.
46. Bevan, *King William III*, 20.
47. Burnet, *History of His Own Time*, vol. IV, 60.

Netherlands and occupied most of the Seven Provinces, the Dutch could only muster an army of 25,000 men.[48] William and his officers prevented the loss of the Republic by opening the sluices of the polders and cutting off Louis's forces. De Witt was murdered and William installed as *stadtholder*, admiral, and captain-general of the Union. Gaspar Fagel, an exponent of Grotius' politics of republic and prince, replaced de Witt. Although the French demanded punitive remunerations, William's new power and popularity placed him in the position to hold out for a surprisingly positive peace agreement. But it meant that the victory over France became the defining basis of William's ongoing leadership. "He had accepted leadership of a country battling for existence against France; he had set himself up as the prime obstacle to Louis's ambitions; and had cemented himself in power on this platform."[49]

3. Defending Multiplied Sovereignty

Throughout the multiplication of sovereignty delineated above, the military role of the House of Orange was central. While the decades in which William III was growing up under de Witt's leadership were years of peace and great prosperity, the lack of the military contribution of the Oranges was exposed by the momentous events of 1672. After this the relationship of the House to the future of Europe was inextricably bound up with diplomatic and military strategies for the defense and maintenance of multiplied sovereignty in the face of pretensions to universal power. As a result the relentless requirements of men and money for war with France became a driving factor for William's relationship with the States-General and finally the motivation for his advance on England. The difference in ambition between Louis XIV and William III has been the subject of much debate.[50] What is clear is that Louis stood in the tradition of the medieval exclusive sovereignty of Innocent III and Frederick II, remarking in 1668, "my dominant passion is certainly a love of glory."[51] Like them he probably had no real pretensions for full universal power. But "the role of arbiter in Europe was one that Louis

48. Bevan, *King William III*, 31.
49. Claydon, *William III*, 20.
50. Lossky, "'Maxims of State' in Louis XIV's Foreign Policy," 7.
51. Bevan, *King William III*, 30.

XIV demanded for himself."[52] William, on the other hand, stood for the promotion of limited sovereignty for the House of Orange's survival and Europe's path to peace. But this made Louis an implacable enemy.

Only one approach to sovereignty could now survive in Europe, a fact that makes the period a defining point for the modern world. An eventual peace with France was formally agreed at the Treaty of Nijmegen in 1678. But for William it was premature.[53] He did not believe that Louis XIV would abide by diplomatic treaties. When his *Réunions* policy demonstrated that Louis had found a way of invading further territories, action was clearly necessary. William used the Association League to pressurize France into keeping her agreements and prepared to enforce them militarily. Originally the initiative of Sweden, it included the Republic, the Empire, Spain, and Bavaria. William tried to include England, unaware that his uncle, Charles II, was in a secret treaty with Louis. It was difficult at points of crisis to persuade the parties to act together. Their ambivalence towards imperial sovereignty inclined them to make independent agreements with France. This came to a head in 1683 when Emperor Leopold I, already at war with the Turks, signed the Truce of Regensburg with the French king. France immediately invaded the Spanish Netherlands and laid siege to Luxembourg. In consequence both Spain and the Empire signed a twenty-year truce with France. For William this demonstrated the critical situation Europe was in, and when the States-General opposed military action, he became convinced that "It is from England that the salvation of Europe must come, without her it must fall under the yoke of the King of France."[54]

In the aftermath of the collapse of Cromwell's Commonwealth and the subsequent restoration of the monarchy, William had married Mary Stuart, the eldest daughter of the heir to the English throne, James, Duke of York. In 1685 Charles II died and James II became king. As already noted, he was a Roman Catholic whom the Bill of Exclusion attempted to prevent from succeeding. In consequence his move to provide greater religious freedom for Catholics by means of his Declarations of Indulgence in 1687 and 1688 was interpreted as a threat to the freedom of British Protestants, especially in the light of the persecution of Huguenots with the revocation of the Edict of Nantes in 1685. Burnet's

52. Troost, *William III*, 71.

53. Claydon, *William III*, 23.

54. Bevan, *King William III*, 99.

invitation to join with William and Mary at this time may have been for diplomatic purposes, but, by the end of 1687, significant changes were influencing their thinking. It was officially announced that James's wife was pregnant, and if the child was a son he would displace Mary from the succession. As a result William's supporters in England began to see the situation as hopeless apart from his military intervention.

In May 1688 the Archbishop of Canterbury and six bishops refused to sign James's second Declaration of Indulgence and he unsuccessfully tried them for sedition. On the day of their acquittal William received the request "to make an armed descent upon England."[55] In the strength of this and in the context of his recently negotiated anti-French coalition of the League of Augsburg, William was able to mobilize "one of the most daring and impressive amphibious operations in history"[56] as the Dutch fleet and army supported his invasion of England. Landing safely at Torbay in 1688, pre-planned defections from James and uprisings by William's allies in the north undermined support for the king, who left the country for France. William was welcomed by a government-in-waiting who called a national convention, which, by February, had offered William the crown in an innovatory joint monarchy with Mary. Ireland's crown followed, being constitutionally attached to England's, and Scotland called a similar convention that recognized William and Mary several months later. James, meanwhile, had joined forces with Louis in support of an uprising in Ireland against William's accession. But William had what he desired, a base from which to challenge and negotiate the containment of the Sun King.

There were several important implications arising from these changes and developments in the sovereign status of the House of Orange and its role in the Dutch Republic. To begin with, they had become willing to give up a considerable measure of sovereignty. This was of course pragmatic, since they were without any real alternative option. But once William III had acknowledged the necessary compromise he steered a manifestly judicious course. Secondly, the underlying soteriological transformations of the cross continued to undergird the movement from universal to multiplied sovereignty. The republican configurations of law that secured the emerging States-General proved capable of safeguarding the survival of the monarchy. They also pre-

55. Traill, *William III*, 25.
56. Claydon, *William III*, 25.

pared the way for its relocation in the emerging constitutional monarchy of a latitudinarian Britain. Thirdly, William's military prowess, or at least readiness to give a lead alongside the republican government in providing protection against the reactions of the imperial powers, also revealed the price William was prepared to pay in order to preserve at least some sovereignty for his House. He was prepared to risk his life, but, more to the point, he was ready to apply his mind to the fact that it was rapidly becoming a price beyond anything that he could personally afford. The overall lesson of the Dutch experience was the need for partnership between surviving monarchy and the emerging bourgeois pretensions for power, particularly in return for the finances required for the military actions necessary for the monarch to defend both their positions. Money rapidly became the grounds for the compromise at the heart of the mutual relationship between the beneficiaries of multiplied sovereignty, and it was as the means to supply the ever-increasing need for resources for this that the banks emerged.

C. THE FOUNDING OF THE BANK OF ENGLAND

This third narrative describes the partnership of William III and Gilbert Burnet, and the enormous financial expense of the war by which they attempted to protect and consolidate the multiplied sovereignty necessary to the new nation state. It shows how the urgent requirement of funds precipitated the discovery of an innovatory money supply that both paid for the war and resolved the conundrum of how to multiply power without losing it. It suggests that this momentous intervention was of soteriological proportions in its impact and of eschatological dimensions in its outworking. It concludes that, as a result, the new agency for the peace became dependent on the long-term maintenance of its own credit rating and thereby opened the door to the lordship of Mammon. The section explores these developments under four subsections, investigating firstly how the pursuit of multiplied sovereignty through war created the circumstances that the Bank was established to meet, and secondly describing the two main provisions of the Bank's foundation, namely the loan for the war and the parallel innovation of civil loans for the same amount. The third subsection demonstrates from the language that William Paterson used to describe his proposal for the Bank, that he recognized, at least subconsciously, that it was a distinctly Messianic, soteriological innovation. As such it actualized the redemptive power of the cross for the acquisition of multiplied sovereignty. The final subsection then shows how the beneficiaries of the scheme were almost completely blind to these theological implications because of their subordination of faith to their desire for at least some measure of sovereign power.

1. The Continuing War and Its Cost

In the first year of his English reign William mobilized a military and naval partnership between the Dutch Republic and Britain and declared war on Louis XIV. In the ensuing twelve years he subdued Louis's threat to Ireland and harnessed British foreign policy into a war against French absolutism that was to last for a century. Together they formed a new Grand Alliance with Austria and Spain in the attempt to stop Louis gaining control of the Spanish Empire through his marriage to Philip IV's daughter, Maria Theresa, on the seemingly ever-impending death of the sickly Carlos II. Eventually, in order to prevent this worst-case scenario, William was prepared to enter into a deal with Louis himself, for the partition of the Spanish dominions between France and the Empire in the event of Carlos' death. When Carlos did die in 1700, his will rendered the diplomacy unnecessary as he left the empire intact to Louis XIV's grandson, Philip of Anjou, effectively combining the two monarchies. Louis's real intentions were clear when, on the death of James in 1701, he recognized the deposed king's son as James III of England. By this time the English parliament had passed the Act of Settlement and affirmed the Protestant House of Hanover as the successors to William after James's daughter Ann. Louis's action was thus viewed as an act of such aggression that when William was himself dying in 1702, "he knew that the English nation would continue his life's work."[57] The place of multiplied sovereignty in pursuit of European peace was guaranteed by the emerging British state.

England's entry into the war against France resulted in an immediate and massive increase in public expenditure.[58] When William came to power in 1688, the total revenue of the Kingdom was less than £1.7 million. Between 1689 and 1702 it varied between £5 million and £6 million per year.[59] Parliament had granted James II and Charles II before him

---

57. Troost, *William III*, 262.

58. Israel, *The Anglo-Dutch Moment*, 13.

59. Andreades, *History of the Bank of England*, 55.

the automatic right to tax revenues. Now, in a determination to avoid absolutism, parliament was involved with every financial demand. The majority of these were met through Customs and Excise and the new Land Taxes. The executive raised £32 million in short-term loans against these taxes between 1688 and 1697. However, of the overall government expenditure of £72 million during William's reign, there was still a short-fall of some 10 percent, and this had to be raised through long-term borrowing.[60] While this may appear a proportionally small sum, it was the critical factor that opened the door to the modern age. In Europe as a whole, the economic milieu had become increasingly conducive to the development of long-term loans for colonial trading projects within a financial climate affected by a contemporary obsession with gambling. This provided an environment in which risk played a large part in the ideas being developed. It was in this context that the concept of tontine loans[61] and annuities sprang up. In December 1692 parliament voted on the supplies for the coming year. In response, the House of Commons appointed a subcommittee to draft a bill for a tontine loan of £1 million. This was passed by parliament on 26 January with the proviso that, if the money had not been raised by May, the outstanding sum should be procured by the sale of 14 percent single-life annuities. Then in March 1694 parliament passed a bill authorizing a lottery of £1 million with £10 tickets, the holders of which were to receive interest for sixteen years. It was in this atmosphere that William Paterson and Michael Godfrey drew up their plan for the Bank of England.

2. Establishing the Bank

Parliament agreed that the Bank should be established on the basis of a £1.5 million permanent loan to the government for the purposes of carrying out the war with France.[62] The actual sum raised from the Bank's depositors was £1.2 million at 8 percent interest. The full amount was raised in less than three months, and was made up of 1,267 individual

60. Dickson, *The Financial Revolution in England*, 47, 343.

61. The tontine was a speculative form of life cover.

62. The official proposals for the setting up of the Bank were appended to a Ways and Means Act that was already in process as the pressure of the needed funds for the war was too great to go through the lengthy process of formulating a separate bill. The Act is now always known as The Bank of England Act 1694. John Giuseppi, *The Bank of England*, 11.

holdings, the maximum allowed being £10,000. This was immediately spent in its entirety on the war. On the strength of the expected interest the Bank issued a further £1.2 million of negotiable paper currency, which in turn was lent at 8 percent.[63] Basically the artifice at the heart of the Bank was that initial investors lent the *same* money to the state and to civil society. The loan to the latter was secured by the former in terms of future taxation. The security of the loan to the government was guaranteed in turn by economic growth in civil society. "It was a brilliant, self confirming system of mutual dependence and benefit."[64] Philip Goodchild notes four counterbalancing forces that combined to make the new banking system work. Firstly, there is the demand made by unproductive government expenditure such as warfare, offset by the opening up of regions for profit and exploitation. Secondly, there comes the provision of a secure source of transportable and convertible wealth, in the form of currency, for paying the military and equipping them with innovative weaponry. This strategic advantage leads to greater territorial success and increased growth in tax revenues. Thirdly, there is the ongoing demand for capital to invest in expectation of further profit and, finally, comes the payment of interest on the borrowed capital from the profits made as a result of the opportunities created. Assets and liabilities tend to cancel themselves out but the overall size of the economy grows.[65]

John Giuseppi delineates seven simple steps in the development of banking that led up to this point. First there was the move from barter to coinage, then the provision of secure storage for people who had more coinage than they required for current purchases. After this, there developed the facility to transfer money without the carriage of actual coin. This led to the judicious lending at interest of monies held and the general trade in bullion and precious metals. This was followed by the mercantile aspects of banking such as the purchase of bills of exchange at somewhat less than their face value. Finally came the issue of acceptable paper money "backed by gold or solid material wealth in one form or another either in the possession of the banker or at his command."[66] This seventh step was the last of the functions to develop and was the

63. Clapham, *The Bank of England*, 21; Giuseppi, *The Bank of England*, 14.

64. Goodchild, *Theology of Money*, 10.

65. Ibid., 9.

66. Giuseppi, *The Bank of England*, 3–4.

particular provision of the Bank of England. The critical factor on which it depended was the quality of the security that undergirded it.

When William Paterson first proposed the formation of the Bank, the parliament accepted the proffer of a loan in perpetuity but objected to the idea that the Bank would issue paper currency on the strength of it, precisely because of its openness to corruption. Giuseppi is of the opinion that this openness to corruption was sufficiently offset by the "honest" approach of the bankers who did not take advantage of it too much.[67] Goodchild points out that a similar use of deposits for loans by which banks effectively created money was developed in Florence, Genoa, Venice, and Amsterdam. The difference with the Bank of England was the interlinking of the government loan and the nation's growth to provide exceptional monetary stability. As the Bank of England's notes were readily redeemed in hard currency, they were not generally presented for redemption. As a result coinage was replaced by credit as the secure basis for the economy. In this way "the Bank gradually took over the money supply and responsibility to stabilize the value of money."[68]

3. Paterson's Economic Soteriology

In his *Brief Account of the intended Bank of England*,[69] William Paterson uses distinctly soteriological terminology to explain the Bank in four ways. He states that it will bring dead money to life; that it will be secured by the effectiveness of English Christendom; that the paper currency will deliver many from oppression; and that it will fulfill the eschatological hopes of the nation. Firstly, in evidence of its power of resurrection Paterson states that ". . . if the proprietors of the Bank can circulate their *fundation* of twelve hundred thousand pounds, without having more than two or three hundred thousand pounds lying dead at one time with another, this Bank will be in effect, as nine hundred thousand pounds, or a million of fresh money brought into the nation."[70] By this means a million pounds of paper money is raised for new lending from a dead two or three hundred thousand. Secondly, the efficacious power of English Christendom is vested in its long-term reputation for protecting

67. Ibid., 15.
68. Ibid., 9.
69. Paterson, *The Writings*, 81–91.
70. Ibid., 85.

property. As Paterson puts it, "there being no country in Christendom where property hath been more sacred and secure for some ages past not withstanding all our revolutions, than in England, it must needs follow, that nothing less than a conquest, wherein all property, justice and right must fail, can any way affect this foundation." In fact the whole purpose of the Bank was the soteriological task of defending not only the nation but the new structures of Christendom from this perceived threat of conquest by the encroaching universal pretensions of France.

Thirdly, the salvation from oppression lay in the Bank's ability to provide secure and inexpensive loans to both the city-dwelling bourgeoisie and the country nobility, who had become increasingly dependent on usurious loans from the rich.[71] At the time of the Restoration, most banking was carried out by the goldsmiths whose financial viability became increasingly volatile in the following decades.[72] By the first two years of William and Mary's reign there was much insecurity surrounding loans although the demand for them had increased.[73] In offering to supply a reliable source of money, both to the monarch in his parliament of Whigs and Tories and to the common men and nobles that they supposedly represented, the Bank offered deliverance from perceived abuse. Finally, the terms of Paterson's argument for the Bank are presented as an apparently perfect example of realized eschatology. The miraculous million pounds of fresh money provide for an immanent manifestation of the hoped for peace, they are connected to a past source, and look for a future fulfillment. He describes the proposals as capable of bringing the "designed work to perfection" and claims that they represent a continuation with a past age of peace "which seems to be reserved for such a time as this the better to enable the Government and people of England to recover, revive, and transmit to posterity the virtue, lustre, and wonted glory of their renowned ancestors." It also promises future greatness, for it will "lay a foundation of trade, security, and greatness within this kingdom for the present and succeeding ages."[74] These statements of Paterson's evocatively expose the origins of the Bank in the ecclesiological drives of sovereignty and peace as they pass to it in order to substantiate the new imperial politics of the nation state.

71. Ibid., 86.

72. Clapham, *The Bank of England*, 13.

73. Ibid., 14.

74. Paterson, *Brief Account of the intended Bank of England*, 87.

4. Blindness to the Underlying Implications of the Bank's Development

The far-reaching implications of the Bank's development appear to have been almost entirely hidden from the church, the monarchy, and civil society. This obfuscation was fostered by three factors: the almost immediate recoinage, the religious legitimation of the regime, and the controversy over Burnet's approach to the doctrine of the trinity. The unprecedented increase in prices and 25 percent fall in the exchange rate[75] caused by the influx of money raised by the Bank were blamed on the poor state of the clipped coins in circulation. The government was faced with two contending remedies. They could either mint new coins of nearly a quarter less value, the preferred cheaper remedy of the Treasury, or replace the debased coinage with new coins of the original content, the recommendation of John Locke, for whom the value of gold and silver was central to his economic theories.[76] Locke's remedy involved supplying the difference, which amounted to some £2.7 million.[77] Locke won the day and the government raised the necessary sums by a tax on windows.[78] However, for all the apparent moral and scientific authority of the argument, the increase in prices had not occurred because of the state of the coinage, but "it was the inflation of paper money that caused the steep increase."[79] While the gold standard provided the sense of security that paper currency could be exchanged for real money, few people asked for their money in coins. As a result Paterson's Messianic money supply multiplied and repayment continued to be deferred to a distant eschatological horizon. The supposed gold standard was in reality a veil over his extraordinary device.

Secondly, the Bank's economic innovations took place against the background of a shift of emphasis from radical politics to godly reform. Initially the new political order was justified by the Declarations of rights and freedoms for both the rural nobility and urban bourgeoisie, but once the new order was established the accent changed. Within a month, Burnet had submitted a memorandum to William suggesting a program of moral reform. Tony Claydon highlights three emphases that drew on themes developed in the earlier Tudor years of the Reformation: God's

75. Vilar, *A History of Gold and Money*, 214.

76. Manent, *An Intellectual History of Liberalism*, 43.

77. Vilar, *A History of Gold and Money*, 219.

78. Davies, *A History of Money*, 246.

79. Vilar, *A History of Gold and Money*, 220.

providence, the monarch as godly Prince opposing the Roman Catholic Antichrist, and Britain as the new Israel.[80] They now reappeared in Burnet's sermon before the king on December 23, 1688. A week later divine providence was the theme of his sermon to the Commons, in which he located William's accession in the context of the battle between the two mystical churches.[81] The picture of apocalyptic victory against the Antichrist foe was heightened by imagery from the Revelation, marked and evoked by the white clothes and white horses with which William marched into London.[82] Burnet's propaganda focused particularly on Queen Mary's saintly behavior and court[83] to justify the image of England as a type of the restored Israel. The resulting impression of William and Mary as godly magistrates incurring divine favor continued to hide from view the transition from dependence on God to money in procuring the peace.

Thirdly, the perspective on the founding of the Bank suggested by this conduit is that it was of crucial significance in the transition to multiplied sovereignty that issued in the conjunction of sovereignty and money and defined the modern world. Nonetheless, it is being argued that this was the corollary of the pursuit of the soteriological instruments of law and war, not the conscious decision to allow the purchase of sovereignty to supersede the propitiatory transaction embodied in the eucharist in securing sovereign power and blessing. At the time, this transformation passed virtually unnoticed because the latitudinarian approach subordinated doctrine to the new configuration of power. Two statements from Burnet's *History,* and his apparent preoccupation with a controversy, unwittingly caused by his views on the trinity in his *Four Discourses,*[84] illustrate this. In the first of these statements he asserts that all those benefiting from the funds created would tend to support the government's reforms "since it was not to be doubted, but that a revolution would have swept all these away."[85] In the second he affirms that "the bank will be an advantage to the nation as it certainly is a great

80. Claydon, *William III and the Godly Revolution*, 31–35.

81. Ibid., 28, 31.

82. Ibid., 55, 57.

83. Burnet, *History of His Own Time*, vol. IV, 248–9.

84. Clarke and Foxcroft, *A Life of Gilbert Burnet*, 320–1, 543.

85. Burnet, *History of His Own Time*, vol. IV, 124, 224.

one to the King."[86] But while he clearly recognizes the important role the foundation of the Bank is playing, he makes no attempt to evaluate it in theological terms. But this is by no means to admit that it had no theological significance. Burnet was preparing his *Four Discourses* for discussion with opponents that he describes as atheists and libertines, Socinians, Roman Catholics, and Nonconformists.[87] These were all those who might disturb the emerging state and so had either to be corralled into the broad church or excluded from it.

The second of these *Discourses* covers the atonement, which, although Foxcroft thinks is "far from clear," certainly maintains the familiar fourth-century position of the "propitiatory and expiatory sacrifice . . . both upon our account and in our stead,"[88] as a consequence of which God offers the world pardon for his offended sovereignty and the blessing of his peace. Burnet was almost casually restating the payment position on the atonement while its economic transformation was being introduced. As Martin Greig makes clear in his commentary on the third of the *Discourses*, concerning the trinity, this was able to happen without difficulty because Burnet's theology was rooted in his pragmatic epistemology.[89] This in turn was directed towards his latitudinarian objective in the cause of multiplied sovereignty. Greig makes clear that, from this point of view, his adversaries did not so much accuse him of denying the divinity of Christ as recognize that his biblical pragmatism could justify a Socinian Christology or a whole range of other heresies. If so, then they were right. His theology was subordinated to the practical purpose of the new politics in the cause of which the acquisition of sovereignty facilitated by the advent of the Bank was tacitly affirmed.

To summarize, the foundation of the Bank of England marked an epochal, yet almost unnoticed, watershed in the genealogy of church and empire. From this point onwards the progress of the peace and its ongoing soteriological transformations of law and war were subordinated to a new Messianic device that operated as the transubstantiated *corpus verum* of the eucharist had at the height of medievality. Just as the mediated sacrifice, which mysteriously purchased the divine favor and made the ongoing progress of the peace an eschatological possibility,

86. Clarke and Foxcroft, *A Life of Gilbert Burnet*, 320.

87. Ibid., 320–1, 543.

88. Ibid., 322.

89. Greig, "Burnet and the Trinitarian Controversy," 632–7.

had emerged as the overt and true Messianic body, now the mysterious device of money, which was really indebtedness, was substantiated by a piece of paper that could acquire the multiplied sovereignty that the growing populace was learning to strive for. From now on, the nation state was set in place in eschatological dependence on the ever-increasing prosperity necessary to repay the loans that undergirded the new currency. By this means increasing opportunities were granted for more and more of the populace to acquire sovereignty for themselves.

D. AN ALTERNATIVE VISION

Thus far the conduit has traced the trajectory of the genealogy of the fourth-century embrace of sovereignty and its multiplication in the latitudinarian policies of Burnet and William and the founding of the Bank. However, it cannot be forgotten that one of the most prolific outpourings of eschatological vision in European history was also impacting England during this same period. The execution of Charles 1 in 1649 had the apparent effect of removing imperial sovereignty altogether and, as Gerrard Winstanley explained in defense of digging up St George's Hill in Surrey, any rights claimed by the Lords of the Manors had been "cut off with the King's head."[90] In the decades that followed, the activities of those variously known as Levellers, Ranters, Diggers, and Quakers paralleled the narratives described so far in this conduit and arguably came nearer to achieving a truly radical breakthrough of constituent power in England than at any other time in history.[91] While they "anticipated and tried briefly to effect some of the ideas most important to nineteenth and twentieth century economic radicalism"[92] their fate in relation to the conjunction of sovereignty and capital prefigured their successors. For although they gestured past and forward in ways to which Part III will return, such apparently radical initiatives proved ephemeral and soon yielded to the desire for multiplied sovereignty. Among them, Winstanley's adventure in constituent power and William Penn's "holy experiment" stand out as bold attempts to promote an egalitarian way of life distinct enough to provide examples of why, like Joachim and

---

90. See Taylor, *Gerrard Winstanley in Elmbridge*, 7.

91. See Hill, *The World Turned Upside Down*.

92. Winstanley, *The Law of Freedom in a Platform*, 1.

Francis before them, they once again failed to provide a lasting alternative to sovereign power.

Gerard Winstanley was probably born in Wigan in 1609 and moved to London as a clothing apprentice. He prospered in his work, becoming a freeman of the Merchant Taylors Company in 1637. However, a combination of high taxation and trade depression brought him into financial difficulties, which caused him to leave London for the Cobham area of Surrey.[93] At this time he believed that he heard God speaking to him in a vision the words, "Worke together, Eat bread together; declare this all abroad."[94] In January 1649, at the same time as the execution of the king, he published the pamphlet *The New Law of Righteousness Budding Forth to Restore the Whole Creation from Bondage of the Curse.*[95] Joining together with the prophetic company of William Everard and half a dozen or so others, on Sunday April 8 Winstanley set about digging and planting vegetables on common land at St George's Hill near Cobham. During the week following, they returned in increasing numbers and began burning off the heath in preparation for growing grain. By the weekend they were at Kingston market buying corn and inviting all the poor to come and help them, with the promise of food, drink, and clothing in return. However, although it genuinely was common land, by the laws developed since the Norman invasion, this only meant that the tenants of the landowners of the manors in which it lay held specific rights in common on it, for which they paid rents and dues. The Diggers argued that this whole system had rested on theft and forcible seizure since Norman times but had come to an end with the execution of Charles. Neighboring landowners, the landlords of the manors themselves, and those stirred up on their behalves, regarded the Diggers' actions as an attack on private property as a whole, and amid appeals to the new Commonwealth military leadership, harassed them with increasing violence. As a result, the "budding forth" of the Diggers' new law on St George's Hill lasted barely a year and Winstanley appears to have settled back into a more conventional style of life. Nevertheless, his courage and uncompromising writings earned him a place alongside Marx and Engels on the first monument of the Russian Revolution erected by Lenin in 1918.

93. Taylor, *Gerrard Winstanley in Elmbridge*, 2.
94. Ibid., 3.
95. Winstanley, *The Law of Freedom in a Platform*, 2.

When Charles was executed and Winstanley was digging up St George's Hill, William Penn, an exact contemporary of Gilbert Burnet, was just five years old. Son of the wealthy Vice-Admiral Sir William Penn and his wife Mary, the extraordinary times in which he grew up had a profound effect on him. At only twelve, while contemplating the turbulence and injustice, he had a profoundly transcendent encounter that led him to conclude that he was being called by God. He was already a student at Oxford in 1661 when the Corporation Act required all municipal officers to participate in the sacraments of the established church, and the Act of Uniformity obligated all clergy to the Book of Common Prayer. In 1662 the Quaker Act made it illegal for Quakers to gather in groups of more than five members. This did not sit well with Penn's direct experience of God and he made no secret of it. By the time he was eighteen he had already been expelled from Cambridge for being too religious and a non-conformist.[96]

Physically chastized and sent by his father to Paris in the company of exemplary young noblemen for two years, in hope of distancing him from his non-conformist contacts and experiences, Penn afterwards spent a brief period studying law before being sent off to manage the family estates in Ireland. However, here he reencountered the Quaker preacher Thomas Loe, whom he had heard while at Cambridge, and consequently went through a defining conversion, embracing the Quaker way of life. Penn soon became a traveling evangelist and prolific writer in the Quaker cause of personal faith and religious and political freedom. By mid December 1668 when Burnet was being appointed Professor of Divinity in Glasgow, Penn was languishing in the Tower of London for publishing *The Sandy Foundation Shaken*,[97] challenging the established order and defending freedom of conscience. He was eventually released, with the influence of his father, the following July. In prison again in 1670 and 1674 and faced with ongoing persecution, Penn and his fellow Quakers began to pursue the possibility of establishing a colony of their own in America.[98] William's father had lent Charles II substantial sums of money to help fund the consolidation of the monarchy during the Restoration period. With his death, the king was indebted to Penn in

96. Fields with Fields, *The Seed of a Nation*, 7.

97. Ibid., 18.

98. Ibid., 21.

the amount of £16,000, a huge sum that he could not afford to pay.[99] So when Penn formally petitioned Charles for a grant of land in the New World in 1680, the king saw the possibility of discharging his debt and getting rid of the Quakers in one move. Penn found himself, at the age of thirty-six, as the sole proprietor of twenty-eight million acres of what is now Pennsylvania. He immediately embarked on what he described as a "holy experiment."[100] At the heart of this was the seed of what was to become the American Constitution, and a fledgling state council put together in a series of unique treaties concluding with the Great Treaty of 1683. By means of these treaties, Penn, entirely unarmed, recognized the Delaware as the host inhabitants and owners of Pennsylvania, purchased the greater part of what is now south-eastern Pennsylvania for the mutual, loving cohabitation of the two nations and included the Delaware in the state council.[101] In contrast to the small Digger colony on St George's Hill, this territory was vast and the experiment lasted for seventy years until his descendants broke the terms of the Great Treaty[102] and the Native Americans were excluded both from the council and their own land.

In the end, both initiatives, small and large, were terminated for the same underlying reason. For, although they represented a categorical alternative to the contemporary conjunction of sovereignty and money, they both remained dependent on the legal component of the Christendom paradigm. For, despite their origins in transcendent vision, neither of these egalitarian endeavors was configured on the originary gospel testimony that had supposedly motivated them, but on received law. Winstanley contrived an understanding of private property as theft directly from the Old Testament story of creation,[103] and Penn argued the basis of his experiment from the unwritten native rights of England, what he called the Great Charter and "our birthright."[104] The problem with making law the foundation is that, as the main narratives of this conduit indicate, it seemingly cannot prevail without being backed up by war. This suggests that unless a kenotic, resurrectional alternative

---

99. Ibid., 25.

100. Ibid., 28.

101. Ibid., 45–50.

102. Ibid., 86.

103. Winstanley, *The Law of Freedom in a Platform*, 59.

104. Murphy, *The Political Writings of William Penn*, 394.

is brought into play, law undefended by military violence is unable to stand against an opposing stronger power, in the Diggers' case Parson Platt, the local Lord of the Manor and his troops,[105] and for the Quaker colony the perfidious greed of Penn's sons and the competing colonial pretensions of the French.[106] This admittedly large claim is taken up and investigated further in Part III.

E. CURRENTS OF MODERNITY; IMPULSES OF BIOPOWER

Through these narratives it has been possible to document the process by which the fourth-century embrace of monarchical sovereignty and its bifurcation and conflict after the fall of Rome, transitioned into multiplied sovereignty without yielding the deep structural principle of imperial power. The interpenetration of church and empire together engendered the nation state as the instrument of the hoped for peace by the soteriological instruments of law and war. In order for this to succeed, a transformative crossover occurred in the appeasement component of the soteriology triad being traced through these conduits. The contrivance of substitutionary appeasement shifted to the similarly unequal device of the Bank of England's new money. Just as the transubstantiated body of Jesus was publicly displayed in the eucharist paying the highest power in return for a measure of sovereign peace, so the new money was invested in the national Bank in return for newly recognized opportunities of sovereignty for the bourgeoisie. In the process, the powerful and rich remained secure, now joined by the newly sovereign entrepreneurs. But just as the multitude in the medieval world became the subservient victims of the sovereign peace of emperor and pope, so now the new contrivance only brought immanent peace to the newly rich and powerful when the new money was compounded with the labor power of the peasantry, who were in reality the victims rather than the beneficiaries of the developing genealogy.

The shift from the substitutionary exchange Christ for the monetary exchange Christ of the new capitalism ensured the necessity of sovereignty to the progress of the eschatological peace even more strongly than before. For the future of the pursuit of peace through sovereignty had now become inseparably linked to the new money. Its agent was

---

105. Taylor, *Gerrard Winstanley in Elmbridge*, 10.

106. Fields with Fields, *The Seed of a Nation*, 95, 107–14.

now the nation state and its savior the Bank of England and succeeding banks modeled on the same contrivance. It followed that the nation state would now have to pursue a policy of encouraging ever-increasing trade in order for capitalist investors to return enough profit to pay back the interest on their loans and enough taxation for the state to pay its own debts to the bank. As the foregoing narratives have indicated, this result was essentially theological and soteriological in origin. It was simply another stage in the genealogy of church and empire. As such, its ongoing affirmation of imperial sovereignty and its implementation through law, war, and money provided the impulse for the future of the West. In this way, it is suggested, the developing nation states inherited their sense of responsibility and agency for the future ongoing peace of the world. The consequent conjunction of sovereignty and money in the continuing drive for peace and its ongoing soteriology became the impulse and engine for the commodification of life itself in the passage to biopower, as the fourth conduit exposes.

5

Conduits of Christendom

Biopower and the Century of the Spirit

THE THEOPOLITICAL IMPULSES ENGENDERED by the partnership of church and empire, as traced in the previous three conduits, carry the expectation of a world of soteriologically empowered nation states, promoting and preserving multiplied sovereignty acquired by money and undergirded by law and war. This fourth study attempts to explicate the contemporary West from this prospect, drawing on neo-Marxist thought to show that the outcome takes us through and beyond the anticipated configuration to a commodification of life itself, or biopower. The advent of the so-called century of the Holy Spirit is then considered as a possible counter expression of transcendence alongside it. The structure of the conduit necessarily differs from the previous three. As these have elucidated, with the arrival of modernity the ontological status afforded sovereign power in the medieval world was reconfigured in a multiplied, limited sovereignty guaranteed by the emergent nation state. As a result the position of church and monarchy underwent a substantial shift in relation to the anticipated peace, which now became the state's primary obligation.

The Western political system itself is therefore positioned in this study as the outcome of the continuing multiplication of sovereignty in the succeeding centuries of modernity. From this perspective the three components that provided the tripartite structure of the previous conduits, church, empire, and the pursuit of sovereign power, can be seen to have combined together to constitute biopower. In consequence this conduit is no longer the overt story of church and empire but rather that

of the ensuing contemporary order, which, it is argued, their covert genealogy continues to sustain. This elicits an account of the current Western
experience of biopower as the fullness of the church-empire embrace of
sovereignty, in which the naked life of the multitude is exposed as its material resource and ultimate destination. The soteriological components
of law, violence, and money are seen to facilitate this consummation of
eschatological promise. The perception of a radical disjunction between
biopower and the society of discipline consequent on medievality and
modernity, such as posited by Foucault, Agamben, and Hardt and Negri,
is explained in terms of the rejection of transcendence as the carrier
and legitimator of sovereignty. The blatantly transcendent character of
the late modern Pentecostal-charismatic movement, whose exponential
growth and primitive rooting in egalitarian constituent power appears to
have the capacity to reconfigure the relationship of *ecclesia* and empire,
is then advanced and its subsequent pragmatic capitulation to biopower
contemplated. Finally, an evaluation of the neo-Marxist recasting of naked life as the potential power to move through and beyond biopower,
and the complementary potential of living by faith that rests at the root
of the Pentecostal-charismatic movement, stands in the place occupied
by Irenaeus and Dionysius, Joachim and Francis, Winstanley and Penn
in the previous conduits.

A. BIOPOWER

This section examines the nature of contemporary biopower from three
complementary angles. The first of these explores the capacity of biopower to bring about the culmination of the pursuit of peace through
sovereignty that has characterized the genealogy of church and empire.
In so doing, it attempts to trace the progress of biopower from its starting point in the conjunction of sovereignty and money described in the
previous conduit. Its outcome in the commodification of the naked life
of the multitude is then delineated. Secondly, the unfolding role of the
transformations of soteriology in the advancement of this biopolitical
fullness is then explicated in terms of the conjunction of sovereignty and
money undergirded by law and war. Finally, the part played by biopower
in the ongoing subsumption of originary transcendence is considered to
consist of a continuity in the operation of sovereignty since the fourth-
century miscegenation, despite the suggestions of a radical discontinuity
between the modern and postmodern worlds.

1. Biopower as Means and Fullness of Sovereign Peace

(A) THE PROGRESS TO BIOPOWER

As the third conduit has described, with the invention of the new debt-money by Paterson and the Bank of England in order to pay for William's war with the Sun King, sovereignty and money conjoined. The new money left the "real" money and the property it signified in the hands of the powerful while at the same time making sovereignty available for purchase. The doubly indebted promissory notes were secured by the necessary future prosperity of the state, which was itself underpinned by the original loan to provide the legal and military support for the whole project. For the opportunity to acquire sovereignty to be ongoing and the necessary support for the whole enterprise to be provided for by the state, substantial profits had to be made. This could only be achieved by combining promissory loans with labor power, ideally cheap or slave labor, together with, and at times instead of, the labor of the investors themselves. In this way labor became the primary means of exploiting the agricultural, mineral, industrial, and commercial sources for multiplying wealth in order to acquire and defend sovereignty. From the neo-Marxist perspective this was simple theft, by which surplus value obtained by the exploitation of labor was transferred to the capitalists and their shareholders.[1] This was compounded in the eighteenth and nineteenth centuries by the enclosure of common land traditionally available for subsistence living, to be put to profit-making use by the landlords, with the resultant pauperization of the peasantry.[2] It reduced peasant labor power itself to the raw material for the exploitation of resources by which to achieve the profits necessary for the acquisition of sovereignty. These profits became the source of the tax necessary to secure the future of the nation state as the agent of the anticipated peace. It may be considered as one of the first steps towards biopower because, as the neo-Marxists argue in terms that will be considered shortly, labor power can be regarded as an attribute of life itself.

From the perspective of the genealogy here proposed, biopower was an inevitable consequence of the convergence of sovereignty and money. The Bank's promissory notes facilitated the multiplication of

---

1. Hardt and Negri, *Empire*, 31.

2. Thomson, *England in The Nineteenth Century*, 14–16; Hill, *Reformation to Industrial Revolution*, 268–74.

increasing autonomy to a whole new category of persons. It began with the rising bourgeoisie but ultimately it opened up the pretensions of individual and corporate power to all with access to the new money. As a result of the ontological status afforded to sovereign power, throughout the transformation from absolute to multiplied sovereignty, the purpose remained the domination of the many by the few for the benefit of the few. As the amount of autonomy necessarily relinquished to others grew more extensive, the remaining power still retained an orientation towards control by the few. It is hard to overestimate just how huge the impact of the reduction of sovereign power on those who yielded it up must have been. In the Christendom partnership, sovereignty was configured as an aspect of being. Hierarchy and superiority were transcendently legitimated. From this perspective the surrender of a degree of sovereignty for another to purchase involved harvesting an intrinsically transcendent element of one's own life for consumption by others and was no less a move towards biopower than the exploitation of the properties of another human life as labor power. The incorporation of both these aspects of being, immanent and transcendent, labor power and sovereign power, into the production process, together provided the necessary initial ingredients for the eventual commodification of life itself.

Viewed along the immanent plane, the potential power made available by the new money was the power to purchase labor. Adding the transcendent perspective, it was the power to purchase labor for the purpose of multiplying sovereignty. In the modern law-based latitudinarian state, what Foucault and the neo-Marxists after him describe as a society characterized by discipline,[3] the populace was ordered for the purposes of exploiting labor power and the multiplication of sovereignty. In the course of modernity this gave way to what is termed the society of control, in which the mechanisms of command became "ever more 'democratic,' ever more immanent to the social field, distributed throughout the brains and bodies of citizens"[4] and everything was reduced to monetary value.[5] Foucault is the first to describe this process as biopower or the power "to invest life through and through."[6] He uses the

---

3. Foucault, *The History of Sexuality*, vol. I, 140; Hardt and Negri, *Empire*, 23.

4. Hardt and Negri, *Empire*, 23.

5. Ibid., 32.

6. Foucault, *The History of Sexuality*, vol. I, 139.

concept to refer to the subsumption of the whole of life, social relations, communications systems, information and affective networks into the process of production. The concept is organized around two basic poles. The first centers on the development of the human body as an identifiable machine, and disciplines its capabilities, forces, usefulness, and docility, what Foucault calls the "anatomo-politics of the human body."[7] The second focuses on the body as a biological species, regulating and controlling the processes of propagation, birth, and mortality, and the level and conditions of health, life expectancy, and longevity, what he calls "a biopolitics of the population." In this way the human body is identified as both the engine of production and its raw material. The proposed genealogy of church and empire adds to this a transcendent perspective and regards Western life as having already been subsumed by sovereignty, at least since the fourth century. From this standpoint, the first of Foucault's two poles already includes the desire for sovereignty as part of the body's anatomo-politics, and biopower thus encompasses the fullness of human being, body and spirit. Put simply, there develops a corporate mindset that consumption is what life is about.

While the disciplinary institutions remain, the state is seen to give way to an internal and embodied commodification of the multitude with no identifiable outside. Instead of the populace needing to be consciously organized to keep the rules, the behavior appropriate to the commodification of life for the pursuit of sovereignty is increasingly interiorized and accepted in the subjects themselves. However, while the bounds of sovereignty for individual rulers diminished with its commodification and spread throughout the populace, its ontological nature as the means to peace remained unchanged. The enigma inherent in the drive to domination is that it ultimately grants the right of everyone to as much sovereignty as they can muster while relinquishing a degree of autonomy, smaller or larger depending on the starting point, for others to purchase. In sum, the terms for peace are the paradoxical circumstances of yielding maximum purchasable power to as many persons as possible commensurate with holding on to as much as possible. In this respect a crucial component of the transition to biopower was the inclusion of the multitude in the pursuit of sovereign power. As Hardt and Negri make clear, this was the impact of "the Golden Age of the New Deal reform of

7. Ibid., 139.

capitalism on the world stage."[8] It is important to emphasize that instead of this resulting in greater freedom, it expedited the incorporation of the multitude into the society of control. In consequence they became subsumed by the *telos* in which life became the acquisition and production of sovereignty from the individual outwards, in and through the whole universe of being.

(B) THE NAKED LIFE OF THE MULTITUDE

The concept of the multitude is basic to the neo-Marxist analysis of biopower and in order to grasp its importance, several points need to be emphasized. Current neo-Marxist literature traces the reemergence of the multitude as a new subjectivity surfacing through the experience of history and the process of production. The historical development arose through the twentieth-century's hard lessons where people's army soon became oppressor.[9] The contemporary multitude is regarded as a recovery of ground lost during the counter-revolutionary resurgence after the renaissance challenged the transcendence of sovereignty with immanence.[10] It is a new subjectivity that includes all those involved in the production process and is distinct from "people," which was subsumed by the counter-revolutionary sovereignty of the state. Hardt and Negri emphasize the multitude's composition as a set of singularities characterized by unresolved difference in contrast to "the people" that arrives at unity by setting aside difference.[11] Agamben describes the distinction in terms of a fundamental split between naked life (people) and political existence (People). The latter constitutes the body politic, while the former remains the excluded class.[12] Virno utilizes the terms "centrifugal" and "centripetal" to capture the difference between the two concepts.[13] The contemporary multitude's centrifugal movements are not centered by anyone; they are spontaneous reactions to the moment, always and only manifesting the One of the many. This is in contrast to the One of

---

8. Hardt and Negri, *Empire*, 244.

9. Hardt and Negri, *Multitude*, 73–74.

10. Hardt and Negri, *Empire*, 74.

11. Hardt and Negri, *Multitude*, 99.

12. Agamben asserts that there is no exception to this and "it surely reflects an ambiguity inherent in the nature and function of the concept of people in Western politics." Agamben, *Means without End*, 31.

13. Virno, *A Grammar of the Multitude*, 42.

the people that makes a centripetal trajectory from atomized individuals to sovereignty, via the unity of the body politic. In sum "the people" serves the imperialism of the state and the multitude is exploited by it.

The consequence of the economic success of the nation state as a result of the conjunction of sovereignty and money, and the course of its progress towards the increasing inclusion of the multitude in the biopolitical process, is that immaterial forms of labor have developed that combine with money to produce biopower. These have now replaced the primary role of traditional productive work such as agriculture and mining and the related industries of food and automobile manufacture and, as Hardt and Negri have argued, have emerged to define labor power in three ways.[14] Firstly, in the communicative labor of industrial production, informational networks transform the production process. Instead of driving the market, production now interfaces and communicates with it. Secondly, in interactive labor, symbolic analysis and problem solving are increasingly interposed between the worker and their object of labor, as in computerized tailoring or weaving. Thirdly, in the labor of the production and manipulation of affects, such as health services and entertainment, actual or virtual bodily contacts produce sensory feelings that generally have no material outcome. This cooperation that is normative to immaterial labor has placed a new constituent power in the multitude's hands. Involving the production of thought, language, communication, and image, it consists in the hybridization of intellect both within the functioning of labor and in political action.[15] Cooperation, centripetal in purpose in the modern world of Fordist labor, is centrifugal in its effects in the biopolitical world of affective labor. Unlike the working class, which was defined by its indispensability to the production process, and could hinder it by withholding labor, the multitude has positive power because it can function as a distributed network. Hardt and Negri describe this as the fullness of the multitude. For Marx, the proletariat referred to those who labored for, rather than benefited from capital, and as such were in direct opposition to it. But now, these binary distinctions break down and the multitude consists of all those who labor and produce under the rule of capital.

Paolo Virno gives clarity to this concept of immaterial labor by describing it as "the aggregate of those mental and physical capabilities

14. Hardt and Negri, *Empire*, 293.
15. Virno, *A Grammar of the Multitude*, 65.

existing in physical form, the living personality of a human being."[16] He describes the propensity of the multitude to yield up these attributes as commodities in the service of the state, as the statization of the intellect.[17] He analyzes this development by means of exploring the dissolution of what he posits to be the ancient and universally accepted structure of knowledge. He maintains that the Aristotelian tri-positioning of labor, action, and intellect as independent categories of life continued right up until the 1960s but that this partitioning has now dissolved.[18] As the previous conduits have indicated, the accepted structure of knowledge was also the carrier of ontological sovereignty. Its dissolution still leaves the pursuit of sovereignty intact as the controlling motivation of being. So when Virno shows that by encompassing the immaterial, this extended labor power subsumes the life of the mind as well as the body, it is important to recognize that this includes the desire for sovereignty. As this potential power has as yet no separate existence, it must be part of the living person of the laborer. This potential power now includes the whole gamut of human capacity and is indistinguishable from naked life. "'Life,' pure and simple *bios*, acquires a specific importance in as much as it is the tabernacle of *dunamis*, of mere potential."[19] This, says Virno, is the heart of biopower.[20]

The phrase "naked life" encapsulates the fusion of capital and sovereignty that characterizes biopower. As translated into English, it represents a semantic family that includes "bare life," "mere life," and "the flesh of the multitude." Hardt and Negri refer both to "naked life"[21] and "the flesh of the multitude,"[22] Agamben opts for the term "bare life,"[23] and Walter Benjamin "mere life."[24] Altogether it is a capacious symbol that denotes the focus of economic activity, the eschatological goal of sovereignty, and the consummate expression of exploitation. It encompasses physical labor power, immaterial labor power, and the degree of personal

16. Ibid., 81.
17. Ibid., 67.
18. Ibid., 51.
19. Ibid., 82.
20. Ibid., 83.
21. Hardt and Negri, *Empire*, 32.
22. Hardt and Negri, *Multitude*, 101, 189.
23. Agamben, *Homo Sacer*, 4–5.
24. Benjamin, *One Way Street*, 151.

sovereignty yielded in order to preserve the remainder. Representing the sum total of the mental, physical, and spiritual capabilities of human life, it is the object of money, what it must purchase in order to multiply itself and the sovereignty it bestows. But it is also the eschatological end of the capitalization of potential power for the sake of sovereignty, for paradoxically it also represents the unrestricted freedom of sovereignty. It is the sum total of what someone has left when they have risked everything for the sake of preserving their own autonomy. In this it is possible to see the actions of the boy Frederick II, ripping off his clothes and even his skin, as an antecedent of naked life and the price willing to be paid for sovereignty. It follows that the concept of naked life is also rapacious, encompassing the Faustian aspect of selling one's own soul.

For the sake of maintaining sovereignty, money is let loose to pay for law and war. But it only brings an adequate return, what Paterson called raising dead money, by purchasing life itself. More and more naked life is consumed to this end until one's own life is the price paid for naked freedom. The impact of this is evocatively portrayed in Naomi Wallace's contemporary drama *Things of Dry Hours*. Set in 1932, the dramatist's choice of a period at the heart of both Pentecostal revival and Communist mobilization suggests their common significance as means to transform the life of the multitude. The central character, Corbin, is depicted at the mercy of the consuming biopolitical hegemony of the Tennessee Coal and Iron Company and the inadequacies of Marxist immanence and Pentecostal transcendence, represented by the African-American Tice who offers him shelter, and symbolized by the sheets of washing that his daughter takes in. To provoke an answer to the question "How far are you prepared to go to make yourself a new man?" Tice gradually entices Corbin to remove his clothes until finally he strips off his underpants and is revealed stark naked at center stage.[25] In place of the naked Christ, emptying out his sovereignty for the life of the world, the end pursuit of autonomous power is revealed as naked humanity devouring its own flesh for the sake of sovereignty. Yet it is at this point that it is possible to glimpse a possible aperture through which naked life might evoke engagement with resistance[26] and become the means to the *katargēsis* of biopower. It is to this effect that Wallace achieves a portrayal of naked victimhood in her play that is also beauty and hope, calling for

25. Wallace, *Things of Dry Hours*, 66.
26. Hardt and Negri, *Empire*, 366.

a recovered transcendence with the capacity to reconfigure naked life as gift. In this sense naked life is both the multitude's constituted capacity to provide capital and the constituent power it possesses against it. This hope for transformation that the neo-Marxists develop is explored as part of the alternative substratum of the conduit in the final section. But first it is necessary to expose the ongoing soteriology within the genealogy of church and Christendom that has led to the point where the naked life of the multitude has become both the fullness of biopower as well as its possible *katargēsis*.

2. Christendom Soteriology and the Advancement of Biopower

The genealogy of sovereign power exposed in the first conduit and traced in this conduit to its fullness in biopower was, it is suggested, legitimized by an Old Testament Christology of imperial kingship. This viewed the Christ as one subordinate substance with the Father for the restoration of sovereignty through a soteriology of atonement in which sovereignty was appeased, the law upheld, and the powers overcome by the violence of Christ's sufferings. The second conduit disclosed the ongoing promulgation of sovereignty through an enlargement of this soteriology in which Christ's appeasement was transubstantiated into a regular public payment in the mass, the affirmation of the law was expanded into the canons of the papacy and the reinstituted Roman *Justitia*, and Christ's sufferings were imitated in the *negotium crucis*. The third conduit described how the regular public liturgical propitiation of sovereignty, reconstituted as a once-for-all payment by the reformers, was transformed to exchange Christ for money with which to purchase sovereignty, while the laws of church and state transitioned into the latitudinarian theopolitics that the violent military business of the cross initiated and defended. By means of this progressive genealogy it is proposed that the necessity of payment for restored sovereignty, both God's and humanity's in relationship to it, together with its legal justification and military defense, was established at the center of Western consciousness.

(A) THE FULLNESS OF MONEY

As this conduit has already described, the conjunction of sovereignty and money is now expanding to fill all things. Contemporary events demonstrate the outcome of this in practical terms. The day that this is being written is Wednesday October 20, 2010, the day of the British Coalition

Government's spending review in the aftermath of the 2008 banking crisis. In order to ensure the survival of three of the major banks, Royal Bank of Scotland, Lloyds TSB, and HBOS, the British Government injected £37 billion on September 13, 2008.[27] On May 11, 2009 the Bank of England injected a further £50 billion into the economy by buying up government and corporate debt in a bid to bring down long-term interest rates. This fullness of the Bank's creation of money from debt, what Channel Four economics correspondent Faisal Islam calls "magic money the bank is assuming into existence,"[28] can be seen as the continuing price of Christendom's pursuit of peace through sovereignty. Two things are happening. The Bank of England has once more created new debt-money secured against the future prosperity of the country, and this eschatological security has been drawn down to ensure that the banks themselves do not collapse. As a result, the future is engulfing the present in indebtedness. There is no longer a permanently deferred outcome to this debt but the public is required to accept £81 billion[29] of real cuts in services that will in many cases excoriate life itself. It will, for example, be instantiated in the £30,000 debt with which average British graduates will begin their working life.[30] In this way the fourth-century assumption, that peace on earth is secured by the operation of sovereignty paid for by the flesh of God's Son and substantiated by the *ecclesia* through soteriological means, has translated into the wholesale consumption of human life and habitat.

(b) Law

In today's political context where power and money have conjoined to produce an unequal sovereignty for all by the consumption of life itself, the underlying function of law is increasingly only the maintenance of the conditions necessary to this commodification. In the same October 2010 response to the economic crisis referred to above, the British Coalition Government imposed cuts in child benefit that set aside part of a sixty-year-old law that had established the universality of the welfare state. These and other financial cuts also broke the unequivocal prom-

27. *BBC Business News*, September 13, 2008.

28. Faisal Islam, *Channel Four News*, transcript from *The Real News Network*, May 11, 2009.

29. *Financial Times*, October 20, 2010.

30. *The Browne Report*, transcript from the *BBC News*, October 14, 2010.

ises of the manifestos of both Coalition parties. This seemingly casual approach to law and politics is justified by party leaders as obviously unavoidable by reason of the economic situation. In other words the maintenance of the ongoing financial sustainability of the state to vouchsafe the acquisition of sovereign power is of such paramount importance as to set aside democratically negotiated laws that established principles of justice. This discloses the status of law as a subsidiary principle belying a covert *telos* that reveals its actual biopolitical function. The law is not primarily there to sustain the principles of justice, but rather the economic conditions that are assumed to be necessary for the continuation of just decrees. This was already discernible in the use of law in the latitudinarian origins of the nation state explored in the third conduit. Today, however, law no longer prescribes the external shape for society, but rather impels its internal dynamic, preserving the biopolitical order and justifying its defense against any kind of threat.

It is the increasing contemporary exertion of this underlying capacity of law that Giorgio Agamben identifies in his adoption of the phrase "state of exception."[31] The concept originates with the writings of Carl Schmitt, who differentiates between two applications of the exception, a reactionary means to reestablish constituted power that he describes as "commissarial dictatorship," and a revolutionary means to release constituent power that he refers to as "sovereign dictatorship."[32] Agamben, however, explains its current application not as the temporary suspension of law in order to prepare for its reconstitution in either direction, but as the permanent affirmation of the conjunction of authority and power. The political power that is represented by law no longer simply prescribes the written or unwritten constitutional, religious, or humanistic ideals of morality and justice, but fuses with the authority that lies behind those formulations. This transpires to be the unrelenting authority of the market. This recognition of the conjunction of authority and power in biopower acutely identifies the initial pathway of the soteriological genealogy of Western law. Although the separation of the two was only apparent, in fourth-century Rome and medieval Europe the dialectic of emperor and senate, *sacerdotum* and *regnum*, could function peacefully until bifurcation and conflict became intolerable. But their combination in the conjunction of sovereignty and money is coming to

31. Agamben, *State of Exception*.
32. Ibid., 32.

a fullness in the nation state and the biopolitical order into which it is now opening out, where they coincide in a single person or system in which the state of exception becomes the rule and "the juridico-political system transforms itself into a killing machine."[33]

In evidence of this, Agamben cites the military order issued by President George Bush on November 13, 2001 to show how this conflation of authority and power manifests in the operation of the state of exception, whereby the law encompasses living beings by means of its own suspension. This provision authorized the "indefinite detention" and trial by "military commissions" of non-citizens suspected of involvement in terrorist activities.[34] The innovation of this provision is the way that it erased any legal status for an individual held under the order, thus producing "a legally unnameable and unclassifiable being." Agamben points out that the Taliban captured in Afghanistan and held in Guantanamo, came neither under the terms of the Geneva Convention on POWs nor under American Law, and are an example of where "bare life reaches its maximum determinacy."[35] It is not hard to see this as a contemporary fullness of the application of Canon and Roman law, as described in the second conduit, where heretics and adversaries were also treated as non-persons. Although Agamben asserts that the modern state of exception is a creation of the democratic-revolutionary tradition and not the absolutist one,[36] an alleged disjunction that will be taken up in the next section, this genealogical connection indicates otherwise. In any event, once the assignment of the outside to the domain of non-persons is identified as the necessary cost of conserving the West, then the West itself is revealed as dependent on the state of exception. In this way the [il]legal reaction to September 11, 2001 exposes the soul of contemporary Western biopolitics. Agamben cites Clinton L. Rossiter to the effect that "no sacrifice is too great for our democracy, least of all the temporary sacrifice of democracy itself."[37]

From the perspective of the theopolitical genealogy being traced here, this fullness of Western law is the climax of the Christendom project. In order to preserve the biopolitical system where money is

33. Ibid., 86.
34. Ibid., 3.
35. Ibid., 4.
36. Ibid., 5.
37. Ibid., 9.

Messiah and the most powerful hold onto their pretensions for imperial sovereignty while granting its multiplication, the state of exception
overwhelms law to affirm biopower. As Walter Benjamin states in his
exchange with Schmitt, "the 'state of exception' in which we live is the
rule."[38] Although, as Agamben recognizes, this was written during the
Nazi era, it remains true of the whole stance of the Western democratic
nation state. As already pointed out with reference to the submission of
law to the biopolitical conditions for the ongoing acquisition of power
with relation to the current banking crisis, Western representative
democracy appears as a transitory dependant of imperial sovereignty
interposed on a continuum of relative power. From this perspective it
cannot be absolutely distinguished from the Nazi era. The potential of
the state of exception can be applied at any time the circumstances are
considered to threaten the ongoing conditions for the promulgation
of normative unequal sovereignty through biopower. In answer to the
question of who or what provides this anomic fullness of law, Agamben,
quoting Schmitt, famously asserts, "Sovereign is he who decides on the
state of exception."[39] For Schmitt the state of exception is miraculous and
the sovereign "identified with God" is capable of eschatological decision.
For Benjamin, who rejects transcendence, the sovereign is "a creature
consigned to a world of creatures" and completely unable to make any
decision, with the result that the state of exception is consigned to ca-
tastrophe. Agamben describes this as "a zone of absolute indeterminacy
between anomie and law."[40] This anomic space is so essential to the juridical order that it demands a relation to it although acts that take place
in it defy legal definition. Agamben attempts to encapsulate this in the
mysterious idea of "a force of not-law" that both constituted power and
constituent power attempt to appropriate. His enquiry into the content
of the exception is reminiscent of the mystics' attempt to enunciate the
space vacated by the lost *corpus verum* and is a further trace of the theopolitical ancestry that preceded this soteriological consummation.

To summarize, the transmogrification of law into the state of exception shows how its operation conflates authority and power as sovereignty, forever producing and devouring itself in the holy of holies of the
biopolitical world. It reveals the urgent need to investigate whether this

38. Ibid., 57.

39. Agamben, *Homo Sacer*, 11.

40. Agamben, *State of Exception*, 53.

ark at the center of the Western system must only be an empty space in which "a human action with no relation to law stands before a norm with no relation to life."[41] For if this is the eschatological fullness to which the church-empire partnership has consigned the contemporary West, then politics is reduced to the blind ally of either constituent power employing violence to create newly vacuous law, or the constituted power to negotiate with existing empty law. Then the only truly radical political action is reduced to a counter-movement that works in an inverse direction in law and in life, always seeking to loosen what has been artificially and violently linked, in order to "ceaselessly try to interrupt the working of the machine that is leading the West toward global civil war."[42] This book proposes an alternative move in which transcendence might yet be reconfigured as a kenotic authority, in relation to which human action might be rediscovered as a fullness of law capable of recreating life as gift. Further important issues surrounding this will be considered in the coming section on biopower and transcendence. But before then it remains to take note of the adverse and violent complement to the state of exception that its function ineluctably opens up.

(c) WAR

From the perspective of the soteriological genealogy that began with the proposed fourth-century lapsis, the violent sufferings of Christ were necessary to deal with two things. The first of these is the anger of God at our failure to submit to his sovereign law and which needs appeasement. This was partly met by the propitiatory payment that has now given place to money. But it also ascribes violent anger to God. In the next section and in Part III the relation of choice to divine being will be articulated. Enough to say here that for God viewed as imperial sovereign, anger is part of his choice of being and therefore of any juridico-political system derived from or legitimated by it. The second issue that the cross had to deal with was the antagonism of the demons identified with the idols of polytheism. Here the physical battle was also a spiritual fight by which the demons were defeated. These were conflated with the political pluralities of temporal kings and governments in Eusebius's writings and in Constantine's military use of the *labarum*. As traced in the second conduit, it was an easy step from this to identify violence enacted against

41. Ibid., 86.
42. Ibid., 87.

Saracens or heretics, in the attempt to recover land and sovereignty for Christendom, as the imitation of Christ's sufferings. In this way suffering and death in war became necessary Christian sacrifice as really as Christ's sufferings to overcome demons and plural government. Once the attempt at preserving the universal sovereignty of church or empire had transitioned into the multiplication of sovereignty for all while conserving as much as possible for the already powerful, exclusive pretensions to sovereignty were seen as opposing it. The imitation of Christ's sufferings in war consequently became identified with fighting the anti-Christ pope or emperor. So violence and war became both defensively and offensively necessary to the hoped for peace through sovereignty and continued to be legitimated by Christ's sufferings.

In the context of biopower the soteriological role of suffering has expanded significantly in two ways. Firstly, just as the shift from the society of discipline to biopower resulted in the internalization of the commodification of sovereignty through statisization, the same process included the assumed necessity of violence both to defend the conjunction of sovereignty and money from the enemies of the system and to sustain the conditions for it. The unavoidability of war is thereby added to the corporate mindset that consumption is what life is about. Secondly, with the emergence of the state of exception, a complementary motivation for violence is disclosed. For if the corollary of "sovereign is he who has the power of the exception" is "sacred is he who can be killed but not sacrificed," then the authority that maintains the conditions for the maximum availability of the universally desired sovereign peace achieves a quasi-transcendence that requires the sacrifice of others to defend it. This brings us to the heart of the question of transcendence. It is proposed that ultimate power can head in one of two directions, either to domination, or to kenotic love, as is taken up again in the next section and developed more fully in Part III. In the genealogy of the choice of sovereignty as the means to peace traced here, domination is the power that has been substantiated, and all forms of sovereignty, personal or corporate, are delegated from it. In this context the state of exception reveals the choice of potential power that now unites authority and sovereignty. If the only possibility of personal sovereignty is delegated by the system, and the authority behind the system can be killed but not sacrificed, then it is necessary to fight and defend the system at all costs if it comes under threat. This step from the investment of naked life to the readiness of sacrificing it altogether is not a large one.

Today a stream of reports of the hitherto unpublished records of thousands of Iraqi civilian deaths and violent experiences of torture has been made available through Wikileaks.[43] It is clear that the degree of violence and sacrificial sufferings of the American and British forces and the civilians involved required to bring about the opportunity for regime change and Western-style democracy for the Iraqi people, is embedded as normative in the corporate Western mindset. But in reality it is not about the freedom of the multitude but about the sovereign decision of the powerful to defend the system from those deemed as non-persons outside it and to maintain the economic conditions for the ongoing multiplication of sovereignty. The commitment of those who have paid the sacrificial price identifies them even more strongly with the system, which is why the real circumstances remain hidden. In this way the contemporary Western system is kept constantly at war. The place of the exception is apparently empty, yet can only be kept that way by constant violence and suffering.

3. Biopower and the Subsumption of Transcendence

It is in order to have a hopeful remedy for what they see as the abuse of transcendence, that Hardt and Negri, with Foucault before them, posit a radical disjunction between biopower and the society of discipline. As has already been intimated in chapter 1, this is a corollary of the rejection of medieval transcendence as a result of the adverse outcomes for the multitude consequent on the papal and imperial conflicts over universal sovereignty such as those exposed in the second conduit. Given that the genealogy put forward by this book draws on the neo-Marxists' analysis but challenges this disjunction by proposing a continuous flow of sovereign power from the fourth-century lapsis to present-day biopower, it is necessary to consider the reasons for their perception and its bearing on the thesis being put forward here. The first of these is their support for what they assume to be a rejection of transcendence by the opinion formers among the resurgent multitude because of its association with imperial sovereignty and the consequent oppression and impoverishment of the populace. Hardt and Negri regard the sixteenth century

---

43. *The Guardian* newspaper, October 22, 2010.

as the crisis of modernity where the counter-revolutionary forces of sovereignty were victorious over the "immanent, constructive, creative forces"[44] of the multitude. From this perspective they see the subsequent Thirty Years War and the peace that followed not as a genuine peace for the multitude, but peace for "the extreme urgency of escaping death."[45] They view the seventeenth century as a more ambiguous period, where "From the abyss of the social world always arose the memory of what it tried to bury."[46]

This leads on to the second point, where Hardt and Negri ascribe the characteristics of these memories to what they perceive as the "transcendental apparatus"[47] of immanent sovereignty. As they see it, theoretical humanists from Descartes to Kant and Hegel configured a modern European sovereignty that brought about "the death of Man" by once again reifying human being above nature. They thereby expose a continuity between the medieval understanding of transcendence that accorded a power above nature to God and the modern "secular" thought that ascribed the same power above nature to Man. As they put it, "The transcendence of God is simply transferred to Man. Like God before it, this Man that stands separate from and above nature has no place in a philosophy of immanence. Like God, too, this transcendent figure of Man leads quickly to the imposition of social hierarchy and domination."[48] These quasi-transcendent configurations of sovereignty serve to compound the neo-Marxist perception of transcendence and their opposition to both its divine and humanistic forms. As a result they reject transcendence.

This leads in turn to the third point, where, having affirmed the vital significance of the Renaissance humanist revolution as the way in which it placed the imperial being of medievality outside the immanent world, Hardt and Negri now attempt to do the same with modern imperialism. By rejecting transcendence they relegate imperialism beyond all legitimacy precisely because without transcendence there is no outside from which to measure it. In this way they are then able to make what they posit to be an objective immanent assessment of the operation of

44. Hardt and Negri, *Empire*, 76.
45. Ibid., 75.
46. Ibid., 77.
47. Ibid., 78.
48. Ibid., 91.

biopower. As they boldly pronounce, "Ni Dieu, ni maître, ni l'homme—no transcendent power or measure will determine the values of our world. Value will be determined only by humanity's own continuous innovation and creation."[49]

Given the previous two points it seems clear that it is on account of their determination to uphold this displacement of transcendence that they maintain the disjunction between the end of modernity and contemporary biopower. It is not difficult to see that this move, however, far from escaping the inroads of sovereignty, relegates the imperial to the status of non-person and is evidence of the ongoing function of sovereignty despite the overt rejection of transcendence. Imperialism is outside now, so they will not give it room or credence. But the precise reason for its rejection manifests within. For although they hold on to the ideological position that allows them to deny biopower transcendent legitimacy, and declare that behind the state of exception there really is nothing, once they set about configuring the immanent potential power of naked life to break through and beyond biopower, it transpires that it is the opportunity for the multitude "to express itself autonomously and rule itself" that they are reaching for.[50] While this is hardly surprising given their practical and theoretical roots in autonomous Marxism,[51] it makes the hoped for move beyond biopower, as will be contemplated further in the final part of this chapter, a form of sovereignty that Sergio Bologna describes as a "eulogy of the power of the political."[52] It follows that the inevitable product of the biopower that is the consummation of the genealogy of the fourth-century choice of sovereignty, is once again the choice of sovereignty. The rejection of transcendence allows sovereignty to survive unscathed after all.

The criticism being made here of Hardt and Negri, and Foucault before them, is not over their characterization of sovereign transcendence or their rejection of it. The reason for their position is easily recognized. The problem is with respect to their assumption that sovereignty is the sole necessary configuration of transcendent power. In this the neo-Marxists display the same mindset as Eusebius before them, and from the perspective of this book present further evidence of the power and

---

49. Ibid., 356.
50. Hardt and Negri, *Multitude*, 101.
51. Steve Wright, "Mapping Pathways within Italian Autonomist Marxism," 112.
52. Ibid., 114.

prevalence of the supposed fourth-century ontological choice of sovereignty and its subsequent genealogy. However, the imposition of social hierarchy and domination that Hardt and Negri assume to be a condition inherent to transcendence is, instead, a condition of sovereignty that is not necessary to transcendence. While their analysis of resurgent sovereignty is unexceptional from the perspective of the genealogy pursued here, it is the superficial and premature rejection of transcendence per se that is problematic. As has already been intimated in Part I, the argument that Part III will attempt to articulate still further, is that transcendence in no way necessitates hierarchy or sovereign domination. The reverse is rather the case, namely that the originary testimony to the human Jesus as the revelation of the essential nature of divine being makes transcendence the opposite of hierarchical domination. Instead of exerting power over others it gives power away to others for their elevation and consequent equalization. Simply put, Hardt and Negri argue that there must be a disjunction between modernity and postmodernity otherwise there is no escape from transcendence, whereas the argument being made here is that if there is such a disjunction then there is no escape from sovereignty. The criticism is not of their argument against sovereign transcendence in its medieval and modern forms with which it essentially agrees, but of the deeper presupposition on which it is based. The thesis presented here is based on a different presupposition of the relation between transcendence and sovereignty.

From the perspective of the genealogy of church and empire put forward in this book, this disjunction is being challenged both pragmatically and objectively. Pragmatically, because once transcendence and sovereignty are disentangled, then transcendence can be drawn on precisely for the purpose of overcoming the oppressive sovereignty with which it has been associated. This is an intended outcome of this study and the orientation of Part III. Objectively, because as has already been exposed in this conduit, it can be shown that the genealogy of imperial sovereignty undergirds biopower and accounts for the authority of the exception behind it. So although Schmidt, unlike Hardt and Negri, Agamben, and Benjamin, still holds on to transcendence and claims that the state of exception is miraculous and opens onto a transcendent sovereignty capable of eschatological decision, the genealogy of sovereignty proposed here reveals the real reason for the eschatological emptiness of naked life. The unmitigated desire for sovereignty is the reason that a human being devouring himself in its pursuit stands behind biopower, not the now rejected transcendence or the quasi-transcendent apparatus that is its memory.

Despite the strength with which Hardt and Negri argue against any transcendent outside, in the climax to *Multitude* they do appear to recognize the limitations of their position. As will be examined in detail in the final section of this conduit, they make a strong plea for the motivation of Judeo-Christian love to complement what they regard as the potential power of naked life to overwhelm biopower from within. While, as might be expected, they stop short of describing this as a form of transcendence, it is a significant motion towards the alternative understanding of the relationship between sovereignty and transcendence configured by this project. In order to be better prepared to consider the full implications of this, it is time to explore the countervailing testimony of claims for a completely different expression of transcendence emerging among the early twentieth-century multitude.

B. THE CENTURY OF THE SPIRIT

The events that gave rise to the inception of the Pentecostal movement were clearly transcendent in nature and yet the circumstances of their origin and the immediate consequences of their impact ran remarkably counter to the supposed characteristics of sovereign power. They appear to have the potential to supply the multitude with love as constituent power and therefore provide a helpful vantage point from which to reconsider the culmination of two millennia of the partnership of church and empire. The fact that the growing movement was soon vulnerable to the covert currents of biopower only serves to emphasize the depth of the impact of the choice of sovereignty as the means to peace and its subsequent genealogy as explored in the dissertation so far. The now generally agreed deficit of the Spirit, manifest in the relative absence of any serious pneumatology in the Western church since the fourth century and until the twentieth, affirms the lack of an adequate concept of transcendence and points to the pressing need for its radical reconfiguration. To this end, the following section of the conduit explores these seemingly antithetical events and considers the consequences of an absence of any adequate pneumatology at their inception to enable appropriate theological reflection on their meaning and significance. The way that this initially left the embryonic movement at the mercy of the Christendom genealogy and its consummation in biopower is then indicated.

1. A Different Kind of Transcendence

The socio-political implications of the egalitarian character of the early twentieth-century transcendent experiences that gave rise to the Pentecostal movement have until recently largely been overlooked.[53] The phenomenon has been relegated to the margins of the biopolitical world and to the even more obscure extremities of the marginalized church within it. Nevertheless, the exponential growth of the movement means that it is impossible to ignore it any longer. Current statistics give the number of Pentecostal-charismatic Christians as more than 520 million,[54] making them the second largest body of Christians after the Roman Catholic Church and consisting of approximately one-twelfth of the current population of the world. Grouped in 740 denominations, 6,530 non-Pentecostal mainline denominations with organized internal charismatic contingents, and 18,810 independent neo-charismatic denominations and networks, they can be found in 9,000 ethnolinguistic cultures speaking 8,000 languages[55] now extending mainly beyond the boundaries of the Western world. As Philip Jenkins surmises, "One way or another, inside the Catholic Church or outside it, Third World Christianity is becoming steadily more Pentecostal."[56] The essentially counterintuitive character of this extraordinary grassroots movement in relation to the church-empire embrace of sovereignty and the modern and postmodern Western rejection of transcendence means that its surprising eruption from left field has to be taken seriously as a significant component of the contemporary story of church and empire.

Almost all the many expressions of the Pentecostal-charismatic movement recognize the ecstatic experiences of the 1906 Los Angeles Azusa Street revival as a primary defining narrative. Since the latter part of the twentieth century, a growing historical, anthropological, and theological corpus of work on the movement has increasingly focused attention on its comprehensive spread and its capacity for indigeniza-

---

53. See Hepden, *The Impact of Racial Inclusivity in the Azusa Street Revival*.

54. Barrett, *The Worldwide Holy Spirit Renewal*, 388.

55. Ibid., 383.

56. Jenkins, *The Next Christendom*, 67.

tion. The University of Birmingham has become a focus for study, beginning with Walter J. Hollenweger in the seventies and Allan H. Anderson in the nineties.[57] As might be expected from a comparatively recent and still contemporary field, there are conflicting schools of thought about the ownership and precise circumstances of Pentecostal origins, what to include, and how far back to go. But as Peter Hocken makes clear, almost all of these still agree on the defining character of the Azusa Street experience. As he states in summary of his comprehensive and international overview of the corpus of study, "when we examine Pentecostalism as a historically identifiable movement, then the evidence does point to . . . Azusa Street playing a major role in the identity and diffusion of the movement."[58] While recognizing that an extensive coverage of the growing field of enquiry is beyond the capacity of this book, the main interest of this investigation can be confined to three areas, the different apprehension of transcendence, its counterpolitical potential, and its rapid but partial accommodation to the covert genealogy of church and empire. As Hocken, speaking of the revival focus of the experience, puts it, "The category of revival . . . expresses the sense of a work of God that exceeds human categories of explanation . . . The revival focus . . . points to a God who cannot be tied down in doctrinal formulae."[59] For the purpose of this study his statement can well be expanded to include the whole imperial genealogy behind such formulae.

The *Los Angeles Times* of April 18, 1906 famously records meetings in what is described as a tumble-down shack. "On Azusa Street, near San Pedro Street . . . coloured people and a sprinkling of whites compose the congregation, and night is made hideous in the neighbourhood by the howlings of the worshippers who spend hours swaying forth and back in a nerve-racking [*sic*] attitude of prayer and supplication. They claim to have the 'gift of tongues,' and to be able to comprehend the babel." Frank Bartleman, a journalist personally involved in the events, describes them from the perspective of a participant: "Divine love was wonderfully manifest in the meetings. They would not even allow an unkind word said against their opposers, or the churches. The message was

57. See Hollenweger, *Pentecostalism: Origins and Developments Worldwide*; Anderson, *An Introduction to Pentecostalism: Global Charismatic Christianity*.

58. Hocken, *The Challenges of the Pentecostal, Charismatic and Messianic Jewish Movements*, 19.

59. Ibid., 7.

the love of God. It was a sort of 'first love' of the early church returned. The 'baptism' as we received it in the beginning did not allow us to think, speak, or hear evil of any man."[60]

Accounts are unanimous that a countercultural, non-hierarchical unity of male and female, black and white, rich and poor characterized the embryonic movement.[61] While William Seymour, a second-genera- tion African-American slave descendant, was clearly recognized as the nominal leader, there was no structured hierarchy. "We had no priest class, nor priest craft . . . We did not even have a platform or a pulpit in the beginning. All were on a level."[62] This paralleled the developing labor movement, pre-dated women's suffrage by more than a decade,[63] and preceded racial equality by more than half a century.[64] The overall politi- cal stance at the beginning was anti-state and anti-war. Charles Parham, one of the most universally recognized, although not the most radical of Pentecostal leaders, who early on struggled with the social diversity of the Azusa Street happenings, nonetheless "consistently resisted any hint of dual allegiance to the Kingdom of God and that of Caesar."[65] Long be- fore the outbreak of war within Europe he berated all so-called Christian nation states, including the United States, for yielding themselves up to the "Moloch God, Patriotism, whose doctrine was honour," whose soldiers were "self-appointed murderers," and whose governments were "imbecile."[66]

The initial counterpolitical orientation of the movement has im- portant implications for the proposed thesis in two particular ways. Firstly, it presents a serious challenge to the idea that biopower leaves no remaining place to stand outside itself. The Azusa Street experience, and the many similar expressions of supposedly divine presence that ensued, facilitated a resurgence of the multitude beyond the biopolitical hegemony of sovereignty and money. This is clear both from the many popular biographies and testimonies from the previously cited Frank

---

60. Bartleman, *Azusa Street,* 54.

61. Synan, *The Century of the Holy Spirit*, 49, 54–55; Wacker, *Heaven Below*, 104–5.

62. Bartleman, *Azusa Street*, 57.

63. Women did not get the vote in the US until 1919.

64. This was the height of the era of the Jim Crow laws of racial segregation.

65. Wacker, *Heaven Below*, 218.

66. Ibid., 218.

Bartleman onwards,[67] as well as the evidence of the growing confidence of third-world Pentecostalism as the church of the poor.[68] Secondly, given the thrust of this book to investigate the relationship between church and empire, the ecclesial and theological impact of the phenomenon on the marginalized and state-subordinated twentieth- and now twenty-first-century church has been profound, and the possible consequences of the impact of another form of transcendence on the future relationship of church and empire cannot be disregarded. The roots of this counterpolitical transcendence lay in the practice of "living by faith," as Karla Poewe so crucially exposes.[69] The financial component of this practice, expressed in an utter abandonment to God for every need, physical as well as spiritual, had the capacity to disconnect the movement from dependence on the capitalist economics of the prevailing sovereign power. This played a central role in the astonishingly rapid spread of the movement and will be further explored in the final part of the conduit. However, this alignment of transcendence and constituent power, what Grant Wacker designates as primitivism,[70] was soon beset by the prevailing Western progress of sovereignty and capital.

What has been argued here to be the underlying structure of ontological sovereignty, and its embodiment in the expressions of church and state of twentieth-century America, inevitably manifested in attempts to consolidate the originary transcendent Pentecostal experiences into the constituted structures of denominations and networks. This consisted either in the inclusion of the experimental initiatives and communities into existing holiness denominations, for example the Church of God, the Pentecostal Holiness Church, and the Church of God in Christ, or into completely new ecclesial structures and networks like the Assemblies of God, the Pentecostal Assemblies of the World, and the United Pentecostal Church.[71] To begin with these tried to maintain the purity of the originary expressions of reconciling love. But before long, these ecclesial formations began to betray evidence of the familiar sovereign forms. One of the first of these was the social subjugation and

67. See, for example, Pullinger and Quicke, *Chasing the Dragon,* rev. ed. (Hodder & Stoughter, 2006).

68. Hollenweger, "The Pentecostal Elites and the Pentecostal Poor," 201, 205.

69. Poewe, "The Nature, Globality and History of Charismatic Christianity," 7–9.

70. Ibid., 12.

71. Synan, *The Century of the Holy Spirit,* 5–6.

segregation of African-Americans. The racial equality common to the primitive beginnings eventually gave way to the racism inherent in the American church and society at the beginning of the twentieth century. The Jim Crow laws had been in effect at Parham's Apostolic Faith Bible School in Houston where Seymour had been obliged to listen to Parham's teachings about the Holy Spirit outside the classroom through an open door. But in Frank Bartleman's words, "the color line was washed away in the blood"[72] in the subsequent ecstatic events of 1906.

The effective disregard for these juridico-political obligations in the Azusa Street experience, however, was relatively short-lived. Wacker nuances what he terms the Edenic model of racial harmony advanced by influential studies of early Pentecostal black-white relations. As he sees it, at the beginning whites and blacks came spontaneously together in mutual affection. However, once the whites reflected on the social and cultural implications, they drew back and the blacks by necessity followed suit. As a result, by 1914 Seymour had decided to restrict director's posts at the Azusa Mission to "people of Color," and by the mid twenties two of the most significant interracial groupings, the Pentecostal Assemblies of the World and the Church of God in Christ, followed the politics of the day and divided along racial lines.[73] Wacker emphasizes racism as the first of three foci at the heart of the move towards pragmatism, to which he adds security and a sustained loyalty to the American pilgrim dream.[74] From the perspective put forward here it was the genealogy of church and empire that lay behind that dream, and racism can be seen as part and parcel of the process towards limited sovereignty where those of another race or culture are relegated further down the hierarchy of relative power. The dependence on the state for security correlates with the soteriology of law and war, together with the driving motivation of entrepreneurial freedom and profit behind it all.

As far as the accommodation of the movement to law is concerned, it is clear from the *Los Angeles Times* report on Azusa Street that the immediacy of the Pentecostals' spiritual encounters could appear decidedly anti-social to their neighbors. The interpretation of their experience as the restoration of the Holy Spirit to the world in preparation for the return of Christ made their testimony and subsequent evangelism

---

72. Bartleman, *Azusa Street*, 54.

73. Wacker, *Heaven Below*, 231.

74. Ibid., 226.

urgent and intolerant. This combined to make them a controversial and sometimes persecuted body. In this they depended upon the police to defend their freedom and attend to their security, as the administrative minutes to their committees and the reports of events in their journals make clear.[75] This reliance on the law was linked to a strong sense of the almost sacred status of America as a righteous nation. While this was at first distinguished from the party political powers of the Washington government, it was rooted in the pioneer expectations of a land where the opportunity for personal sovereignty was protected by the constitution and the flag. This increasing dependence on the law of the land was accompanied by a sense of obligation to support the violent defense of the nation.

With its initial institutionalization, the movement still attempted to maintain its original irenic stance such as in the proscription against war handed down by the General Assembly of the Church of God.[76] But this was inexorably adjusted to the wider mores of contemporary politics. By the time America entered the First World War in April 1917, the proscription against war had been called into question. It disappeared from the minutes of the Church of God in 1921, reappeared in modified form in 1928, and disappeared for good in 1945.[77] Overall the public accommodation to contemporary racism, the reliance on security enforcement, and the increasing veneration of America as a special nation accorded with the unequal multiplication of sovereignty and the soteriological operation of law and war on the part of the nation state consistent with the now familiar path to biopower. It is hardly surprising that under this lay theological roots that also left them vulnerable to the drive for universal autonomy through money.

As Wacker points out, the pragmatism of the emerging Pentecostal movement was directly connected to the "classically American sentiment"[78] of the pursuit of autonomy, manifest in the generally individualistic entrepreneurial approach to work.[79] The research of André Droogers on the later charismatics similarly recognizes the influence of

---

75. Ibid., 236–7.
76. Ibid., 248.
77. Ibid., 248.
78. Ibid., 29.
79. Ibid., 213–16.

individualism.[80] There appear to have been two particular points of vulnerability. Firstly, the practice of living by faith, while counterpolitical at root, carried a propensity for accommodation to other people and cultures, as Poewe articulates by tracing its roots back to non-Western, Chinese, Asian, and African cultural influences connected to the practices of Pietists and Jesuits.[81] Poewe's analysis discloses a dual capacity in this attitude of accommodation, which, while partly responsible for the capacity of the new transcendence to overwhelm biopower with a kenotic attitude of spirit, was also vulnerable to the cultural mainstream and its orientation to individual autonomy. Subordinated to an underlying ontological sovereignty, such faith practice becomes a covert, at best unconscious, at worst conscious embrace of the Messianic conjunction of multiplied sovereignty and money. In this context ecclesial life, charity, and mission can become deeply parasitic on contemporary biopower.

Secondly, the prevailing influence of premillennialism[82] in the worldview of many early Pentecostals, with its under-realized eschatology, tended to divert attention away from the importance of applying the new transcendence to everyday political life. Instead of a responsibility to serve the needs of the world, it looked for a removal out of it that left the multitude subject to a conflagration from which the church escapes. Dayton's investigation into the genesis of this eschatological position offers significant insight into its role in accommodating biopower. According to Dayton's argument, the early American Methodist and Holiness traditions "had little interest in eschatology" and inclined to the postmillennial position.[83] But when the bold nineteenth-century social justice agenda of Holiness protagonists such as Charles Finney and Oberlin College failed to deliver the expected freedom and equality for women and blacks that was expected, hope shifted to the imminent direct intervention of God and a heavenly eschatological future rather than an earthly one.[84] This perspective conjoined with the accepting and affirmative aspects of living by faith to accommodate the burgeoning capitalization of American society. Effectively the primitivism of their immediate spirituality combined with under-realized eschatological

---

80. Droogers, "The Normalization of Religious Experience," 34.

81. Poewe, "The Nature, Globality and History of Charismatic Christianity," 7–9.

82. Ibid., 23.

83. Dayton, *Theological Roots of Pentecostalism*, 146.

84. Ibid., 155.

hope and diverted their primary attention. The problem resided at least in part in the acute lack of an adequate understanding of the work of the Holy Spirit. While the initial transcendent experiences ascribed to the Spirit carried strongly egalitarian countercultural implications, there was little or no existing theology of the Spirit by which to interpret them.

2. A Pneumatological Deficit

The work of the Spirit has not so far featured as a pronounced theological current within the genealogy of church and empire traced by this book. This is for two reasons, the first of which is historical: the doctrine of the Spirit has not featured prominently in the formulations that have been crucial to the partnership of church and empire before the twentieth century. The second is theological: pneumatology has not been central to the theology of Western Christendom in either its medieval or modern expressions throughout the same period. These are crucial factors for understanding and evaluating the way that the new expressions of transcendence were soon vulnerable to subsumption by sovereignty. They provide further important insights into the effects of the covert genealogy traced by this book.

In his recent and comprehensive overview of pneumatology, Veli-Matti Kärkkäinen proposes the concept of a deficit to describe this lack of place for the Holy Spirit in Western theology since at least the fourth century. As he puts it, citing Hilberath,[85] "Rather than speaking of a *Geistvergessenheit*, (oblivion of the Spirit), we should speak of a pneumatological deficit."[86] As Rowan Williams similarly states, "Many writers have remarked a certain poverty in theological reflection on the Holy Spirit in Western Christianity over the last decades."[87] Kärkkäinen suggests that this has been the result of two interrelated factors, a unilateral preference to Christ in Western Christianity, and a subordinate and controlled role for the Spirit. The apparent overbalance of emphasis on the Son was noted by Eastern theologians at the tenth-century division and a millennium later in the ecumenical deliberations around the Second Vatican Council.[88] The subordination of the Spirit seems to have devel-

85. In Schneider, *Handbuch der Dogmatik*, 1: 445–452, cited in ibid., 17.

86. Kärkkäinen, *Pneumatology*, 17.

87. Williams, *On Christian Theology*, 107.

88. Kärkkäinen cites Nikos A. Nissiotis, "The Main Ecclesiological Problem of the Second Vatican Council and Position of the Non-Roman Churches Facing It," in *Journal*

oped as the result of four contributing trends. The first is a depersonal-
ized role for the Spirit, which has been attributed in particular to the
influence of Augustine and his idea of the Spirit as *vinculum amoris*. The
second is what Kärkkäinen regards as a directly biblical New Testament
testimony to the Spirit's self-effacing or kenotic role, which makes his
apparent subordination an almost unavoidable characteristic. Third is
the possible consequence of an ecclesial fear of charismatic-prophetic
freedom as the result of an overreaction to negative experiences during
the second- and third-century Montanist movement. The final suggested
influence is the dialogical nature of theology. Here the example given is
from the World Council of Churches (WCC) where pneumatology only
seriously emerged onto the theological stage from the 1980s onwards.[89]
Kärkkäinen can find only two reasons for this late twentieth-century correction of the deficit: the impact of the entrance of the Eastern Orthodox
churches into the WCC, which, not to be underestimated, is clearly the
lesser of the two and outside the remit of the thesis articulated here, and
the impact of the Pentecostal-charismatic movement over the last century.[90] The section that follows indicates ways in which the two probable
general causes of the deficit of the Spirit may be explained in the light of
the thesis so far, and considers the four trends outlined above.

The first of the two initial factors, an overbalance towards the role
of the Son in the agency of the Godhead and the functioning of the *ecclesia*, seems somewhat ironic given the alleged eclipse of the human Jesus
consequent on the partnership of church and empire. However, once
this is reflected on in the light of the supposed work of the subordinately
sovereign Word in the advent of the Roman eschatological peace, it is
apparent that any alleged Christomonism[91] of the fourth-century church
was rooted in a decidedly pre-incarnational Old Testament Christology.
The important role that this perception of the Christ played in legitimating the interpenetration of church and empire has already been discussed
in Part I and the first conduit. Given the defining role of this sovereign
Christ for Western Christendom and Christianity, as displayed in these

---

of Ecumenical Studies VI (1965), 31–62.

89. Kärkkäinen, *Pneumatology*, 18–19.

90. Ibid., 12.

91. Terminology articulated by the Greek Orthodox theologians Nikos Nissiotis
and Vladimir Lossky to describe the perceived exaggerated position of Christ to the
detriment of the Spirit in Western theology. Ibid., 17.

very Christocentric nomenclatures themselves, the Eastern Orthodox allegation of the deposition of the Spirit is not so surprising.

With regard to the second factor, the apparent subordination of the Spirit, this can be understood even more obviously as the outcome of the supposed fourth-century lapsis. If the Nicaean resolution of the fourth-century Christology controversy is likely to have subsumed a hierarchical relationship between the Father and the Son, the subordination of the Spirit may be considered to proceed from this formulation. This is the implication of the first of the four trends put forward in further explanation of the alleged deposition, the depersonalization of the Holy Spirit. Kärkkäinen cites Hilberath again to the effect that Augustine's approach to the Spirit as the bond of love between the Father and the Son "laid not only the theological groundwork for the *filioque*, the view that the Spirit proceeds both from Father and Son, but also divested the Spirit of full personality."[92] The perspective already pursued on *homoousios* in the first conduit tends to a practical if not theoretical subordinationism. The consequent formulation and attachment of the *filioque* to the Nicene Creed in 589 CE would seem to bear this out.[93] The theological implications of this will be investigated in more depth in chapter 6 at the beginning of Part III, but it certainly makes general sense of the suggested subordination of the Spirit.

It might seem that the second trend to subordination, the kenotic aspect to the Spirit's role, could explain how the person and work of the Spirit were inevitably closeted from general view. But even if this is the case, such a suggestion has profound implications for the genealogy proposed here. It does not only explain the apparent reclusiveness of the Spirit, but has significant repercussions for the ontology of sovereignty. It indicates a counterpolitical characteristic of power and raises the question of why such an alternative did not materialize to challenge imperial sovereignty. Possible answers to this question are that the ontological status of sovereignty and the de-eschatologization consequent on the embrace of the *pax Romana* as evidence of the desired peace precluded the lasting success of any such challenge. This connects directly with the third- and fourth-century tendencies to obscure the Spirit, the fear of

92. Ibid., 18.

93. It was appended to the Nicene Creed at the Council of Toledo in 589 but not ratified by Rome until 1014. It was a contributory factor in the East–West schism of 1054.

loss of ecclesiastical control in reaction to Montanism, and the dialogical bent of theology. The pre-fourth-century emergence of Montanism makes an accurate assessment of its nature and impact difficult. Outlawed by the ecclesiastical hierarchy by the end of the third century and viewed through the lens of Eusebius's ontological sovereignty, the orthodox perspective is of a decidedly heretical sect. However, its embrace by Tertullian and the accessibility of his extant writings have safeguarded a degree of clarity over its character and content. While scholarly sources advise caution,[94] two significant characteristics stand out. The first is that it was a highly charismatic-prophetic movement claiming direct access to revelation without the mediation of the church or state,[95] and the second is that it identified the church as independent of the sovereign power of both hierarchical orders. Tertullian himself wrote, "Where but three are, and they of the laity also, yet there is a church"[96] and "one state we know, of which all are citizens—the universe."[97] On this basis one way of understanding the fate of Montanism is that it was outlawed primarily out of fear that its emphasis on direct access to the Holy Spirit would undermine the imperial sovereignty of bishops and increase suspicion of the church among the Roman imperial authorities. From this perspective the fourth-century affirmation of the strength of ecclesiastical sovereignty and the *pax Romana* as evidence of realized eschatological peace inevitably increased the deficit of the Spirit.

The fourth-century combination of over-realized and under-realized eschatology tended to a long-term de-eschatologization of Western theology with the resultant loss of counterpolitical impact for the gospel testimony. This will be explored further in Part III. Here it is sufficient to point out that this has serious relevance for evaluating the approach of dialogic theology that assumes a passive and reactive role for the *ecclesia*. From the perspective of the proposed genealogy of church and empire, this passivity is a likely sign of de-eschatologization, where the church

94. "Montanism cannot be appropriately characterised as a clash between a power-hungry hierarchy and ordinary believers set on freedom of expression." Davidson, *The Birth of the Church*, 183.

95. "They taught a rigid asceticism over against the growing worldliness of the Church . . . and the universal priesthood of believers (even female), and their right to perform all the functions of church officers, over against the growing sacerdotalism of the Church." McGiffert, "Notes to the Church History of Eusebius," 229, n. 1.

96. Broadbent, *The Pilgrim Church*, 13.

97. O'Donovan and O'Donovan, *From Irenaeus to Grotius*, 26.

is denied its active counterpolitical agency. Given the strong association of the Holy Spirit with realized eschatology throughout the gospel narratives and Acts, the fourth-century de-eschatologization made the subsequent deposition of the Spirit almost inevitable. However, it is the strong implication of the impact of the Pentecostal-charismatic movement that, despite its pragmatic accommodation to the covert subsumptive power of sovereignty, it nevertheless provides a radical challenge to the dialogic approach. Instead of the *ecclesia* waiting for the world, the possibility for the reconfiguration of the *ecclesia* and its theology is presented by the new orientation of transcendence.

C. THE POTENTIAL POWER OF IMMATERIAL LABOR AND LIVING BY FAITH

The analysis of biopower that forms the large part of this conduit demarcates the fullness of the church-empire genealogy of Christendom. But if the neo-Marxist perception of the ironic and paradoxical potentiality of life itself, on which biopolitical production depends, can be brought together with the potential of the new transcendence among the multitude, it is possible that the fullness of Christendom might yet provide the opportunity for radical transformation. It is this hope that provides the radical substratum to this conduit of contemporary empire. Beginning with the neo-Marxists' perspective, it is certainly the case that they look to naked life as the ground of struggle through which the multitude will emerge from imperial domination. Locating it within a semantic field that marks it as both subject and object of desire and driven by the struggle for true democracy, they describe the resultant emerging multitude as a new Davidic champion[98] and Joseph's many-colored coat.[99] As they see it there are two possibilities: on the one hand is biopolitical sovereignty with no outside; on the other is the new immaterial and cooperative creativity of the multitude. They perceive this as a growing and positive crisis, from which can emanate a resistance that becomes love and community.[100] Today's multitude needs to become a posse of self-valorization, cooperation, and political action.[101] This posse will

98. Hardt and Negri, *Multitude*, 50.

99. Ibid., xiv.

100. Hardt and Negri, *Empire*, 361.

101. Ibid., 410.

operate through the militant action of those who constantly resist capitalist exploitation, collectively construct and exercise a counter power, organize struggle and die if necessary, seeing themselves as constituent power, not merely representative power.

For what they see as the necessary motivation for such resistance, Hardt and Negri make recourse to love. They draw on the figure of Francis of Assisi to point the way forward. "Once again in postmodernity we find ourselves in Francis' situation, posing against the misery of power the joy of being. This is a revolution that no power will control—because biopower and communism, cooperation and revolution remain together, in love, simplicity, and also innocence."[102] Finally in the last pages of *Multitude*, they define constituent power itself as love and make a plea for the kind of love rooted in the pre-modern traditions of Judaism and Christianity: "Christianity and Judaism, for example, both conceive love as a political act that constructs the multitude . . . There is really nothing necessarily metaphysical about the Christian and Judaic love of God: both God's love of humanity and humanity's love of God are expressed and incarnated in the common material political project of the multitude. We need to recover today this material and political sense of love, a love as strong as death."[103]

They regard this as an extension of the love of spouse, mother, and child that provides the basis for political projects in common and the construction of a new society. They express it in Christian vocabulary and eschatological terminology. "When love is conceived politically, then, this creation of a new humanity is the ultimate act of love. Without this love, we are nothing."[104] Time is split between a present that is already dead and a future that is already living while waiting for "the real political act of love."[105] The multitude will either be reenlisted by capital, or else "developing its productive figure based on the common, the multitude can move through Empire and come out the other side, to express itself autonomously and rule itself."[106] Or to conclude, "These common singularities will organize themselves autonomously . . . in line with the

---

102. Ibid., 413.

103. Hardt and Negri, *Multitude*, 352.

104. Ibid., 352.

105. Ibid., 358.

106. Ibid., 101.

long philosophical tradition that stretches back at least to the apostle Paul of Tarsus."[107]

However, this autonomous aspect of the neo-Marxists' view of constituent power and their tendency to reach into the Christian heritage for its past evidence and future sustenance raises two important related issues. The first is the already identified problematic of configuring constituent power as autonomy, and the second is their almost inevitably obscured reading of Christian origins. Suffice it to say at this point that they are right to be careful to distinguish the constituent power of the multitude from the constituted power of the people because they recognize it as a form of sovereignty. But then they proceed to identify constituent power and autonomy in a way that it would seem only the sense of freedom from sovereignty accompanying their rejection of transcendence could allow them to do. As a result they appear impervious to the way that their embrace of autonomy as the fullness of the multitude coincides with the same kind of power as the sovereignty from which they believe themselves to be escaping. Similarly, despite the obvious attempt to disentangle it from sovereignty, their reading of the Christian configuration of constituent power in the apostle Paul continues this connection with autonomy. But if the theological genealogy of individuated autonomy is simply the universalization of sovereignty, or everyone's opportunity to be sovereign rather than its opposite, then de-eschatologization has its full end. If constituent power is a voluntarily received gift, it cannot be subjugated to another absolute obligation, not even the autonomous self or the autonomy of the multitude. This is the problem with Negri's unequivocal statement, "The absoluteness of sovereignty is a totalitarian concept, whereas that of constituent power is the absoluteness of democratic government."[108] Constituent power, if configured as love, has no such right to insist on its own way. Negri, of course, argues against this synonymy of absolutes. The apostle Paul, apparently following on the gospel testimony, proffers otherwise,[109] as Part III attempts to explicate. His configuration of the body of Christ, the new humanity, is a body identified by the mutual surrender of autonomy between God and humanity in Jesus and consequently among humanity in him.

107. Ibid., 159.
108. Negri, *Insurgencies*, 12.
109. 1 Corinthians 13:5.

The radical transcendence represented by the originary experiences of the Pentecostal-charismatic movement carries just such egalitarian motivations for love among the multitude that the neo-Marxists look for. The suggestion of this conduit, in line with the general direction of the alternative substrata of the previous three, is that the genealogy of church and empire indicates that transcendence can be separated from sovereign power. The implications of this move then leave open the possibility of an alternative configuration of transcendence capable of providing the loving motivation for the activation of the life of the multitude. It is being suggested here that the practice of living by faith that Karla Poewe recognizes to be at the roots of Pentecostal-charismatic spirituality carries a potential power in parallel with and complementary to the potential power of immaterial labor. As has already been noted, she traces the exercise of living by faith, or what she also terms "faith prayer,"[110] to the nineteenth-century faith missions and their practice of accommodation, by means of participant observation and mirroring, culminating in their embrace of the indigenous culture of the host community. Classical examples of this are indicated in the founding tenets of the China Inland Mission in which the adoption of Chinese dress and lifestyle was a requirement for missionary work.[111] As she describes it, the exercise is a form of accommodation to God and other people based on surrender and receptivity, in which the direction is from the "non-rational to the rational, from happening to doing, from experience to talk, from sign to metaphor, from spiritual gifts to utility, from receptiveness to action, from demonstration to theology and from indigenization to globalization."[112] The result is a reversal of "the centrality of the rational, of calculated doing, of articulate verbal skills, of doctrine, and of things Western" that are basic to modernity.

Poewe emphasizes the impact of this operation of faith in relation to financial and material provision in a way that provides particular insight into the economics of Pentecostal-charismatic primitivism. From this it is possible to demonstrate both the vulnerability and the potential of the Pentecostal-charismatic experience of the Spirit in relation to the developing theopolitical genealogy of biopower. Although it is not difficult to see how this accommodated the burgeoning capitaliza-

---

110. Poewe, "The Nature, Globality and History of Charismatic Christianity," 10.

111. Grubb, *C. T. Studd, Cricketer and Pioneer*, 54.

112. Poewe, "The Nature, Globality and History of Charismatic Christianity," 12.

tion of American society, Poewe's analysis discloses the dual capacity of this accommodation, which, while rendering Pentecostal-charismatic primitivism vulnerable to biopower, at the same time recognizes that it is originally imbued with a kenotic attitude of spirit in which living by faith yields up autonomy and in so doing challenges the ontological sovereignty inherent in the genealogy of biopower.

In this way living by faith is analogous to immaterial labor in its twofold faculty. For in the same way that immaterial labor has the potential power to become either the constituted object of biopower or the constituent power to overcome it, so the accommodatory character of living by faith has the vulnerability to affirm multiplied sovereignty on its path to individual autonomy but also the potential to challenge biopower with kenotic surrender and receptivity to the Other. If the kenotic potential of living by faith is conjoined with the potential power of immaterial labor and directed counter-politically at the biopolitical system, it is possible that together they can issue in the empowerment of the multitude to give themselves in unconditional love to God and therefore one another. The eschatological ethos of living with empire today is momentous from the perspective of neo-Marxist and neo-Christian alike. The challenge of the times and the potential for mistaking again the fullness of the peace for its opposite, makes the moment especially poignant in the light of the cautionary application of the proposed fourth-century lapsis. It makes the evaluation of kenosis and the attempt to reconfigure transcendence from the originary gospel testimony that is the focus of the third part of this book, the more pertinent.

PART III

Reconfiguring the Divine

6

Kenotic Theology

THE PURPORT OF THE preceding two parts of this project has been to expose the fourth-century affirmation of sovereign power as the identity of transcendence throughout the Western European partnership of church and empire. They concluded with a presentation of the contemporary biopolitical West as the consummation of this, Christendom's defining decision. The implication of the whole has been that a Christology consequent on this choice framed the theology of incarnation, and, in so doing, disfigured the portrayal of Jesus and with it the subsequent representation of divine transcendence. As a result no adequate transcendent tool remains by which to criticize or change the present world. Part III now attempts to remedy this situation by offering a means of reconnecting with an originary counterpolitical Jesus. It consists of two chapters, the first of which considers kenotic directions in contemporary theology that parallel the lapsis theologies considered in Part I. It shows how the proposed primary fall may be answered by the complementary development of a particular kenotic Christology to provide a present resolution to the problem initiated there. The final chapter then attempts to configure an eschatological hermeneutic and an accompanying narrative exegesis that points the way to the operation of a kenotic theopolitics. As has already been intimated, these objectives require a major reorientation both of christological work and the nature of theology itself beyond the scope of the thesis of this book, in preparation for which this third part can only hope to provide some important signposts.

To this end it is helpful to recall Paul Fletcher's three crucial challenges, which formed the conclusion to the first chapter of Part I. These were the call to interrogate how faith became subject to juridico-political force, the need to achieve the eschatological reconception of time, and the attempt to reconnect with the counterpolitical Jesus. The four conduits have addressed the first of these challenges through the exposure of the miscegenation of church and empire and its subsequent genealogy. Part III now draws on the possibilities of kenosis to point towards a reconfiguring of the divine in such a manner that it can be liberated from its subordination to imperial time and restored to its counterpolitical potential. The concluding sections of the fourth conduit suggested that the originary experiences of the Pentecostal movement may be identified as a new kind of transcendence among the multitude, which, together with the parallel reemergence of pneumatology, points towards a necessary reconsideration of gospel Christology. This chapter now takes up the complementary initiative of kenotic theology, which has gained such momentum in recent years that "by the latter half of the twentieth century most major theologians had come to speak of kenosis as lying at the very heart of the life of God as Trinity."[1] Current directions in kenotic theology are explored and a distinctive kind of kenotic theology, or kenarchy,[2] is developed in hope of achieving an effective alignment of potential power and initiating the reconception of time.

A. KENOTIC CHRISTOLOGY

Given that the result of the supposed subsumption of the character of God by sovereign power was the displacement of the *corpus verum*, the aim of these concluding chapters is to set out a possible way of understanding the incarnation of God in Jesus of Nazareth without any such identification with sovereignty. In consequence the unapologetic approach taken in this chapter is to employ the modus operandi of moving from the gospel testimony of Jesus of Nazareth to the nature and character of divine transcendence. The crucial effect of this approach is that it applies the kenotic demeanor of Jesus directly to deity. It is this that distinguishes the understanding of kenosis proposed here from the notion as generally developed. Instead of putting the emphasis on the concept of God and explicating kenosis as the emptying out of the sup-

---

1. David Brown, *Divine Humanity*, 3.

2. This is an invented word for the particular kenotic theology configured in this chapter, as the initial section explains.

posed attributes of divine power, it puts the accent on the self-giving, loving behavior of Jesus and, rather, reinvests that into the nature of transcendence. As a result, the meaning of "emptied himself," as found, for example, in the *carmen Christi* of Philippians 2, is not interpreted as referring to Jesus' equality with God, as if it were his divinity that Jesus poured out, but as emphasizing that it is the nature of divinity to empty itself out in love. The significance of his equality with God is then related to his kenotic lifestyle, which is taken to mean that the divine life is therefore definitively kenotic life. Understood in this way, the term "kenosis" is taken to be an appropriate depiction for the overall tenor of the whole Jesus narrative, from the nativity to the crucifixion, resurrection, and ascension, and the final days of the story are simply seen as its consummation. The particular advantage of this interpretation of kenosis is that, by being thus placed at the opposite pole to imperial sovereignty, it provides for its effective dismissal. This, as the following sections will make clear, is not the case with most kenotic theology. The advantage of reconfiguring incarnation in this way is that it positions Jesus, and therefore God, in confrontation with the powers, with which, in the course of Christendom, divinity has been increasingly aligned.

By bringing together the move from Jesus to God and the identification of Jesus with kenotic love, this chapter extrapolates from the Jesus of gospel faith to the defining demeanor of deity, which it configures in terms of kenosis. It makes the claim that the gospel figure of the Christ is properly exhibited as one emptying out his life for the sake of the poor in body and spirit. It is not difficult to see that such an approach answers the imperial genealogy traced through the preceding conduits and in so doing resonates with the alternative subplots depicted alongside them. With this in view, the chapter first delineates the contours of the distinctive form of kenotic Christology proposed by this project. The overview that then follows takes note of the impact that the directly configured kenosis expounded here could have had on the genealogical stages of church and empire indicated in the four conduits. Its concord or discord with the development of kenotic theology is then used to clarify its timbre in confrontation with imperial power. This exposes firstly the contradiction between the gospel Jesus and the Christ of Roman Christendom, secondly the "two Gods" of the territorial pope-king and transubstantiated propitiator, thirdly the constrained latitudinarian sovereignty of the benevolent modern monarch and its multiplication by money, and fourthly the rejection of transcendence and its transformation into the commodification of life itself as embodied in contemporary biopower. This is then followed by a consideration of kenotic love as a qualitatively different kind of power to imperial sovereignty, the purpose of which is to substantiate the capacity of the configuration of kenosis devised here to overcome the obligation of faith to juridico-political force.

1. Kenarchy

In order to distinguish clearly between the configuration of kenosis proposed here and the various other contemporary approaches, the new word "kenarchy" has been contrived and deployed as part of this project.[3] It is a composite of the Greek words *kenō* to empty and *arkhō* to rule. It brings together kenosis and rulership from a particular understanding of kenosis and authority that draws on their use by the apostle Paul in Philippians 2 to describe the manner in which Jesus emptied himself (*kenoō heautou*) and the way that this resulted in him being given the highest position in the cosmos. Many configurations of kenotic theology use kenosis in the attempt to reconcile imperial sovereignty and humility in God, so that his humility becomes a moral component of his sovereign power on the continuing assumption that sovereign power is necessary to divine transcendence, as the coming sections discuss. Kenarchy, however, proposes that the behavior of self-emptying love described in the *carmen Christi* is the fullness of divine rule. Rather than seeing the downward and upward movement of the Christ as reasserting hierarchical sovereignty, it regards the incarnation as permanently emptying out sovereignty and thereby rendering the gift of potential power for the blessing of the others, the primary attribute of God, humanity, and the whole universe of being. The effect, expressed in colloquial terms, is to turn the hierarchical domination system of empire on its head. Life-laying-down loving becomes the *telos* and motif from which all cultural, political, and creational life is ordered. Hence the ultimate expression of rule described as "highly exalted . . . above every name" (*huperupsoō . . . huper pas onoma*) is permanently kenotic and by no means implies a

---

3. Google and Twitter reveal another use of the word "kenarchy," which is a form of student action and bass rhythm evolved by one Kenny Woods in 2008. The "ken" is seemingly based on Kenny not kenosis. While this has nothing to do with the development of the word "kenarchy" configured here, it lends it a grassroots feel.

return to a place of imperial sovereignty. Its effect is to turn all imperial configurations of rulership and political relationship upside down by making the lowest place the highest place, and the exercise of power the emptying of it out.

Paul Fletcher has described the current condition of Christianity as in "the midst of its occupation by capitalism."[4] He characterizes the accompanying normative theological position as an "anti-eschatological accommodation with the ascendancy of guilt." With these descriptions he calls for "the activity of identifying and reconstructing a genuinely Christian form of temporal existence, an undertaking which begins from the point at which the God of capital is not only identified but from which the practice of giftedness and kenosis is intensified within the very heart of the dream-world of the system." Kenarchy attempts to develop this practice of giftedness and kenosis in the recognition that the existing mainstream forms that take the Western political system for granted need to be deconstructed and replaced by the choice to donate one's own naked life, by emptying out potential power in love. At its heart is an understanding of the exception as the fulcrum of divine grace and outpoured love where God's choice to love abolishes[5] the whole soteriological genealogy of church and empire expressed today as biopower. This identifies Jesus' choice to love as the heart of the gospel testimony. This kenarchic love is regarded as the disposition of transcendence behind everything at all times, which came to its consummation at the cross. It identifies the place where this fullness now needs to operate as the heart of daily life within the biopolitical world.

2. From Jesus to God

The proposal to argue from Jesus to God derives unexpected support from one of the most renowned detractors of the traditional theory of the incarnation of the last century. Don Cupitt, in his famous chapter "The Christ of Christendom" in *The Myth of God Incarnate*,[6] clearly recognizes both the imperial function of the traditional formulation of the incarnation and its radical variance with the gospel tradition. His exposition of the classical doctrine effectively characterizes the hierarchical Christ

---

4. Fletcher, *Disciplining the Divine*, 158.

5. What Giorgio Agamben configures as *katargēsis*. See Agamben, *The Time That Remains*, 108.

6. Cupitt, "The Christ of Christendom," 133–47.

that ratified Constantine's role as God's earthly counterpart described in the first conduit. From the perspective of kenarchy configured here he is emphatically right to call this into question. Even from his modern, diminished view of the capacity of the gospels to provide a view of the real Jesus, he is still able to contrast the Christ of Christendom with the "not quite unreachable" figure behind them.[7] In so doing he clearly connects the "ecclesiastical Christ" to the proposed fourth-century lapsis and provides an exposition that underlines the displacement of the gospel testimony. His primary argument shows how the synthesis of the divine and worldly was at the cost of the moral opposition of Jesus and gentile kingship. As he clearly states, "Christ's lordship was originally eschatological, and manifest in this age . . . by ironic contrast with temporal lordship. But the dogma of the incarnation brought it forward into this present age. As the manifest Absolute in history, Christ became the basis of the Christian Empire and of political and ecclesiastical power in the present age."[8] From this perspective, as Cupitt underlines, if the tradition of Jesus' own teaching were to be taken seriously, "Chalcedon and later dogmatic systems derived from it would have to be abandoned."

Despite his unusual clarity about both the form of the imperial Christ and the contradictory nature of Jesus of Nazareth, Cupitt moves to reject incarnation altogether rather than moving to argue from Jesus to God. But there is a real danger that, despite his insights into the Christendom Christ, his criticism of kenotic theology just prior to the emergence of its more mature phase, carries the same ontologically imperial view of transcendence as that which he exposes and rejects in the classic formulation of the incarnation. This shows itself, firstly, in his claim that "a metaphysical kenosis is incompatible with theism"[9] and then in his secondary suggestion that kenotic theology is derived from the class system. To begin with this secondary criticism of kenosis, Cupitt observes in Charles Gore and H.P. Liddon what he considers to be a condescending, culturally relative, and class-bound attitude in their formulations.[10] But to align kenosis only with this view suggests

7. Ibid., 145.

8. Ibid., 141.

9. Ibid., 137.

10. Cupitt cites Liddon, *The Divinity of our Lord and Saviour Jesus Christ*; Charles Gore, *The Incarnation of the Son of God, Bampton Lectures 1891*; Charles Gore, *Dissertations on Subjects Connected with the Incarnation*. Ibid., 137.

an inability to grasp the complete reversal of rank that kenotic theology is also able to conceive. There is nothing condescending about a nullification of hierarchical superiority that, far from being dependent on the class system, calls for its dismissal. This amounts to an egalitarian identification with the multitude, not class-bound condescension.

To return to the primary basis of Cupitt's statement of the incompatibility of kenosis and theism, this consists in his apparent acceptance of Aquinas' understanding of divinity, namely that "the divine attributes belong to God not contingently but analytically."[11] From this viewpoint it is understandable that Cupitt sees sovereignty as already a necessary aspect of God and so cannot be put off "like a superfluous piece of clothing." However, this may be no less an example of an imported hierarchical understanding of the nature of transcendence than the imperial theology he is exposing. The fascination of kenosis consists in its capacity to challenge the deep structure of sovereignty, which is where the requirement of analytical theory itself lies. If the connection between deity and humanity is relational and not essentially theoretical, then the discovery that God has chosen to exchange domination for love overcomes the necessity and power of analytical theory, and renders dependency on it a form of predication on the genealogy of sovereignty. However, while recognizing that there are challenges in conceptualizing an all-powerful being who continuously gives away power, arguing from Jesus to God means relinquishing analytical conceptions of metaphysical possibility as much as it does setting aside the official canons of church councils. It follows that Cupitt's rejection of Christendom's understanding of the incarnation is not only rooted in its obligation to imperial power, but betrays an underlying theological objection to reconciling immanence and transcendence. His proposed "fresh start"[12] claims that, in any case, to argue from Jesus to God leads to a cult of Christ and anthropomorphism, as if such conclusions were self-explanatorily in error. As he puts it, "God is with man, in man, only in his transcendence . . . Christology . . . must be theocentric, not Christocentric."[13] While this clarifies his position, it in no way precludes the alternative standpoint presented here, which is that God is with man only when he is present both transcendently and immanently.

11. Ibid., 137.
12. Ibid., 141.
13. Ibid., 146.

The unavoidable implication of arguing from Jesus to the divine is that old formulations are experimentally jettisoned only to be restored, if at all, when once they have been evaluated in the light of the gospel testimony. These include, as has been indicated, the assumption of imperial sovereignty together with its overt or covert expression within deity. But there follow other familiar, apparently defining characteristics of God such as the usual omnipotence, omniscience, omnipresence, impassibility, and creation *ex nihilo*. Some at least of the significant theologians that have worked with a concept of kenosis since the middle of the last century, have taken, or are beginning to risk, a path tending in this direction. Jürgen Moltmann follows the Lutheran scholar Paul Althaus in his view that the type of God revealed in the incarnation is such that it must put in question any notion of divine immutability and with it the axiom of the impassibility of the divine nature.[14] He notes positively that "we have the kenoticists to thank for at last having made the contradiction plain."[15]

Karl Barth affirms the need "for a different understanding of omnipotence," although his dialectical way of approach involves his insistence on the notion of divine obedience on the part of the Son even within the life of the trinity, which may continue to imply notions of subordination.[16] Kevin Giles makes clear that in this Barth is not positing a simple subordination between the hypostases, but rather in the inner life of God's own self, or what he terms "Godself."[17] But most significantly, Barth states unequivocally of our understanding of deity that "it cannot be gathered from any notion of supreme, absolute, non-worldly being. It can only be learned from what took place in Christ" and asserts that we must "learn to correct our notions of the being of God" in the light of the incarnation.[18] John Milbank makes a similar point when he suggests that to point to the narrative of the life of Jesus is the only certain way we can say anything definite about God.[19] N.T. Wright explains that it is "not that we know what the word God means and can discover the extent to which this God was present in, or revealed through, Jesus; rather that,

---

14. Brown, *Divine Humanity*, 227.

15. In Polkinghorne, *The Work of Love*, 137–51, esp. 141–2, cited in ibid., 227.

16. Barth, *Church Dogmatics*, IV, I, 202.

17. Giles, *The Trinity and Subordinationism*, 89.

18. Barth, *Church Dogmatics*, IV/1, 177 and IV/1, 186.

19. Milbank, "Postmodern Critical Augustinianism," 55.

by close attention to Jesus himself, we are invited to discover, perhaps for the first time, just who the creator and covenant God was and is all along."[20] Bruce McCormack's work affirms the direction advocated here when he suggests "reversing the *genus maiestaticum* ('the genus of majesty') of classical Lutheranism and its *genus tapeinoticum* ('the genus of humility'), now to be applied directly to God the Son: instead of divine attributes given to the human, the communication of human attributes to the divine."[21] He has further developed this thinking in a series of lectures and a promised forthcoming book to suggest that the theologian's task is not to consider first what it is to be divine and then think about the incarnation but, rather, to "consider first the particular history of Jesus Christ, and then discover such ideas of divinity as emerge from that particular pattern of events."[22]

3. Reconciling Two Gods

An obvious outcome of arguing directly to a kenotic God from Jesus is that it voids the approach to incarnation that juxtaposes an imperial sovereign Father and a propitiating kenotic son. In so doing it sets aside the underlying complications necessary to reconciling two contradictory characters as one substance as manifest in the machinations of church councils such as Nicaea and Chalcedon. It also answers the bifurcation and conflict of sovereignty delineated in the second conduit and the inversion of the *corpus verum* and the *corpus mysticum* consequent on it. From the standpoint of kenarchy, the whole endeavor to recover and maintain temporal peace through sovereignty was utterly misguided. Instead, the role of the church was to welcome the fall of Rome and, as agents of love and justice, to serve and encourage emerging leadership gift among the people, sacrificing their own lives in the process if required. It also follows that the configuration of the eucharist as the place of resolution of God's sovereign power and man's failure to submit, by the appeasing interposition of Jesus' death and blood, was similarly misconceived, together with its legitimating function of hierarchical mediation between cleresy and people. It is seen to embody instead the

20. N.T. Wright, *The Meaning of Jesus: Two Visions*, 214.

21. McCormack, "The Humility of the Eternal Son," 243–51.

22. Brown, *Divine Humanity*, 233.

fullness of God's life laid down in loving confrontation with, and over-coming of, imperial power.

While the examples of kenotic theology referred to above, in com-mon purpose with the burden of this book, have begun to indicate ways in which transcendence might be reconfigured in response to the endemic subsumption by sovereignty, many kenotic theologians still distinguish between an imperially sovereign God and the human Jesus of the incar-nation and utilize kenosis as a device to resolve the ensuing interplay of the kenotic and the unkenotic. The work of two magisterial proponents of kenotic theology, Bulgakov and Balthasar, still moves from the trinity to the Son and not the other way round. As a result Bulgakov maintains monarchical hierarchy within transcendence,[23] and Balthasar refers to "here" and "beyond" in a way that seems to make the God of beyond greater than the God who is incarnate here. Indeed, Balthasar's whole concept of meta-drama may contribute to this, because it could suggest that the real is the meta-drama and the part is just an episode, rather than recognizing that the real might equally be God's stage here.[24] This is clearly not Balthasar's intent, as is evident from his description of Jesus as "The matrix of all possible dramas" for "he embodies the absolute dra-ma in his own person."[25] However, whereas the concept of incarnation contemplated here posits a time when transcendence and immanence are overlaid one on the other, the analogy of a meta-drama of which the incarnation or even the whole creation is just an important scene could appear to subordinate the episode to the whole for its full explanation. This may prove to be a general problem with making arguments from analogy the primary route to the knowledge of the divine, as the coming section on difference and otherness will develop. In the kenotic theol-ogy being proposed here, the incarnation is regarded as more than an episode or an analogy, but rather the actual intrusion of transcendence on the immanent plane. This is perhaps better displayed by Balthasar's language of a scission in time, discussed in the next chapter.

As David Brown makes clear, this potential duality of an imperially sovereign God and the human Jesus of the incarnation characterizes the British kenoticists from Gore to Hebblethwaite. Among these Brown ob-serves two parallel strands to the life of God the Son, the one permanently

23. Bulgakov, *The Lamb of God*, 307.

24. Healy, *Church, World and the Christian Life*, 61.

25. Balthasar, *Theo-Drama: Theological Dramatic Theory*, vol. II, 62.

part of the heavenly divine life, the other fully kenotic in the incarnation and thereafter, each thus directed to different but overlapping eternal goals in fulfillment of divine life and human life. These two strands are sometimes conceived with recourse to particular analogies such as in the example of Richard Swinburne, who uses the paradox of whether an omnipotent being has the power to create a stone too heavy for such a being to lift, to show that divine omnipotence must include the ability to limit its own omnipotence.[26] Others put the whole thing down to mystery, or explain it away by sleight of hand as in Forsyth's observation: "if the infinite God was so constituted that he could not live also as a finite man then he was not infinite."[27] But Brown is of the view that something is missing imaginatively, and offers a most revealing analogy of his own that serves to encapsulate succinctly the tension being referred to here. The analogy Brown offers is the practice of Method Acting developed by Konstantin Stanislavsky.[28] The basic idea of this technique is that realistic portrayal is achieved through total absorption in the character's identity: seeing the world through the particular character's eyes such that, while the film or drama is being produced, the actor actually lives the part both on and off stage. While strongly emphasizing the exercise of the actor's imagination, also relevant is close observation of others and drawing on what is already known from personal experience. The aim is so to infuse one's own self with the thoughts, emotions, and personality of the character that one actually becomes that character for the duration of the film or play. Brown suggests that the role of God in the incarnation is like that of the Method actor.

The difficulty here is not with the analogy itself, which works well to illustrate Brown's point. Rather the problem is that the analogy is so good that it discloses exactly the position that kenarchy aims to avoid. It puts God in the position in which he is not really kenotic but just pretending, or putting on an act, which he later relinquishes when once he has made his point. But from the perspective being set out here, it is not the case of a non-kenotic, or partly kenotic God acting as if he is kenotic for the purposes of incarnation. God is not acting a part; rather he is revealing his heart. There is no other God than the one incarnated in the kenotic Christ. The tension that characterizes Brown's position

26. David Brown, *Divine Humanity*, 245.

27. Ibid., 247.

28. Ibid., 251–3.

is underlined by the ingenuousness of his reference to the kenotic and non-kenotic aspects of God the Son,[29] and his affirmative use of Austin Farrer's statement that "God cannot live an identical godlike life in eternity and in a human story," but that above, the Son's life is "a co-operation in sovereignty and an interchange of eternal joys."[30] This is contrasted with his incarnate life below where the appropriate response is "an obedience in inspiration, a waiting for direction, an acceptance of suffering, a rectitude of choice, a resistance to temptation and a willingness to die." In the end, and in line with his dramatic analogy, Brown concludes that not all divine action is kenotic and that some aspects of the divine promise do depend on unqualified power. He particularly asserts that something more than kenotic power is necessary to raise the dead and that "the attempt to follow Christ in this world should not always take the kenotic path. Sometimes power is the right instrument to use."[31] But in the concept of kenosis being put forward here, it is precisely the decision to lay life down in love that consists in the power to raise the dead and unkenotic power that kills. This returns again to the problem of whether kenosis can be configured as the true power of love, which is taken up in the discussion of John Caputo's work in section B below.

4. Kenosis and Sovereignty

The assertion of kenosis consequent on arguing from Jesus to the divine, confronts the inception of the nation state and its responsibility for the multiplication of sovereignty through law, war, and money detailed in the third conduit. Instead of justifying the limitation of universal sovereignty in the cause of trading the remainder through the device of money as debt, kenarchy configures power as its unconditional release by the choice to love. As already noted, the deep structural aspects of love as power are explored further in the second main section of this chapter. For now let it suffice to note that the choice to love and the choice to give away power are so closely aligned that their effect would be to rearrange society from the bottom outwards, forgiving enemies, empowering the poor, re-instating the marginalized, and giving the maximum honor to children. Rather than conserving the optimum measure of sovereignty

29. Ibid., 254.

30. Ibid., 256.

31. Ibid., 264.

commensurate with yielding up just enough to preserve it, kenotic love would motivate the yielding of power and access to property in the cause of humanitarian justice and love, not economic investment and profit.

However, the perception of incarnation as a resolution of the tension between the unkenotic omni-power of deity and the kenotic power manifest in the human Jesus is developed by some kenotic theologians to point to a voluntary constraint within God. As Giles suggests is the case with Barth, this is either portrayed as taking place between the persons, or perhaps within the shared substance of the Godhead itself.[32] These kinds of arguments for kenosis continue to contribute to the complex theological solutions necessary to the continuing affirmation of transcendence as sovereignty, paralleling the move from absolute to multiplied sovereignty. From this perspective kenosis can be regarded as a means of ameliorating universal sovereign power and making its multiplication acceptable. Incarnation is presented as an explanation of the way in which an absolute sovereign God graciously gives place to the sovereignty of others by living among them in Christ and forgiving their sinful competition with him. God is seen as emptying out a degree of sovereign power in order to allow others a real but limited measure of it. Both Brown and Ward trace the genealogy of kenotic theology back to Luther whose understanding of the incarnation exemplifies this. He sees the divine attributes as being emptied into the human Jesus, who, aware of the divine form as well as the human, "does not take it up nor use it to lord himself over us, rather he serves us with it."[33] From this perspective the divine form could be used to lord over, but instead it empowers, or multiplies power. This is a decisive shift away from the medieval hierarchical view where God is the heavenly Lord, and the pope and emperor are his vicars lording on earth. Now incarnation configures a human being who has omni-power that he willingly restricts, thereby making room for the sovereignty of others. So in his exposition of the *carmen Christi*, Luther states of the reformist monarchs, "Let the prince then empty himself of his power and supremacy in his heart and concern himself with the needs of his subjects as though they were his own needs. For this is what Christ has done for us, and this is a genuine work of Christian love."[34]

32. Giles, *The Trinity and Subordinationism*, 89.

33. Ward, "Kenosis: Death, Discourse and Resurrection," 26.

34. Brown cites *Luther's Works*, German ed. 11, 273; American ed. 45, 120. David

The seventeenth-century kenoticists that succeeded Luther continued in this vein. Hence, on the one hand, the Giessen school propounded
the view that in what was termed the *exinanitio* (emptying out), Jesus
only partially refrained from employing his omniscience, omnipotence,
and omnipresence. Thus they drew a distinction between the potential
possession of majesty and the conscious restraint in exercising it. The
Tübingen school countered with the view that Jesus did exercise his majesty as the Son of God but it was concealed from those who did not at first
believe.[35] In both cases sovereignty was upheld while others were made
room for in a way that aligned with the shifting role of the monarch in
relation to the burgeoning bourgeoisie in seventeenth-century economics and politics. In the same way the nineteenth-century kenoticists such
as Gottfried Thomasius and Charles Gore seem to have been following
the contours of modern thought in the rejection of transcendence and
the elevation of immanence, in the attempt to prevent sovereign power
from limiting the freedom of rational human expression. As Ward sees
it, they connected kenosis with historicism, biography, and *Bildung*,
thereby providing a theological aspect to the humanly orientated search
for the historical Jesus and the evolution of his Messianic consciousness.[36] Given the rejection of transcendence it was, of course, unlikely
for this to disclose an historically transcendent kenotic Christ.

In line with this, Thomasius viewed kenosis in the incarnation as
the emptying out of the perceived sovereign transcendence of the divine
nature, the omni-powers that he distinguished as relative attributes only
existing in God in relation to the creation, as distinct from freedom, holiness, absolute truth, and absolute love. The impact of this distinction,
however, was used to emphasize the moral character of finite humanity
rather than to free God from imperial power. Charles Gore continued to
develop kenosis in a way that bound humanity to the immanent plane
and explained that even Christ experienced contingency and possessed
an historically governed consciousness. With them both, rather than
developing kenosis as a central aspect of the character of God derived
from the incarnation in a movement away from domination within God,
kenosis is simply regarded as an affirmation of human finitude.[37]

Brown, *Divine Humanity*, 28.

35. Ward, "Kenosis: Death, Discourse and Resurrection," 28.

36. Ibid., 29.

37. Ibid., 30.

Once incarnation is either rejected as sovereignly transcendent or denounced as anthropomorphic, the Death of God and the atheology represented by the writings of Mark C. Taylor and Thomas J.J. Altizer appear to be the only viable alternatives. These radical forms of kenosis do not describe attributes of God but are theories that, as a consequence of the identification of transcendence with domination, empty out the divine nature altogether. Kenosis in this context is the emptying out of God. This is the opposite of the move being attempted here, where the kenosis manifest in the Jesus of the gospel testimony is taken to be the apotheosis of the character of God. From this standpoint kenarchy expresses the fullness of God's power and is the complete opposite of imperial sovereignty. While the emptying out, or death of an imperial, dominating omni-powerful God may be reckoned to be a good thing, without an alternative articulation of transcendence nothing remains save what Ward describes as local, transient, relative, and superficial.[38]

5. Difference and Otherness

Kenarchy challenges the modern and ongoing postmodern rejection of a transcendence equated with imperial sovereignty, with its repression of human freedom and the propagation of bigotry and prejudice. Instead it meets it with a complete reconfiguration of transcendence in terms of Jesus' life laid down in love and validated by resurrection, standing behind the exploited and depleted planet and its people as the true power of the exception, ready to re-empower the multitude with love. It similarly responds to the quasi-transcendent conjunction of sovereignty and money and its consummation as the commodification of life itself in biopower. The form of kenosis proposed here answers this by the presentation of life as gift, able to transform the fullness of biopower manifest in naked victimhood into the potential power for the re-creation of a kenotic way of life accessed by faith. This form of kenosis connects God inextricably to his creation. It flows from a view of incarnation that circumscribes the image of God and embeds the divine in his creation by making the incarnation the starting point for understanding transcendence. As the next chapter suggests, it provides a narrative hermeneutic that can inform a practical standpoint for understanding the whole of life.

38. Ibid., 37.

This brings into focus a recurring contrary trait of contemporary kenoticism, which is a particular emphasis on difference and otherness. While the result of arguing from Jesus to God certainly confronts all human selfishness and desire to dominate with the breathtaking polar opposite of his love, aspects of this tendency to oppose identification and difference may stand in the way of the impact of a fully transcendent human Jesus once again. Working from the gospel Jesus to God, it is comparatively straightforward to affirm difference as necessary to love and relationship between the persons of the trinity, or divine and human, male and female, Jew and gentile, bond and free. All this can be argued from the relationship between Jesus and the Father, the seemingly deliberately wide spectrum of political and character orientation among the disciples within the all-male starting point, and Jesus' subsequent honoring of women, gentiles, and slaves. However, there is a more problematic thread running through some accounts of kenosis, particularly where there is a strong motivation to hold to an orthodox position on Nicaea or Chalcedon. Even Ronald J. Feenstra qualifies his radical approach by setting it within the context of these councils and proposing a merely temporary quality to the Son's kenotic deity within the incarnation.[39] It is perhaps the case that these credal statements do not unequivocally require the maintenance of ontological otherness in deity, but in the light of the proposed lapsis it seems the most likely reading, as has already been intimated in relation to Nicaea in the first conduit.

The difficulty concerns the role of analogy in the apprehension of divine transcendence. The nature of the problem for the kenotic approach being pointed towards here is the potential of analogy to proffer ways of configuring the divine outside of the proposed direct trajectory from Jesus to God. Brown, Ward, and Balthasar all tend at times to ascribe otherness to deity in this way. Brown's view is expressed in the Method Acting analogy already referred to. From that, it is clear that he is unwilling to jettison ontological otherness although he admits that it is difficult to maintain. Attempting to place the incarnation "midway between the projection of another self within the divine life of the Trinity and projection of the world as wholly other in creation," he himself protests that "the created order is not 'wholly other'"[40] and cites the

39. Feenstra, "A Kenotic Christology of the Divine Attributes," 153.
40. David Brown, *Divine Humanity*, 247.

willingness of Augustine of Hippo and many others to speak of nature as the second book of revelation and the scriptures' testimony that humanity was made in the divine image. Brown attempts to justify holding to otherness by recognizing a key role for kenosis alongside it as a divine self-expression that discloses signs of God's creativity and love. Kenotic power is here seen to modify, qualify, and complement omnipotent otherness. Such power is now "properly moderated by creativity and love."[41] But it is surely unnecessary to assert the otherness of God's power in order to disclose signs of his creativity and love. The difference between God's power and ours can be one of quantity rather than quality.

Ward's discussion of Balthasar goes a stage further and attempts to make the *imago dei* itself a reason to assert divine otherness. Ward draws attention to Balthasar's use of the concept of a hiatus, distancing the image of God from a direct reference to God's nature and human nature, and complicating the concept in a similar way to the obfuscation of incarnation that is argued against here.[42] A danger with emphasizing otherness in God in this way is that, just as incarnation is made into a device for the potential solution to an ontological contradiction between sovereign power and kenotic love in God, so creation in the image of God is made to include an ontological otherness between God and humanity. The problem is not with the assertion of divine otherness as a means of emphasizing the extent in which God's love exceeds human love, in order to point the direction in which our shared life can now take us in the light of the incarnation. Rather the problem lies in the assertion of a separation or *diastasis* between the divine and the human,[43] and the expansion of the *analogia entis* with which they resolve it. Ward identifies this as the "ineliminable aporia, an eradicable secondariness, a following after, which is the hallmark of human figuration ultimately understood as discipleship."[44] This move appears to undermine the practical potential of the incarnation by rendering it subsidiary to the *analogia entis*. However, if the incarnation was not the actual conjunction of divine and human life, then its availability for reactivation is called into question.

The kenotic lifestyle being developed in this chapter depends on a real abandonment of Godself to humankind in Christ that can be mu-

41. Ibid., 265.

42. Ward, "Kenosis: Death, Discourse and Resurrection," 44.

43. Ibid., 44–45.

44. Ibid., 45.

tually reactivated by their reciprocal abandonment to him. This is not to ignore that it is precisely in order to recapture a participation in the divine, supposedly lost by the impact of the univocity of being, that contemporary kenotic theologians make recourse to the analogy of being. Their argument is that the univocity of being lost divine otherness and therefore, because God is essentially other by definition, lost access to God. For them the reintroduction of an absolute otherness recovers God and the *analogia entis* restores participation in his otherness. However, the open question left by the proposed earlier fourth-century lapsis is to what extent this radical difference is a characteristic of the imperial sovereignty with which transcendence has been subsumed. It has already been intimated in chapter 1 that the moves by Duns Scotus, William of Ockham, and the nominalists can perhaps be understood as attempts to evade the dominating sovereignty of imperial theology rather than to suborn God's transcendence. The importance of the proposal to argue directly from Jesus to God is similarly an attempt to avoid continuing to carry characteristics of empire on into contemporary attempts to reconfigure transcendence.

The point here is not to deny any hermeneutical role to analogy, but to submit it to the Jesus of the originary testimony rather than the other way round. However, there seems little doubt from Ward's understanding of Balthasar that, rather than arguing kenosis from the Jesus of the incarnation, he uses a prior configuration of the nature of the trinitarian community based on an understanding of *homo symbolicus*. From this perspective Ward explains that "Creation is made possible by intra-trinitarian difference. Creation is completed in the incarnation just as the incarnation is completed in the eucharist. God becomes form and he, the Son, becomes the transcendental signifier, the name above all names."[45] However, the form of kenotic theology being contemplated in this chapter aims to develop the primary understanding of trinity, creation, and eucharist from the Jesus of the gospel testimony. Once this move is made, then a secondary use of analogy is unproblematic. It will be configured in terms of the kenarchic Christ. However, if it is only possible, as Ward expresses it, to live analogously to Christ's kenosis and if it is true that his trinitarian life is forever "an unassimilable alterity," then vestiges of imperial sovereignty may still be imported through the existing theological tradition, which may continue to obscure the *corpus*

45. Ibid., 45.

verum, not least through the existing institutions of the church and its accepted doctrines.

B. KENOTIC LOVE: WEAKNESS OR STRENGTH?

1. Incarnation as Event

In the proposed process from Jesus to God, the incarnation ceases to be a theological device rooted back to medievality, where doctrine functions as the legitimation of empire and requires unity of truth, embodiment of hierarchy, and curtailment of counterpolitics. Rather than conceived as a doctrine, foundation, or meta-narrative, the incarnation is regarded as an originary eschatological event embodying a kenotic, counter-imperial way of life appropriate to both humanity and divinity when operating in unity. It calls for present and future events to overcome empire and bring salvation to the poor in body and spirit. The incarnation is thus construed as the narrative testimony of an event that introduces the reader into a relationship with a person whose disposition is said to have transformed a past historical, socio-economic, and juridico-political situation. In this way it proffers a potential means to engender a counterpolitical outbreak of incarnational life in the present time and continues to call for its eschatological consummation. Given this role for the incarnation, the disciple can remain happily agnostic about theoretical matters of universal epistemology because kenosis is praxis not dogma, and the hegemony of ontological certainty is something it empties out, not something it grasps after.

This approach to the incarnation is illuminated by exploring several affinities with John Caputo's recent work on the theology of the event, as well as by taking note of significant divergences. Commencing with the affinities, the distinction between name and event is central to Caputo's insight and has particular application to the name "God" and the events that it carries but yet cannot fully contain. As he states, "There is always something unconditional and uncontainable about an event, whereas names, like 'God,' belong to conditioned and coded strings of signifiers. The event is the open-ended promise contained within a name, but a promise which the name can neither contain nor deliver."[46] This stripping away of the theological denotations of the name "God" fulfills the

---

46. Caputo, *The Weakness of God*, 2.

need to set aside the imperial subsumption that occurred in the course of Christendom. Caputo's emphasis on God as a name that calls for an event, encourages the emphasis to be on the event as the qualifier of the name instead of what, in the history of Christian theology since the proposed lapsis, has generally been the other way round. As Caputo perceives it, just as the excoriated name only harbors the event and cannot be precisely captured by it, the event itself is not amenable to being tied down rationally or quantified by Platonic, Hegelian, or Heideggerian logic. This is because the event carries emotional and experiential truth rather than definitive theoretical knowledge. As he puts it: "By the truth of the event, I mean what the event is capable of, the open-ended and unforeseeable future that the name harbours, its uncontainable possibilities, which may contain bad news . . . On that accounting, the truth is something one needs to have the heart for, the courage to cope with or expose oneself to . . . That is also why the truth for me is a matter of prayer, not epistemology."[47] This casts the event, and in this case the incarnation, outside both medieval theological restrictions and modern theoretical *mathēses* that might otherwise reduce its significance. In so doing it supports the re-casting of the incarnation attempted here. By freeing it from theoretical definition in this way, it is possible to express the event itself as a dynamic experience rather than an objective and inflexible construct. By aligning event and prayer, Caputo incorporates the disciple into the truth of the event, not in terms of its theoretical meaning but its socio-political and eschatological possibilities. This exposes the close connection delineated between living by faith and incarnational kenosis in the chapter that follows.

This brings us to the divergences from Caputo's approach, two main differences relating to the specificity of the incarnation and the function of kenosis as power. The view of the Jesus event being put forward here is that the socio-political and eschatological possibilities contained in it encourage the prayerful, by faith application of the incarnation to the now excoriated name of God. This hermeneutic activity, configured in depth in the next chapter, unapologetically deploys the Jesus event to rename God, while gladly acknowledging that the consequence of this will continue to be that the event overflows the semantics of the newly configured name. The specific result is the identification of the uncontainable divine-human kenotic way of life manifest in the human life,

47. Ibid., 5–6.

death, and resurrection of the person named Jesus with the operation of divine transcendence. Instead of connecting back to the old memories that adhered to the name "God" during the period of the church-empire genealogy, the name from now on calls for, and together with the Holy Spirit engenders, new eschatological manifestations of the Jesus event. By this means the event truly is an advent that comes, not as Caputo puts it, "independently of me,"[48] but is incarnated by me and the Holy Spirit working in unity together. So while each related event becomes uncontainable immediately it emerges, it is not therefore an uninitiated event. This has the effect of strongly qualifying Caputo's awkwardness with the idea of presence, as expressed in his bold re-rendering of Paul's citation of Isaiah[49] as "I will deconstruct the metaphysics of presence of the strong onto-theologians, sayeth the Lord God" and his definition of Christendom as "the coin of being and presence."[50] Instead it introduces a radical, uncontainable, kenotic presence, now completely separate from what Caputo rejects under the term "presence." The old church-empire conjunction of money and sovereign power, which he rejects as false presence, is thereby rendered as such, in contrast with the true presence configured by a faith hermeneutic based on kenotic love. This connects to the second main contrast with Caputo, which concerns the understanding of the nature of power itself.

2. Kenotic Love as True Power

Caputo does not regard the weakness of God as an altogether different kind of power to imperial sovereignty, such as D.Z. Philips, for example, intimates when he states, "'All power' cannot be attributed to God, since some kinds of power are to be contrasted to God's power."[51] Instead Caputo appears to oppose the permanent weakness of God to power per se. It is not that Caputo totally eschews all possibility of configuring kenosis as power; indeed he affirms it as such in his statement that the transcendence of God is "the power of the spirit, not of the sword" and in his conclusion that "it is the weak force of God."[52] However, in his

---

48. Ibid., 4.
49. 1 Corinthians 1:19.
50. Caputo, *The Weakness of God*, 30, 44, 48.
51. Philips, *The Problem of Evil and the Problem of God*, 33.
52. Caputo, *The Weakness of God*, 38.

concern to make clear that the kenosis of the cross was real, and to reject the abuse of God's power as "spectacular presence,"[53] Caputo challenges the way in which the apostle Paul sets the *carmen Christi*, "his eulogy of the weakness of God," in a "larger economy of power."[54] His concern is that the apostle's development of love as power might continue the validation of imperial power. While the need to disclose and maintain the full implications of kenosis is granted, to do so at the loss of the authority that belongs to the life of faith, is to exchange one misconception for another. Although weakness names crucial aspects of the incarnation event, it also overflows in directions that are not indicative of the impact of kenosis manifest there. Other effects of weakness can leave the world unchanged, the poor undefended, and evil unchallenged.

Caputo invokes the "hyper-realism of the event"[55] to qualify his assertion of God's weakness with passion and intensity. He makes this emotive intensity very clear when he describes the way that "as an event, the name of God overtakes us and overturns us, uprooting and unhinging us, and leaves us hanging on by a prayer."[56] The existential consequence of disconnecting God from all predetermined ontological order and casting the theologian unknowing onto the event is undeniably exhilarating. But unless this can actually reactivate counterpolitical action, its capacity for transformation remains uncertain. In the kenarchic understanding of the incarnation propounded here, a complete abandonment into the fullness of the self-emptying, life-laying-down power encountered in the incarnation event is proposed. Rather than assuming that the apostle Paul's perception of the wider field of power is the Roman imperial one, it is assumed that Paul's naming of power refers to his own existential experience of this kind of power in his faith abandonment to the Jesus of the gospel testimony. Then, rather than reading the apostle as empowering the powers when he assigns the fullness of power to God, as Caputo intimates by citing Paul's infamous seeming affirmation of imperial power, it sets the *ecclesia*'s relationship to the powers in the light of an event that unquestionably overwhelms and disempowers them. Paul's admonition to "be in subjection to the governing authorities"[57] can then

53. Ibid., 44.
54. Ibid., 48.
55. Ibid., 9.
56. Ibid., 11.
57. Romans 13:1.

be read as the way to behave towards oppressive powers after a clearly contrary stance has already been publicly demonstrated.

This reading of Paul and the powers is taken up in the final chapter in relation to Jesus' advice to his critics to "render to Caesar the things that are Caesar's; and to God the things that are God's." This goes beyond the seeming passivity of weakness and poses a confrontation between two different kinds of power, imperial sovereignty and kenotic love. Set in the context of Jesus' confrontation with the powers, the incarnation is displayed as an overwhelmingly loving manifestation of power in direct confrontation with the Roman regime. The Jesus event thus names and calls for an ongoingly kenotic manifestation of power in direct contrast with hierarchical authority. In this context Paul's configuration of power is that which the epistle to the Colossians describes as being fulfilled at the cross where having "disarmed the rulers and authorities, He made a public display of them, having triumphed over them through Him."[58]

Caputo's main difficulty appears to be with those actions within the incarnation narratives such as stilling storms, feeding crowds, healing the sick, and raising the dead that he relegates to "rouged"[59] spectacular presence and "profane magic."[60] For Caputo these imply a return to ideas of omnipotent being and therefore render kenosis temporary, recalling those ontological configurations of transcendence that the name of God needs freeing from. But the question is what stands behind these alleged acts of power within the incarnation event. The point maintained here is that kenotic love is both the motivation for the acts and the actual creative dynamic behind them. This perspective is illustrated further in the coming exegesis of the events leading up to the cross. Suffice it to say at this point that it underlines one of the central tenets of the thesis of this book, already given initial consideration in chapter 1, and discussed again in the fourth conduit, namely the crucial role of a genuine choice as necessary to both the operation of love and the function of God's power. This is the heart of the decision to proceed from Jesus to God in articulating the character of transcendence and is grounded in the testimony to Jesus' consummate choice to love and believe in the human multitude. This is not offered as a rational a priori, but rather as an overwhelming economy of response within a theological standpoint.

58. Colossians 2:15.
59. Caputo, *The Weakness of God*, 42, 44.
60. Ibid., 40.

The chapter that follows takes note that this step may be explicated with reference to Graham Ward's standpoint theology from where this terminology is taken, and that N.T. Wright's critical realism and Ward's own acknowledgment of anthropological and historical findings can undergird it in a secondary fashion. Arguing from Jesus to God interposes a moment of revelation where a love is encountered that calls for a response, and, that for the love that is being responded to, to be love, it involves a decision that cannot be forced or involuntary. This is the crux of the distinction between the power of empire and the power of kenotic love or kenarchy.

The freedom to love, seen in this way as the heart of kenarchic life, breaks imperial power, whether encountered either as agreed doctrine or mathetical theory. When the ensuing choice is to accept the gift of love, it prevents the new freedom from defaulting to the continued hegemony of the self. Choice and love together undo domination. Faith, in this context, is the exercise of freedom to choose the loving Jesus as the definition of transcendence. Standpoint theology and critical realism can help provide its hermeneutical grounds, as the next chapter will argue, but the faith embrace of the choice to love in the way manifest in Jesus is where it begins. From this perspective, the larger economy of power to which the apostle Paul appeals does not therefore imply that the local expressions of kenosis, such as seen supremely when Jesus hangs on the cross, are only temporary displays of weakness because they are voluntary. When the synoptic writer claims that Jesus could have called for twelve legions of angels,[61] but did not, a choice is described that measures the distance between the involuntary power that can only be imposed by juridico-political force and the voluntary power that can release the multitude to love. It is this kenotic choice to love that arguing from Jesus to God makes permanent. God, understood in this sense, is the God of the eternal decision to love.

From this perspective the incarnation event demonstrates that the *telos* of God and creation is fulfilled when God and humans exist in a relationship of kenotic love. It shows Jesus making a permanent choice to love and offers the same divine-human connection. Jesus' weakness, in imperial terms, manifests as the reversal of sovereignty and reveals the real power by which the world was made and consists. This understanding of transcendence continues to draw on Agamben's concept of

61. Matthew 26:53.

the power of the exception, which is here advanced as the disclosure of the decision to love as the true authority behind things. The incarnation event is construed as the revelation of the nature of the power of the exception, with the cross at its heart. If the one who has the power of the exception is potentially sovereign, but freely chooses to empty out that power for the purposes of loving collaboration with humanity, and if the sacred one who can be killed but not sacrificed, chooses to give his own life in love for the world, then God's kenotic love is disclosed as the abiding constituent choice behind the cosmos. This is marked out as the fullness of transcendence, worthy of worship and discipleship precisely because it is not held onto but emptied out kenotically for all. It is to a consideration of the possible components of a working hermeneutic that might engender the reconception of time, access the incarnation, and substantiate such a kenotic theology that the final chapter turns.

7

Towards a Kenarchic Hermeneutic

THE CONCLUDING SECTIONS OF the fourth conduit raised the question of the potential of immaterial labor and living by faith to conjoin and overcome biopower with love. However, the enduring power of the church-empire partnership has been so strong that a theology is needed that is able both to excise sovereignty and reactivate a kenotic Jesus before there can be any hope of such a transformation. In pursuit of this the preceding chapter has configured a form of kenosis, or kenarchy, which sets out some of the qualities necessary to reframe a theology with the capacity to induce this level of change. At its heart is the prospect of accessing the incarnation event as the eschatological exception that can undo the conjunction of sovereignty and money that empowers the life of the contemporary West. As the concluding substratum of the fourth conduit intimated, this hope is reliant on the operation of living by faith characteristic of the nineteenth-century missions, which, as intimated by Karla Poewe, mirrors the kenotic behavior of Jesus and gave rise at least in part to the Pentecostal-charismatic renewal. As the founder of the Worldwide Evangelization Crusade, C.T. Studd put it: "If Jesus Christ be God and died for me, then no sacrifice can be too great for me to make for him."[1]

This abandonment to God's kenotic life confronts the selfish desire for personal sovereignty and makes other people the potential recipients of identification and kenotic love, thus positioning the life of faith as an antidote to biopower. Emerging alongside naked life with its potential, as understood by neo-Marxists, for a breakthrough of interactive power on behalf of the multitude, it is its obvious partner. The coming together of these at first unlikely, but actually obvious bedfellows can accomplish

1. Grubb, *C. T. Studd, Cricketer and Pioneer*, 141.

two important redirections for each. Firstly, when living by faith is added to the operation of immaterial labor, it breaks it free from bondage to capital. By trusting the intrinsic power of love to supply provision, it divests labor power of its primarily economic function, reinvests it in objects of justice and transformation, and moves to transmute all labor into a resource for blessing and peace. Secondly, living by faith breaks potential power free from the deeper bondage to sovereignty that lies behind the commodification of life itself. The life of faith pursues kenotic life, emptying out all sovereignty, including the autonomous individuated sovereignty of the multitude. Conversely, the potential power of immaterial labor challenges the separation of the *ecclesia* and society, reorientating faith to the political issues of justice and equality in the context of the needs of the multitude. It brings the recognition that those whose concern is for the liberation of the multitude are "children of peace,"[2] and co-laborers for the kingdom of God. It is proposed that such a partnership can provide the necessary impetus for overcoming the de-eschatologization brought about by the Christendom partnership and instigate a reconception of time. Such an alliance has important possibilities for empowering the current eruption of the multitude across the Middle East and North Africa to ensure the creation of new political forms that might avoid defaulting to the traditional predominance of imperial sovereignty and autonomy. This in turn could point the way ahead for the transformation of Western democracy.

One of the most significant outcomes of arguing from Jesus to God is the recovery of pneumatology, and in particular the revolutionary potential of the Pentecostal-charismatic movement. It imagines that the Spirit of the excoriated God, who fully engaged and overcame empire in Jesus, is immanently present with the *ecclesia*, suggesting that to engage with him is to disassociate from Western imperial time and to enter eschatological time. It means that the temporal life of Jesus, in its kenotic encounter with empire from the birth narratives to the ascension story, is carried by the Holy Spirit and may be immanently engaged with by the disciple as transcendent experience that liberates her or him from imperial time. This is the supposed source of the potential power of living by faith. It is the conjunction, not of sovereignty and money, but of kenotic love and labor power.

2. See Luke 10:6.

The deliberate abandon of the totality of life skills, summed up in immaterial and material labor, into the transcendent power of kenotic love issues in acts of love in the cause of the multitude, poor in body and spirit, that instantiate the experience of incarnation. Without this kenotic abandon, the Spirit is not engaged and incarnational time is not entered. But when this investment of potential power is enacted, transcendence and immanence connect, and as the resurrection demonstrates, the political situation utterly changes. It follows that if the Holy Spirit carries the temporally incarnated transcendent life of Jesus, then the testimony to the incarnation event is crucially complementary to its engagement. So it is necessary to know what actions will engage his activity. A further corollary is that the Spirit is available to facilitate this knowledge. As the Johannine tradition has it, "But when He, the Spirit of truth, comes, He will guide you into all the truth; for He will not speak on His own initiative, but whatever He hears, He will speak . . . He will take of Mine and will disclose it to you."[3] It is in the cause of engaging and activating the fullness of the incarnation in the contemporary world that this final chapter attempts a reconception of time, an engagement with the Spirit, and an accompanying hermeneutic of the text that can hopefully activate the incarnation and initiate political transformation.

A. INITIATING A FULLNESS OF TIME

1. The Reconception of Time

This book has attempted to show that modern and postmodern approaches to understanding the contemporary Western world tend to be predicated on assumptions about immanence specific to modernity, which are in turn predicated on the medieval equation of transcendence and imperial sovereignty. Behind these various theories lies a particular perception of time. The very term "postmodernity" carries the idea of "after," a time word, and is in part a rejection of modernity, another word that describes a period of time. This modern period, in turn, was quite consciously a rejection of the medieval world, otherwise known as the middle ages, two other very time-sensitive titles. Many historians, as Karl Löwith demonstrates,[4] have assumed that this whole time-sensitive

3. John 16:13–14.
4. Löwith, *Meaning in History.*

way of conceptualizing reality is the result of the incarnation, described
in the Epistle to the Galatians as the coming of Christ at the fullness of
time.[5] As a result they refer to the period between the end of the New
Testament and the beginning of the medieval world as the early church or
patristic period, all time-orientated descriptions. The designation of the
Old and New Testaments with their old and new covenants has simply
been regarded as a further example of this time-sensitive view. However,
the genealogy pursued by this research suggests that this whole progressive view of time is based not on the incarnation of Jesus, but on the assumption that the fourth-century conjunction of the church and empire
was the beginning of the eschatological peace that the Old Testament
prophesied and Jesus proclaimed. Since then Western life has become
an attempt to bring about this universal peace by means of hierarchically
shaped monarchies or republics based on property and money, and legitimated by temple-based worship cultures of various kinds. Right now,
this age-long project is in crisis. As Paul Fletcher enunciates so clearly, if
contemporary theology is to move beyond irrelevance or merely parasitic status, it is necessary to re-conceive time in a wholly new way.[6] The
understanding of the incarnation as event elucidated in the previous
chapter liberates the gospel story out from this imperial time frame and
sets it as an originative eschatological event, or advent. As a result it does
not require a theory or system to fulfill it, but is itself a fullness of time,
an altogether uncontainable event that reveals, embodies, and facilitates
a way of life that it is possible to access at any time and practice accordingly. From this standpoint, Jesus confronted imperial time, flooding the
present with the substance of his kenotic peace. The practice of living
by faith accesses this kenotic way of life and quite literally reconceives
time. Through it the economics, hermeneutics, and politics of this world
can be inseminated with the deconstructive and re-creative seed of the
gospel.

There appear to be two main uses of the word "time," what might
be called a general use and a practical use. The general use is to signify
temporality; that the universe and living things are subject to inception,
change, and decay within a wider enduring context. The practical use
is as a means to separate specific periods from each other for measuring purposes, implementing the common human experience of day

5. Galatians 4:4.

6. Fletcher, *Disciplining the Divine*, 178.

and night to do so, such as to calculate how long a task might take to complete or how old something or someone might be. This usage can be either releasing or controlling dependent on the situation in which it is being employed. The impact of de-eschatologization has been to corral the practical use of time into the service of empire. Its application has been subjected to the subordination of the many by the few or, in modernity, the rights of as many people as possible to exploit the environment and the remaining multitude. In this situation, time becomes a tool of domination at almost every level, no longer a releasing gift in which to share the benefits of the cosmos, but a means to seize the day and impose authority on the creation and other human beings.

The reconception of time advocated here has two outcomes related to this. It re-conceives time as liberator and thereby escapes the determining power of modern historicist theories that define what can and cannot happen in history. But it goes a step further and suggests that a particular kind of encounter with temporality can act as an aperture into the transcendent context in which the general understanding of time is located. Fletcher describes a number of dissociative phenomena such as winks, blinks, gestures, orgasms, and play that are "temporal displacements that reveal the destructive promise of the eternal instant."[7] In the same way as these interrupt the seemingly inevitable onward march of time through the narrative of temporal life, so a revelatory interception of the transcendent life of God might be triggered, which would redirect the future story. God's time would become part of human, immanent time without ceasing to be part of the transcendent life of God. Fletcher explores the way that this transcendent quality of the instant places us between time as history and its future fulfillment. He makes what may seem to be the audacious move of suggesting that this "time between" times can connect us to the incarnation and is the temporal context of the experience of the New Testament *ecclesia*. Fletcher looks for a reconception of time along these lines that will lead beyond the insights of Kierkegaard, Barth, and Balthasar and reinterpret the apostle Paul. For despite their important recognition of the eschatological moment, as Fletcher points out, Kierkegaard tends to limit the instant to the domain of subjective experience, Barth qualifies it with otherness and dissimilarity, and Balthasar squanders the urgency of its penetration of history.[8]

7. Ibid., 160.
8. Ibid., 161–4.

Only the apostle Paul seems to grasp the full importance of the incursion of eschatological time in the midst of world-time and the manner in which its "summons to inconformity" transforms the whole of life.[9] This has the effect of positioning the incarnation as the embodiment of what the apostle refers to as an "administration suitable to the fullness of the times, the summing up of all things in Christ, things in the heavens and things on the earth."[10]

Despite the ease with which Fletcher connects from a wink and a blink to the eschatological politics of Jesus, it does not follow that all experiences of temporal displacement end up there. A vital issue is clearly what a specific temporal displacement is likely to connect one to. All are familiar with experiences that temporarily disconnect the participant from the urgent demands of time as a means to fulfill the legal, cultural, and financial expectations of Western life. It is not that any necessarily moral character is attached to these experiences but that their existence points to the possibility of a different apprehension of time. It is because they disconnect the recipient from the immediacy of the familiar controls of temporality that these apertures in time may be described as basic experiences of transcendence. It is not such a great step from these to the incarnation, which, as Balthasar suggests, can be described as "a scission that Jesus Christ has introduced into the world"[11] or, as previously noted, "a fullness of time"[12] when another perspective on time intercepts imperial time. This is not just an existential leap into the unknown if it is guided by relational and realistic hermeneutics such as those elucidated with recourse to Ward's economy of response and Wright's critical realism in the next section. For with the help of these it is possible to evaluate and select instigators and exercises of the instant that can helpfully evoke the incarnation.

By this means it is possible to understand that a variety of liturgies, sacraments, exercises, testimony, and preaching originally operated as triggers of transcendence. The use of particular words and stories that spoken, sung, or chanted can evoke the instance of transcendence,

9. This is with reference to the apostle Paul's announcement of a foreshortened, contracted time in 1 Corinthians 7:29. Ibid., 168.

10. Ephesians 1:10.

11. In *Word and Redemption: Essays in Theology* 2, trans. A.V. Littledale, 154, n. 3, cited in Fletcher, *Disciplining the Divine*, 163.

12. Galatians 4:4.

points the way to a whole discussion of the function of meditation, liturgy, and the arts that is well beyond the scope of this chapter. While
the profound theological implications of this may provide the content
for serious future theological investigation, what is important here is to
highlight the particular eschatological triggers that became the mixed
subsumptive signifiers of the church-empire genealogy. As the previous
conduits have intimated, the most obvious of these candidates for de-
contamination are the eucharist, particularly for the Catholic tradition,
the preaching of the word for the Protestant and evangelical tradition,
and the operation of spiritual gifts such as glossolalia, interpretation, and
prophecy in the context of the Pentecostal-charismatic movement. It is
clear from Part II that the eucharist came to include the embodiment
of the inversion and displacement of the *corpus verum* (conduit two),
the preached word became the cover for the transference of the agency
for the peace to the nation state and money (conduit three), and the
charismata were pragmatically adapted to entrepreneurship and commodification (conduit four). In order to contemplate the reinstatement
of these core components of Christendom as initiators of the incarnation without, at the same time, downloading the legal, hierarchical, or
economic components of imperial sovereignty, the next section utilizes
William Cavanaugh's development of the eucharist as a means to the
"more radical imaginings of space and time."[13]

2. Transubstantiating Kenotic Love

William Cavanaugh's insightful recognition of the imaginary nature of
cultural and political structure, that things could be otherwise than the
way they are, effectively relativizes imperial temporality. Into the volatile perception of time that remains, he ventures to reinsert an *ecclesia*
configured in terms of the eucharist as a means of re-conceiving a new
temporality for the multitude. Reflecting on torture and disappearance as an ecclesiological problem, with reference to the actions of the
Catholic Church under General Pinochet's totalitarian regime in Chile,
Cavanaugh presents the evocative proposal for what he terms a "kind of
Eucharistic counter-politics which forms the church into a body capable
of resisting oppression."[14] As he more recently describes in the specific

13. Cavanaugh, *Theopolitical Imagination*, 4.
14. Cavanaugh, *Torture and Eucharist*, 14.

context of re-imagining an alternative to the Western nation state, the liturgical character of the eucharist enables it to enact an alternative kind of public body in space and time. This confronts the obligation of faith to the state with a local community of mutual participation that is connected to the universal community of the church. It re-imagines the purpose of space away from imperial endeavor, and re-conceives time by simultaneously remembering the past kenotic death of Jesus and anticipating the future fullness of the kingdom of God. As he puts it, "this interrupts the uniform march of time on which both capitalism and the nation state depend."[15] That this is a radical recasting of the eucharist is expressly affirmed by the intentional direction of his innovatory move. As he clearly states, the object of this development "is not to politicise the Eucharist but to eucharistize the world."[16] In contrast to the church's operation as the legitimating partner of empire, he posits its fullness as the political antagonist of oppression and torture. The crucial importance of his innovation for the thesis of this book is its re-investment of the celebration of the Mass with counterpolitical power. As a result it functions as the embodiment of divine kenosis and effectively re-empowers the mystical church as the true body of Christ.

However, despite the exciting possibilities of this development, without a parallel repudiation of the accruements consequent on the church-empire genealogy, it conflates the recovered role of the eucharist as the true kenotic body with the ongoing properties of its liturgical role as symbol of the mediated imperial presence. As a result the new space and re-conceived time still carry the hierarchical mediation of the ordained priest who alone has the right to celebrate the sacrament, and the connection with the church universal still retains the hierarchical succession of bishop and pope. From the perspective of the genealogy of church and empire consequent on the supposed fourth-century fall, this is highly problematic. The monarchical role of pope and bishop together with the mediatory transaction of the priest is apparently not re-imagined and remains unreformed to continue the legitimation of sovereign power. In the end the refigured eucharist is similar to the attempt to reconcile the imperial and the kenotic, and at a deep structural level continues to justify rather than confront the status quo. So although Cavanaugh's bold attempt at temporal re-imagination extends

15. Cavanaugh, *Theopolitical Imagination*, 5.
16. Cavanaugh, *Torture and the Eucharist*, 14.

the eucharist beyond the institution to the "real" presence, it fails to fully re-conceive the incarnation eschatologically. It remains embroiled in the institutional and imperial power represented by priestly mediation and ecclesiastical hierarchy.

However, by taking Cavanaugh's attempt a step further it is possible to develop an understanding of the eucharist at once weaker and stronger than the Roman Catholic view. This elucidates a kind of transubstantiation of the true incarnate body of Christ beyond the communion table altogether and out into the midst of each sphere and experience of everyday life. Here the community of faith itself activates incarnational time by acts of loving identification with the poor in body and spirit. The real presence is now less in the sacrament than in the crucified and risen kenotic Christ in the body of believers. The two conflate: wherever the church, the body of Christ, is, there is the true body of Christ *corpus verum* and the invisible, real presence *corpus mysticum*. Transubstantiation takes place, not in the act of mediated appeasement conducted by the hierarchical priest, but in the political space of everyday temporal reality, when the people of God non-violently lay down their lives by faith against oppression and injustice as Jesus did. This is not to devalue the symbolism of the broken bread and poured out wine, but to liberate it from the imperial framework and to point it outwards to the fullness of love for and among the multitude and, in this way, to more fully eucharistize the world. Continuing with and expanding the creative thinking and vocabulary behind Cavanaugh's move, it is possible to apply a similar strategy to the function of Protestant preaching and the operation of the Pentecostal charismata. Rather than preaching being confined to the proclamation of the word by the licensed preacher raised to the hierarchical pulpit within the liturgy of the gathered church, the activity of declaring the "at hand" good news of the immanence of the counterpolitical incarnation is extended into politics, media, and marketplace and becomes the opportunity to kerugmatize the world. Similarly, lifted out of the generally mediatory structures of home group or worship event and applied throughout the various experiences of daily life, spiritual gifts release the presence of the kingdom to charismatize society. In these ways the reconception of time is not a theoretical conception so much as an actual insemination of immanence with the seed of the incarnation. It is in support of the fullest possible facilitation of this reconception and transubstantiation of the real presence of

Jesus throughout the biopolitical world that the following sections take up aspects of N.T. Wright's critical realism, Graham Ward's economy of response, and recent research into the counterpolitical context of the gospel accounts.

B. A HERMENEUTIC SUITABLE FOR A FULLNESS OF TIME

While the reconception of time has the capacity to reconnect transcendence and immanence, in order for living by faith to be as incarnational as possible it is important to reconnect with originary gospel testimony. This requires appropriate interpretative tools with which to access the written texts and the historical and theological contexts in which they are contained. To avoid falling back to predication on medievality and modernity and importing the components of empire into the reading of the texts, these need to be complementary to and supplementary of the exercise of living by faith and its eschatological potential to escape imperial time. The attraction of N.T. Wright's critical realism and Graham Ward's standpoint theology is that both contain ways by which the twin dangers of predication on modernity or bondage to contemporary immanence might be avoided. On the basis of their partly eschatological approaches, they present complementary hermeneutics that provide crucial tools necessary for engaging with the originary material, in such a way as to further the release of kenotic love.

1. Critical Realism

Wright suggests that there are four ways of reading the gospel narratives: pre-critical, historical, theological, and postmodern, which correspond broadly to the pre-enlightenment period, modernity, a late modern corrective period, and postmodernity.[17] In order to address what he regards as an obvious distortion of the gospel story by all of these, he proposes a critical realist approach that attempts to draw on their strengths while restoring greater clarity to our knowledge of the originary events. This recognizes two primary reactive modes of knowledge that lie behind the three post-medieval positions, and that can be broadly categorized as positivist and phenomenalist. Critical realism, as developed by Wright, affirms the realism of positivism in the existence of the thing known as something other than the knower, but also grants the necessity of a phe-

---

17. N.T. Wright, *The New Testament and the People of God*, 7.

nomenal approach because the only access we have to the thing known is the ongoing dialogue between the knower and it.[18] The conversation between the knower and the thing known varies from person to person, not only because of the differing locations from which they engage the thing known, but because it is interpreted through distinct individual and corporate worldviews.

This notion of worldview is essential to Wright's development of critical realism.[19] He regards it as the "basic stuff of human existence, the lens through which the world is seen, the blueprint for how one should live in it, and above all the sense of identity and place which enables human beings to be what they are."[20] The interface between the knower and the thing known takes place within the confines of four interacting functions of the worldview, which are comprised of story, questions, symbol, and praxis. Worldviews provide the stories with which humans view reality, which in turn answer the basic questions that determine human existence such as identity, environment, problem, and resolution, anecdotally expressed as "who are we, where are we, what is wrong, and what is the solution?"[21] These stories and the answers they provide to the questions are expressed in symbols, which can be both cultural artefacts and events such as "festivals, family gatherings and the like." The basic questions, and particularly the "implied eschatology"[22] of the resolution of "what is to be done," involve action, which is expressed, at least partially, in the lifestyle or praxis of the person holding the worldview.

Wright uses this framework as a principal interpretative tool in his exposition of what he describes as the three reading stages involved in engaging the gospel narrative: the relation of readers to the texts, of the texts to their authors, and beyond that to the realities they purport to describe.[23] The strength of his approach lies in its capacity to provide practical access to the sources while exposing the individual and corporate context of the writer and reader alike. Before activating this framework to better arrive at a critical realist view of the text, Wright first of all recommends an intelligent approach to what he calls the "grammar"

18. Ibid., 32–35.
19. Ibid., 36.
20. Ibid., 124.
21. Ibid., 123.
22. Ibid., 124.
23. Ibid., 64.

of the story. Utilizing the work done on the narrative structure of stories by A.J. Greimas and Vladimir Propp,[24] he recommends a careful theoretical approach to the analysis of the story by means of which he purports to explain how the story actually works and the means to avoid its misinterpretation.

The theory builds on the proposal that a basic and typical story can be divided up into three moments resonant with the three types of mimesis in Aristotle.[25] These comprise an initial sequence in which a problem is set up or created, a topical sequence in which the central character tries to solve the problem thus set up and eventually succeeds, and a final sequence in which the initial task is completed.[26] Stories can be analyzed as a series of variations on this initial structure. Wright emphasizes the helpful way in which this slows the reader down and limits the tendency for the interpreter to jump to false conclusions. The method provides a meticulous practical complement to the eschatological reconception of time, and is exemplified in more detail in the coming expositions of the Passion week narratives with which the chapter culminates.

Wright helpfully recognizes the need for caution in the exercise of this practice in order to avoid importing unexamined presuppositions.[27] This is important to heed as there remains a difficulty with Wright's theoretical approach as it stands, that marks a general vulnerability to modern rationalism running throughout his epistemology. For while the theoretical procedure he adopts allows him to demonstrate that a story has a particular origin, shape, and reference or meaning, it is difficult to evade the prescriptive impact of asserting a definitive grammar to story. The same trace of predication on modern presuppositions is also carried by his partial maintenance of positivism and phenomenalism, and in the universalizing and normative nature that he ascribes to the overall function of the worldview.[28] However, while this tends to expose his hermeneutic to the interrogatory challenge of obligation to the ongoing impact of sovereignty, it is ameliorated by the

24. Wright cites A.J. Greimas, *Sémantique structurale* and *Du Sens*; Vladimir Propp, *The Morphology of the Folktale*, trans. L. Scott. Ibid., 70.

25. Ricoeur notes the connection between this structure and that put forward by Greimas and Propp. See Ricoeur, *Time and Narrative*, vol. I, 56.

26. N.T. Wright, *The New Testament and the People of God*, 71.

27. Ibid., 73.

28. Ibid., 41.

eschatological aspect of his hermeneutic and its capacity to insert the transcendent instance into the central topical sequence or *muthos* of the narrative. This resides in what he develops as his approach to the gospel as literature. Here Wright advocates a relational attitude to the text as the thing known analogous to the way we value and necessarily take for granted the separate existence and significance of the person we love.[29] By activating the affective response of the reader in this way, he increases the hermeneute's sensitivity to the movement towards resolution within the central component of the grammar of the story. As a result he can describe critical realism as a hermeneutic of love, and offset the way in which it is otherwise vulnerable to the importation of ideas predicated on modern rationalism. This makes even more sense once the grammar of story is opened up to the eschatological instant by the application of the complementary approach to the text offered by Graham Ward's development of the economy of response.

2. The Economy of Response

As Ward clearly states, "History (of Jesus) and narrative (of Jesus) are inseparable . . . All discipleship is readership—the participation in the reading and rereading of this one man's representative life and work and teaching as it is narrated. All serious reading engages in an economy of response."[30] The idea of the economy of response locates in Ward's wider configuration of standpoint theology, which, in common with Wright's critical realism, makes recourse to the notion of worldview as the context for knowledge. However, it offsets the dangers of modern positivist and phenomenalist pitfalls by offering a greater degree of conditionality, what Ward refers to as a syncretic approach to other standpoints. Drawing on the work of Marxist and feminist thinkers,[31] he emphasizes the way in which the emergence of a standpoint is concerned with minority perspectives associated with the domination and marginalization consequent on the operation of the mainstream political status quo. In line with this he notes that Christianity could only emerge as a standpoint after Christendom. As he puts it, "the (Christian) standpoint can only emerge within a deeper cultural atheism and the advance of the

29. Ibid., 64.

30. Ward, *Christ and Culture*, 59.

31. Ward, *Cultural Transformation and Religious Practice*, 73.

secular worldview."[32] From the perspective of the genealogy traced here, which still regards the secular worldview as resourced by the ongoing genealogy of the fourth-century fall and thereby still a covert manifestation of Christendom, there are some difficulties in seeing Christianity as a whole as a minority standpoint in this way. However, if the idea of standpoint is applied to the narrower definition of a subversive kenotic Jesus, then the economy of response proffers an attractive hermeneutical tool. Alongside Wright's more intentionally rational approach to the sources, as with his unwillingness to give god a capital letter,[33] Ward's approach is more obviously amenable to the immediate engagement of transcendent presence. He recognizes that the transcendent operation of God "in, through and upon the immanent orders of the world does not translate the enunciative site from which theology speaks *out of this world*"[34] and in so doing affirms with Wright the necessary conversation between the knower and the thing known. But his introduction of the economy of response brings a more directly eschatological dimension to this dialogue.

Taking as his starting point a challenging warning in Mark's narrative of Jesus' teaching, "Take care what you listen to. By your standard of measure it will be measured to you; and more will be given you besides,"[35] Ward describes the mimetic process whereby the hermeneute, "the one engaged in hearing and recreating the story," moves out to reappropriate it. "The 'measuring' is the act of engagement in an economy of response."[36] In this way he shows how the narrative itself engages us in the mimetic process in a way that opens up the eschatological moment. As he describes it, "mimesis is therefore the measure of our understanding of the Christ."[37] Ward expounds the way that the transcendent and the immanent connect within the reading of the story with reference to two sets of complementary gospel narratives,[38] exposing the impor-

---

32. Ibid., 77.

33. N.T. Wright, *The New Testament and the People of God*, xiv.

34. Ward, *Cultural Transformation and Religious Practice*, 14.

35. Mark 4:24.

36. Ward, *Christ and Culture*, 31.

37. Ibid., 59.

38. The first set is the story of the woman with the haemorrhage (Mark 5:25–34), the story of the deaf man with the impediment (Mark 7:32–37), and Mary's act of gratitude in John (John 12:1–8). The second focuses on John's narrative of Mary's and Thomas's

tance of the bodily intimacies of touch, flows, and relation, and asking how difference and affinity, distance and proximity are established. He notes the play of absence and presence, states of knowledge, modes of address, and finally acclamation and testimony before witnesses. In this way the reader, if willing, is drawn intimately into the narrative, finding their own place in the spatial arrangement of the action and connecting relationally with the events as they are played out. The effect of this is to locate the hermeneute at the eschatological intersection of transcendence and immanence in a way that makes their positioning towards the world integral to the grammar of knowledge and communication. This goes beyond the proposal of a theoretical structure to story, and forms a creative grammar that makes the hermeneute him- or herself the coincidence of transcendence and immanence. From this perspective Ward can state that neither the gospel nor the world can be accessed without the other.[39]

The experimental hermeneutic developing here is worked out in relation to the exegesis of the text along the following lines. Firstly, the practice of living by faith and the reconception of time as eternal instant encourage the hermeneute to embrace the text with a predisposition to consider the originary testimony of Jesus as an eschatological fullness. Secondly, the relational component of Wright's critical realism positions the hermeneute towards the gospel narrative as to a loved-one. Thirdly, with this attitude in place, the hermeneute takes up the tools contained in Wright's understanding of worldview as story, question, symbol, and praxis, ready to depict the seminal story as accurately as possible by means of his application of structural grammar, while remaining all the time open to the breaking in of transcendent presence. Finally, this hope is enlivened by the application of Ward's affective economy of response.

As this book draws towards its conclusion, the final section of the chapter will begin to apply these three hermeneutical steps to five events of Passion week in order to demonstrate the potential of this approach to disclose seminal incidents of originary Christian testimony. The purpose of selecting the events leading up to the cross is their capacity to reveal the political impact of the contentions between Jesus and imperial power as the narrative testimony approaches its culmination. In order to disclose the revolutionary counterpolitical impact of these confron-

---

post-resurrection encounters (John 20:11–18; 20:26–29).

39. Ward, *Cultural Transformation and Religious Practice*, 11.

tational narratives as fully as possible, it is important to consider first of all the recent research into the historico-political context in which the gospel narratives as a whole are situated.

C. HISTORICAL AND ARCHEOLOGICAL INDICATIONS OF A COUNTERPOLITICAL JESUS

Ward, drawing on Bourdieu, deploys the term *habitus* to refer to the whole complex of dispositions that a person or group inherit and into which they are socialized and from which text and theology speak.[40] This opens up the possibility of relocating the exegesis of the gospel narrative away from the normative imperial time frame and recasting it in a definitively counter-imperial setting. It is in this respect that Wright's historical expertise comes to the fore. By his use of critical realism, worldview, and the structural analysis of story, he is able to show how both the content and milieu of the gospel narratives are to be found in Hebrew eschatological prophecy. Bringing together his work with recent historical and archeological research, it is possible to substantiate two important conclusions with respect to the likely political context of the gospel accounts. Firstly, the Hebrew tradition of eschatological prophecy operated as a subversive medium that provided an important antecedent to the proclamation of the kingdom of God. Secondly, the gospel testimony emerged at a critical moment as a direct counterpoint to Rome's move to subsume transcendence with imperial sovereignty.

1. Hebrew Eschatological Hope and the Good News of the Kingdom of God

Drawing on Wright's work,[41] supplemented by others such as Wes Howard-Brook and Anthony Gwyther,[42] it is possible to show that the gospel proclamation of the kingdom of God stands in the Hebrew apocalyptic tradition, which was itself an outgrowth of traditional Hebrew prophecy. Possibly from 800 BCE, and certainly from the fall of Samaria onwards, the subject of a coming eschatological peace began to emerge in the writings of the Jewish prophets whose work now forms the latter

40. Ibid., 18.

41. In particular N.T. Wright, *The New Testament and the People of God; Jesus and the Victory of God;* and *The Challenge of Jesus.*

42. Howard-Brook and Gwyther, *Unveiling Empire.*

part of the Old Testament. They may be described in general terms as prophesying a divinely initiated temporal harmony in which Israel would be the agents of universal justice. Typical examples are the Isaiah visions, of the nations coming to the mountain of the Lord and hammering their swords into ploughshares and spears into pruning hooks, and the wolf lying down with the lamb with a little child leading them.[43] The Jeremiah prophecy of the restoration of Israel and Judah to the accompanying sound of the joyful voice of bridegroom and bride,[44] and the Zechariah predictions of the lowly king riding on a donkey and speaking peace to the nations[45] are in similar vein.

The classic view that the prophetic motivation behind prophecies such as these was withdrawal from the world, prevalent from the nineteenth century to the mid twentieth, is now largely discredited. Julius Wellhausen's nineteenth-century understanding of the post-exilic restoration as withdrawal from the world into a form of religious legalism, through to Paul D. Hanson's conception that eschatological visionaries were those who gave up politics in favor of the direct intervention of God,[46] can no longer be upheld. Brook and Gwyther cite Stephen L. Cook's critique of Hanson in which he establishes convincingly that the post-exilic prophets were by no means limited to the politically powerless. Their own view is that a controversy can be discerned between those anti-imperial prophets, such as those they term Third Isaiah, Second Isaiah, and Second Zechariah, who take issue with the so-called empire-accommodating Zadokites: Ezra, Nehemiah, First Zechariah and Haggai. While it might be possible to place these latter prophets in a more favorable light, it would seem that the temporal political focus of the prophesied peace is no longer in doubt. Brook and Gwyther's assessment of Isaiah's vision of the lion lying down with the lamb sums up this connection between the major biblical prophets and the later apocalyptists that they gave way to. It is intended to "confront those who would accommodate to the Persian Empire in much the same way as

---

43. Isaiah 2:3–4; cf. also Micah 4:1–3; Isaiah 9:1–7; 11:1–9.

44. Jeremiah 33:10–11.

45. Zechariah 8:12; 9:9–10.

46. This was based on the deprivation theory developed by Karl Mannheim and Ernst Troeltsch, grounded in the work of Max Weber that suggested that millennialism was confined to conditions in which segments of society deprived of power looked for an event that would turn the tables on their oppressors.

Daniel does for his own time."[47] Current scholarship affirms that Hebrew prophetic vision operated as a transcendent critique of immanent political, socio-cultural, and religious behavior of both Israel and its perceived imperial enemies.

Wright's comprehensive application of his fourfold hermeneutical framework to the Hebrew worldview that characterized first-century Israel supports this perspective. Firstly, story, symbol, and praxis answered the four characteristic questions of identity, environment, problem, and resolution in a manner that focused attention on Israel's distinctiveness as God's chosen people, located in the holy land, centered on the temple, and firmly focused on the immanent plane.[48] Secondly, the contemporary theological milieu at the advent of the gospel testimony was a network of beliefs, further summarized by Wright as monotheism, election, and eschatology. These were worked out by means of a controversial conglomeration of opinions that were nonetheless generally connected through the basic worldview of one creator God, who has chosen Israel as his people, giving her his law and the holy land. He will act for her and through her to reestablish his shalom throughout the world.[49] All this continued to emphasize Israel's ongoing temporal agency as the people of God despite the adverse circumstances. Thirdly, it was this worldview and these beliefs that undergirded the apocalyptic genre that the second-temple prophets evolved particularly in the period following the Maccabaean revolt in 164 BCE.

The genre contained within it the means by which language could *both* refer to past events within Israel's history *and* invest them with the full significance that, within that worldview, they still possessed.[50] It displays three main characteristics, the personal location of the visionary prophet, the social location of people disadvantaged by the socio-political leadership of the day, and the historical location from which apocalyptic can be deployed for the reversal of both personal and social circumstances. This latter function was achieved through the technique of representation. This operated firstly in the use of a literary or rhetorical figure within a complex metaphor or allegory to represent a person, a nation, or another relevant particular. Secondly it acted through to

47. Howard-Brook and Gwyther, *Unveiling Empire*, 59–62, 70.

48. N.T. Wright, *The New Testament and the People of God*, 243.

49. Ibid., 279.

50. Ibid., 283.

the practice of social representation where a person or group is taken to represent another person or group, and thirdly in the metaphysical representation where heavenly beings and their conflicts represent parallel confrontations taking place on earth. The idiom can be quite complex because it is possible for these three different senses of representation to be used simultaneously. So, for example, a metaphorical monster and an actually perceived transcendent spirit can occur in the same passage.[51] As Wright makes clear, this is fully in line with the established tradition of Amos's plumb-line and Jeremiah's boiling pot in the primary prophetic tradition.[52]

These characteristics combine together to show that the literary form of standard apocalyptic writings contains a linguistic convention, the roots of which are consonant with classic Hebrew eschatological prophecy. Its "complex, many layered and often biblical imagery is used and re-used to invest the space-time events of Israel's past, present and future with their full theological significance."[53] By this means the apocalyptic genre was well suited to facilitate the subversive application of the Hebrew vision of peace in the Roman imperial present of first-century Palestine. This eschatological context to Jesus' message and ministry has the effect of positioning it as the proclamation and embodiment of a reign of peace that called to account the contemporary political scene. From this perspective, the originary good news of the kingdom of God can be viewed as both the introduction to the eschatological reign and the means to call to account the internal and external political powers of the day. The subsequent identification of the eschatological peace with the empire of Rome is thereby revealed to be a substantial misalignment.

2. Locating the Originary Material within First-century Roman Palestine

Utilizing generally accepted work on Rome's history as well as taking particular note of recent research into the historical and archeological context of the gospel story by John Dominic Crossan,[54] Jonathan L.

---

51. In Daniel 10 and 7, for example.
52. Amos 7:7–8; Jeremiah 1:13.
53. N.T. Wright, *The New Testament and the People of God*, 286.
54. Crossan, *God and Empire*.

Reed,[55] Richard Horsley,[56] and Warren Carter,[57] it is possible to expose with new clarity the likely socio-political *habitus* surrounding the advent of Christ, in particular the impact of the emperor cult, and to locate more precisely the imperial context to which the apocalyptic prophetic message of the gospel testimony was directed. The property-based colonialism of Greece and Rome appears to have been in distinct contrast to the general pattern of empire common to highly organized civilizations as various as Bronze Age Greece, the New Kingdom of Egypt, and the Inca Empire. In these a bureaucratic hierarchy descended from a monarch to administrative districts governed by royal functionaries and fiscal officials, who extracted surplus labor from subject villages of peasant producers for redistribution up the hierarchical chain.[58] The Greek and Roman Empires sprang originally not from monarchy or bureaucracy, but from city-states governed by communities of citizens with a significant level of self-government and minimal state infrastructure. While politically various, with Athens a democracy and Rome an aristocratic republic, land was the principal source of wealth for large landowner and peasant alike. Although both empires resorted to a monarchical center as they developed, the hierarchical authority went from the monarch to the city and its surrounding land, not down a chain of offices. This municipal organization was universally adopted, even in rural areas, strengthening local propertied aristocracy and creating them where they did not yet exist.[59]

While the Roman Empire was resourced in a variety of ways as it expanded in the years leading up to the *pax Romana*, when booty, whether of land or slaves, was a primary source of wealth, and trade and usury became important sources of income,[60] direct taxation lay at its heart. Warren Carter cites Kautsky: "To rule in aristocratic empires is above all to tax."[61] The need to maintain this capability was central to Rome's structural development. To this end, by the death of Julius Caesar in 44 BCE, the move to centralize military and economic power had de-

---

55. Crossan and Reed, *In Search of Paul.*

56. Horsley, *Jesus and Empire.*

57. Carter, *Matthew and Empire.*

58. Wood, *Empire of Capital,* 27.

59. Ibid., 33.

60. Rawson, "The Expansion of Rome," 57–62; Wells, *The Roman Empire,* 143–6.

61. Carter, *Matthew and Empire,* 134.

veloped to such a degree that the path was already prepared for Octavius to become Caesar Augustus and establish himself as supreme monarch. But in consequence of the long-established municipal infrastructure, his sovereignty was not something imposed via a distant chain of command from outside its occupied territories. Rather it was a political culture diffused through the power bases of the local propertied elites.

It is now generally agreed that, by the time of Christ, Roman imperial rule was integrated in this way into the theocratic leadership of Israel, as in other similarly occupied lands. It is clear that the High Priestly family of Annas and Caiaphas were Rome's local elite in the south of Israel alongside Herod in the north. Warren Carter underlines that this can be seen from their first appearance at the beginning of Matthew's narrative as the allies of Herod,[62] and in their final appearance as allies of Rome's governor and army against Jesus at the crucifixion.[63] While Carter bemoans the failure of New Testament scholars to recognize that the Jewish leaders of the gospel narratives are the dependent elite of empire, the work of the last few years has provided additional evidence. Speaking of the historical period immediately prior to the gospel narratives, Richard Horsley spells out the new world order and its impact on Judea and Galilee: "The Romans installed their own client rulers, the Herodian kings and the Jerusalem High Priests, who both controlled the area and built an increasingly lavish lifestyle in rebuilt or newly founded cities such as Jerusalem, Sepphoris and Tiberias."[64] Carter describes this time as one where the ruling elite acquired vast wealth through local and imperial taxes, tributes, rents, and services. Compliance was achieved through threat of military punishment, loss of land, and increased tribute and taxes. Laws, political offices, and officials normalized the transactions and peasants were forced to produce a surplus to meet the elite's demands.[65] The impact of this integration of Roman rule and Israel's internal leadership was powerfully strengthened by the emergence of the emperor cult by which, in the interests of economic and political consolidation, the sovereignty of the emperor increasingly included the transcendent realm. By the time the New Testament narratives were

---

62. Matthew 2:4–6.

63. Matthew 27:62–66; 28:11–15.

64. Horsley, *Jesus and Empire*, 34.

65. Carter, *Matthew and Empire*, 13.

written, imperial power was already being legitimated by emperor worship throughout Rome's territories.

While Augustus Caesar was not officially deified in the West until his death in 15 CE, he had already been recognized as a god in the dominions of the East, where the Pharaohs had been deified long before,[66] and the Greek Emperor Alexander had also been recognized as divine.[67] It seems that the association of transcendence and sovereignty present in the Eastern worldview was strengthened by these aspects of the contemporary socio-political process under Augustus.[68] Michael Mann has argued that this association configured an ideological power that pervaded the empire and shaped its progress. "Ideological organization is sociospatially *transcendent*. It transcends the existing institutions of . . . power and generates a 'sacred' form of authority . . . set apart from and above secular authority structures."[69] The practical impact of introducing the imperial cult, at the same time as establishing theocratic leaders in Israel as imperial puppets, was to submit the cult of Yahweh to the worship of Caesar in the interests of the Roman cause.[70] While there has been a tendency to underestimate the imperial cult,[71] the work of Crossan and Reed on the wealth of surviving contemporary artefacts and architecture demonstrates that the titles the New Testament narratives give to the Christ are almost without exception the titles ascribed to the Roman emperors on many contemporary monuments and temples.[72] They note that one such example is "son of God," pointing out the way in which Latin makes a distinction between *deus*, an eternal god like Jupiter, and *divus*, a deified human like Julius Caesar, but that Greek translates both terms with the same word, *theos*.[73] "Christians must have understood, then, that to proclaim Jesus as Son of God was

---

66. Stockton, "The Founding of the Empire," 162.

67. Wells, *The Roman Empire*, 244.

68. Garth Fowden points out that the sacralization of the imperial rule was reignited under the tetrarchy. Fowden, *Empire to Commonwealth*, 89.

69. Mann, *Sources of Social Power: A History of Power from the Beginning to A.D. 1760*, 22.

70. Looked at in this light, the Jewish establishment's objections to Jesus' claims were more political than theological, they having already surrendered to the Roman imperial "son of God" and his claims to deity.

71. Wells, *The Roman Empire*, 244.

72. Crossan and Reed, *In Search of Paul*, 74–104.

73. Latin titles like *dei filius* ("Son of a God") and *divi filius* ("Son of a Divine One") are not distinguished in Greek and appear as *theou yios* or *theou hyios* ("Son of God").

deliberately denying Caesar his highest title."[74] It seems clear that it was into this theopolitical context of the imperial bid for transcendence that the counterpolitical announcement of the good news of the kingdom of God was interposed and the contrast made between Jesus' authority and the imperial sovereignty of the Roman lords of the nations.

D. TOWARDS A KENARCHIC THEOPOLITICS

This concluding section of the chapter applies the hermeneutics of living by faith to the gospel testimony of five events of Passion week in the context of the prophetic and historical *habitus* set out in the chapter so far. In so doing, it anticipates the *telos* of the cross and resurrection in culmination of the incarnation event as a whole. This, in turn, is taken to exemplify the fullness of church and gospel in relationship to temporal politics and points forward to the praxis of contemporary post-Christendom theopolitics. The incidents concerned are the demonstration in the temple and the three contentions that followed, which are narrated in all three synoptic gospels.[75] To these are appended the uniquely Johannine account of Jesus washing the disciples' feet. The purpose of these expositions is to reevaluate Jesus' actions in the so-called cleansing of the temple, and to consider the implications of his responses to the contentions created by them. The outcomes are then expounded to indicate the direction of theopolitical activity in the context of contemporary Western biopower.

For the sake of space, rather than including the whole text of the stories, detailed knowledge is assumed that can otherwise be remedied with reference to the relevant scriptures. While slavish adherence to the hermeneutical approach developed here is not being advocated, its capacity to provide the substance for a genuinely eschatological twenty-first-century apprehension of a counterpolitical God is proffered as a means to undergird the kenarchic politics attempted here. Again for the sake of brevity and to maintain the clarity of argument, the detailed hermeneutic is only applied to the Markan narrative of the demonstration in the temple and the Johannine account of the footwashing. In the other expositions the expository method is left in the background.

---

74. Crossan and Reed, *In Search of Paul*, 11.

75. The use of the word "contention" and the expository direction of these incidents is derived from the unpublished study outlines of author and practical theologian Roger T. Forster. Cf. Forster and Marston, *God's Strategy in Human History*.

Critical perspectives on the text that are predicated on modern assumptions about transcendence, while not discounted, are not utilized here for the obvious reason that they belong to an alternative hermeneutic with its own expertise and purpose.

1. The Demonstration in the Temple

Deliberately investing the text with relational worth, and open to eschatological encounter, the hermeneute can now step into the narrative of the incident in the temple alert to the grammar of the story and aware of three sets of relationships in which to apply the four characteristics of worldview. The relationship of the writer to the text and the narrative to the events it supposedly describes are considered before the relationship of the reader to the text, which is then activated by the economy of response. The four characteristics of worldview embedded in the narrative, as explicated in B.1 above, are the context of the wider corporate *sitz-im-leben*, its deep cultural questions, and the related symbols and praxis.

The grammar of the story can be parsed quite simply as an initial sequence that depicts Jesus in the temple driving out those buying and selling, overturning the tables of the money changers and the seats of those selling doves, and obstructing those who were carrying merchandise. The ensuing topical sequence consists in Jesus' rhetorical instruction of the people, "Is it not written in the prophets, 'My house shall be called a house of prayer for all the nations?' But you have made it a robbers' den."[76] The final sequence then describes the frightened and murderous reaction of the chief priests and scribes towards Jesus, provoked by the amazement with which the multitude greets his teaching. In seeking out the first of the aspects of worldview underlying this simple story, the previous section of the chapter on the prophetic, historical, and archeological context of the gospel testimony gives a good indication of the deeper narrative in which it sits. From the writer's perspective the people of God are likely to be viewed as God's chosen people, located in the holy land, centered on the temple. He will act for her and through her to reestablish his shalom throughout the world, in opposition to the voracious empires of Syria, Assyria, Greece, and now Rome, and the Jewish leaders' political compromises with them. In terms of the reali-

76. Mark 11:17.

ties the story seems to describe, this presents a capital city and religious cult occupied by, and at a leadership level integrated with, the imperial system so as to legitimize occupation, with a subversive apocalyptic prophet confronting them. Continuing on to the "what is to be done" aspect of the worldview of the writer, and referring again to the recent research, the question becomes one of how the oppressive sovereignty of Rome and its infiltration of the society and politics of the day might be curtailed. In terms of the events the testimony depicts, the radical behavior of Jesus fulfills the dramatic actions of Jeremiah who stood in its gate and declaimed a temple without justice[77] and Ezekiel who dug through its wall to reveal the abominations it contained.[78]

Moving to focus on the symbols, these are Jerusalem, the temple, the symbolic connotations of language and action, and in particular the background to the biblical quotations from Isaiah 56:7, "For My house will be called a house of prayer for all the peoples," and Jeremiah 7:11, "Has this house, which is called by My name, become a den of robbers in your sight?" The juxtaposition of these prophecies of Isaiah and Jeremiah, alongside the symbolic power of Jerusalem and the temple, positions the gospel author over against the political powers of Jesus' day. In terms of the realities they assay to signify, the symbols serve to strengthen the portrayal of Jesus as counterpolitical prophet. The conflated prophetic declarations align him with the radical vision of the Hebrew prophetic tradition in which Isaiah regards the fullness of the temple's purpose as a house of prayer bringing blessing and belonging to eunuchs and foreigners,[79] thus setting aside the law denying full access even to Jews with damaged genitals.[80] In this light it is the contemporary leaders' failure to fulfill this intended purpose that makes it a den of robbers. The issue is not just that they are profiteering out of a legitimate appeasement system, but that they have failed to realize the greater goal of mercy towards the poor in body and spirit. In this they are stealing from God and the multitude. The den of thieves' quote allies Jesus with the prophet's view that temple worship is only acceptable as long as the deeper practice of justice is in place. The concluding aspect of praxis or

77. Jeremiah 7:2.

78. Ezekiel 8:8.

79. Isaiah 56:3–5.

80. Leviticus 21:20.

lifestyle, which Wright calls the "implied eschatology"[81] or resolution of the underlying question of "what is to be done?", would be viewed by the writer in terms of the prophetic counterpolitical stream of first-century apocalyptic thinking. It would manifest in an attitude of disdain for the quisling Jewish monarchy, religious elite, and Roman political hierarchy, and the purpose of the story can be seen to be to encourage this subversive orientation.

It is now possible to complete the quest for the contemporary counterpolitical application of this brief but groundbreaking narrative. The eschatological potential of the hermeneutic can be increased at this point by adding the exercise of the economy of response with its foci of touch, flows and relation, difference and affinity, distance and proximity; the interplay of absence and presence, states of knowledge and modes of address; acclamation and testimony before witnesses. It is important to recognize that Ward's approach is not offered as a theoretical hermeneutic in quite the same manner as Wright's. Rather he is indicating the general direction that a mimetic relationship with the content of the story might take. As the reader begins to penetrate beyond the surface of the text, the affective impact of Jesus' intensely physical intervention is soon felt. The driving pressure of his hands or scourge, the tumbling stacks of money, the reek of urine and excrement from the disturbed livestock, and the insistent accents of the Galilean preacher all reverberate through the temple. The words of the ancient castigations resound above the tumult of heaving tables, bruised traders, flying birds, and fleeing customers, contending with the established powers and embroiling the reader within Jesus' apocalyptic demonstration against the imperialized temple system. Paul Fletcher's ease of move from the immanence of the eschatological instant to the radical politics of the incarnation is not so incredible within such a hermeneutic.

In terms of the radical reader's broad picture, in which the miscegenation of church and empire is perceived to be at its fullness, Jesus' actions expose an earlier parallel fullness of law, sovereignty, and money, displacing the kenotic service of the poor and marginalized of the nations. Given that the consequent contemporary question is "what is to be done to resolve it in a kenarchic way?" then Jesus' demonstration against the system indicates the manner in which the *ecclesia* today needs to disclose the fullness of empire in similarly carefully timed ways. For the

81. N.T. Wright, *The New Testament and the People of God*, 124.

kenarchic reader, the symbols of Jerusalem and temple correlate with state and church and represent ways that the underlying religio-political system affirms the sovereignty of empire. The quotations from Isaiah and Jeremiah reveal the impact to be the displacement of the loving purposes of God for the migrant and marginalized. The overall application of the symbols in the story to the symbols of state and church in the context of contemporary biopower is to underline the manner in which the nation state and money affirm sovereign right whether of global organizations, nation states, or individuals. Finally a praxis is indicated, along the lines already explored in terms of a transubstantiated kenosis of loving subversive acts, which amaze the multitude but risk the life-threatening opposition of the powers. As an example of this, at the time of writing, Roman Catholic activist Chris Cole has today been sentenced to prison for incarnating just such an act in demonstration against the arms trade.[82]

2. Three Contentions

Three ensuing incidents are narrated directly after the altercation in the temple by all three synoptic writers. The contentions that they describe serve to expand the counterpolitical praxis of kenarchy being developed here. They affirm the interpretation of the incident in the temple as a demonstration against the whole religio-political system, by showing the implications of such behavior then and its likely fullness now. With the inclusion of John's footwashing story, this is revealed as a kenotic approach that deliberately confronts and draws out the powers of empire without regard for the personal consequences to the initiator, but then helps the representatives of sovereign power to understand the import of the demonstration and the implications of their own choices. It then freely submits to the imperial authority rather than insisting on its own way, while disclosing ongoing ways of revealing the positive power of kenotic love to those open to it.

The first of these contentions concerns Jesus' authority. Raised, according to the three synoptic writers, by the main representatives of leadership, the disciples of the Pharisees, and the Herodians,[83] the

---

82. *Ecclesia* online daily report for January 20, 2011.
83. Matthew 22:16.

chief priests, the scribes, and the elders[84] asked, "By what authority do you do these things?" Each gospel has Jesus answering with a further question: "Was the baptism of John from heaven or from men?" The background story to this question can be drawn from all three synoptic texts, which describe the crowds who came to be baptized by John.[85] Both Matthew and Luke report his "you brood of vipers" speech, which Luke has directed to the multitudes, while Matthew specifies Pharisees and Sadducees. Luke states that they all asked John what to do in order to repent with integrity, and reports John's answer in terms of the redistribution of wealth, an end to corrupt economic practice, and the restriction of military violence.[86]

In the likely knowledge of this background context, the leaders' are left in a quandary. They reason among themselves and decide, "If we say, 'From heaven,' He will say, 'Why did you not believe him?' But if we say, 'From men,' all the people will stone us to death, for they are convinced that John was a prophet." So they answer that they do not know where John's authority came from and Jesus replies, "Nor will I tell you by what authority I do these things."[87] All three questions, the leaders' to Jesus, his back to them, and theirs to each other, clearly present contending political agendas. Their initial question manifests a perception of power based on imperial sovereignty, and their discussion among themselves shows their concern to hold on to their own delegated authority. Jesus' question exposes the choice underlying the nature of authority, which was declared by John the Baptist not to be about the imposition of personal or corporate will at all, but the kenotic sharing of life with the poor. It follows that if John's authority was from God, then the divine will is the choice of kenotic love, and that this was the authority by which Jesus operated.

The next contention was the question about the poll-tax, which all three synoptic writers agree was a trap, instigated by the Pharisees,[88] the Herodians,[89] and the chief priests and scribes.[90] Luke specifies it was "so

84. Mark 11:27; Luke 20:1.
85. Matthew 3:7ff.; Mark 1:4ff.; Luke 3:7ff.
86. Luke 3:10–14.
87. Luke 20:5–8.
88. Matthew 22:15–16.
89. Mark 12:13.
90. Luke 20:19–20.

that they could deliver Him to the rule and the authority of the governor." Once again all three record the same question with little variation, "And they sent their disciples to Him, along with the Herodians, saying, 'Teacher, we know that You are truthful and teach the way of God in truth, and defer to no one; for You are not partial to any. Tell us then, what do You think? Is it lawful to give a poll-tax to Caesar, or not?'" All three make clear that Jesus recognized the trap, with Matthew and Mark recording him asking why they are testing him, while Luke cuts to the chase with the request for the coin used for the poll-tax, which all three identify as a denarius. They all similarly record his question, the leaders' answer, and his response. "And He said to them, 'Whose likeness and inscription is this?' They said to Him, 'Caesar's.' Then He said to them, 'Then render to Caesar the things that are Caesar's; and to God the things that are God's.'"[91]

The historical research described in the previous section confirms the puppet status of at least the majority of these leadership groupings in relation to Caesar's rule. In the context of the altercation in the temple there is surely no way that his request for the coin and his further question to them could possibly be read to indicate Jesus' support for the separation of his loving kenosis and their imperial power, as has so frequently been argued. It would indicate instead "the things that are Caesar's" to be a destructive system of imperial domination for the purposes of trade and taxation. To follow the contours of the demonstration in the temple, already developed at some length, then "the things that are God's" would refer to a kenarchic strategy for engaging with Caesar's system by deliberately drawing the powers out by direct action at a strategic time. Jesus' subsequent behavior, as exemplified in the first contention, and now here, would suggest that this would be complemented by then remaining freely subject to them while operating in an entirely opposite spirit.

As intimated in the previous chapter, the apostle Paul's well-known advice in the Epistle to the Romans, "be in subjection to the governing authorities"[92] needs to be understood in this light. The same applies to the similar injunction in the First Epistle of Peter, "Submit yourselves for the Lord's sake to every human institution."[93] It is significant that

91. Matthew 22:21–22.

92. Romans 13:1.

93. 1 Peter 2:13.

the writer of the Acts clearly depicts Peter and Paul behaving in exactly the manner that the gospel narrative describes Jesus as doing, when he portrays the way that the apostles take direct action in word and deed against the powers, but subsequently submit to them in life and when necessary in death.[94] Taking both the Acts accounts and the advice of the Epistles together arrives at a very similar position to the one being exegeted here.

The third contention was instigated by the Sadducees who, as all three gospel writers remind us, did not believe that there would be a resurrection of the dead. All three record that they addressed Jesus as teacher, quoted the Mosaic law of Levirate marriage, and put to him the convoluted example of the woman who as a consequence married seven brothers, with the question "in the resurrection, which one's wife will she be, for all seven had her as wife?"[95] Both Matthew and Mark record Jesus' immediate response that the Sadducees "are mistaken, not understanding the Scriptures nor the power of God." Luke does not record the initial response but agrees with the others in their account of Jesus' explanatory reply, "in the resurrection they neither marry, nor are given in marriage, but are like the angels," to which he adds the descriptions "the sons of this age" and "the sons of God, being sons of the resurrection" which they become. All three record Jesus' affirmation of resurrection with similar accounts apart from slight textual variations with the statement, "But regarding the resurrection of the dead, have you not read what was spoken to you by God: 'I am the God of Abraham, and the God of Isaac, and the God of Jacob?' He is not the God of the dead but of the living."[96] Mark adds, "you are greatly mistaken" and Luke, "for all live to Him."

Clearly the Sadducees understood time quite differently to Jesus. For them "this age" was the only context for human life. As Matthew and Mark emphasize, from Jesus' perspective the source of their misconception was their failure to understand either the scriptures or the power of God. Jesus' use of the scriptures in the narrative is revealing. Two things stand out. Firstly, his citation of Moses, the scriptural authority for their story, and his encounter with the three-generational I AM of resurrection in a past age, emphasizes God's direct statement of his power to deliver

94. Acts 4:19–20; 23:1–3.
95. Matthew 22:23ff.; Mark 12:18ff.; Luke 20:27ff.
96. Matthew 22:31–32.

the Israelites from the imperial persecutors of Moses' then present time. Jesus points out that the Sadducees do not understand the scriptures like Moses did when he encountered the God who was immanent to his forefathers. The Sadducees' this-worldly, over-realized eschatology means that they are unable to experience the God immanent to Moses in his ability to confront the imperial powers of their time. As a result they were incapable of receiving Jesus as the current revelation of God's name.

Applied to today, it underlines that a theology of immanence without the possibility of a present transcendence endorsed by resurrection can provide no alternative to apathy, suppression, or collusion with the imperial powers of the present age. In contrast, openness to the revelation of a God alive to those living by faith across the ages, facilitates a larger counterpolitical revelation of God. Secondly, Jesus' own exegesis of the scriptures that the Sadducees were indirectly citing, allowed him to use their question to show how the counterpolitical character of the eschaton exposed the gender hierarchy of the law's attitude to women and his expectation that it must come to an end in the resurrection. As a result the narrative uses the idea of resurrection to emphasize the equality of the sexes in a manner that Ray Mayhew, drawing on N.T. Wright, describes as "the politically charged potential of the doctrine of the resurrection."[97]

3. Jesus Washes the Disciples' Feet

The footwashing episode is being offered here as a concluding intimate insight into the heart of the incarnation.[98] For the Johannine author it was the preparation for the public manifestation of the cross. For the concluding deliberations of this book it delineates the eschatological power of the exception that the cross consummated. Taken together with the preceding contentions, it sets the direction for a counterbalanced praxis of incarnational life. But firstly there are important differences between the Johannine writer's use of narrative and that of the synoptic writers that it is important to notice. To begin with, in the story of the footwashing, a hermeneute is already overtly at work. The writer's opinions of Jesus' self-awareness, motivation, and knowledge of his eschatological

97. Mayhew, "Turning the Tables, Resurrection as Revolution," 1.
98. John 13:1ff.

trajectory are contained within the story, together with the source and certainty of Judas Iscariot's future betrayal. So in order to enter the passage and expose its eschatological capacity to engender kenotic life, it is important to apply the developing hermeneutic more intentionally.

The attempt to parse the story soon reveals a far more complex structure than the synoptic narratives. The hermeneute's perspective couches the initial sequence as Jesus' challenge to find a way to love his disciples completely. The topical sequence sets up Jesus' footwashing as the metaphor with which he attempts to solve the problem thus set out. This contains a second inner story in which the unwillingness of the disciples to embrace his act presents a further topical sequence that also needs to be overcome. The resolution is now dependent on both Jesus' action in washing the disciples' feet and Peter's willingness for him to do so. The final sequence in which the initial task is completed becomes both Peter's acquiescence and the imperative of Peter and the others following his example into the future. In this way eschatological involvement on the part of Jesus' disciples becomes part of the grammar of the story, just as Ward intimates when he observes that mimesis positions the hermeneute in a manner integral to the grammar of knowledge and communication, something that has clearly already happened to the Johannine author. The effect of the two levels to the story is to elevate the inner story of the inversion of sovereignty to the transcendent context of heaven and the cosmic confrontation between God and the devil. The structural inclusion of the ongoing activity of the disciples in this drama has the effect of drawing the hermeneute into the narrative even before deliberately connecting with the affective aspect of the hermeneutic.

The answers to the questions intrinsic to worldview are operating at two levels, that of the inner story and the interpretative gloss of the narrator, which is now also part of the narrative. Characteristics of worldview can be discovered at both levels. At the narrator's level his understanding of the larger cosmic story is expressed in his description of Jesus as "come forth from God and going back to God," locating Jesus both in and out of temporality. His description of Judas as the one the devil has subverted recognizes a demonic battle, which is also intersecting the immanent realm. At the inner story level, the intersection of the two time frames is revealed in Peter's two reactions to Jesus' move to wash his feet. He first rejects this because he sees Jesus on the human, imperial level as too great to perform such a menial task for him and then conversely rushes to embrace it because Jesus is too important for him to miss receiving from, and he realizes that Jesus is reinstating the act of footwashing from uncleanness and meniality to holiness and transcendence. The problematics in need of resolution are the powers embodied by the devil at the transcendent level of the story and people's unwillingness to take the lowest place at the immanent level. The redemptive resolution is both the anticipated form of Jesus' departure out of the world at the cross that involves him loving his "own who were in the world" to the uttermost, and the preparatory act of humility embodied in washing his disciples' feet and inviting them to do the same.

The account is replete with symbols, most obviously the Feast of the Passover, supper, footwashing, bathing, and laying aside of garments. The word for "lay aside" (*tithēmi*) denotes the act of laying something down, and is the same word that the writer uses in the earlier narratives and later in this chapter for Jesus laying down his life on the cross.[99] While the footwashing and bathing seem to connote a reversal of ritual cleansing from the servant or worshiper to the one served or worshiped, the Feast of the Passover, the laying aside of garments, and the possible resonance with Paul's kenotic Philippian hymn,[100] mark the shift from sovereign power to kenotic love. The praxis in the external story is the interpretative hermeneutic itself, and in the internal account it is the actions of servant humility and the imperative to follow in the same manner.

Following the economy of response into the text, the reader is immediately drawn into the intimacy of the supper table and an intensely relational interplay between Rome's demonically transcendent sovereignty consuming the life of Judas, Jesus' friend and disciple, and Jesus' conscious confrontation of imperial power with the contrary spirit of transcendent love in the intimate act of footwashing. The act is set among words of transition—"before," "his hour," "depart," "come forth," "going back"—that position Jesus in movement from God to God, from transcendence to transcendence via immanence. The source of love is unmistakably presented as divine transcendence. The reader is pulled

---

99. This Greek word for life, *psuchē*, is distinct from both *bios* and *zōe* and indicates the life, literally the breath, of a distinct individual. Cf. John 10:11, 15, 17, 18 and here in John 13:37, 38.

100. The Epistle to the Philippians is generally dated around 67 CE whereas John is unlikely to have been written much before the end of the first century.

into this trajectory of immanent transcendence that Jesus is described as moving within, as he "got up from supper, and laid aside His garments; and taking a towel, He girded Himself." In identifying with the disciples and especially Peter, the reader is confronted as to their own readiness for the transcendent Christ to take off his outer clothes and under tunic (*himation*)[101] and wash their feet, in confrontation of all pretensions to personal sovereignty. It seems that, in this intimate act, Jesus stripped completely or very nearly naked except for the towel with which he then girded himself. He then proceeded to pour water into a bowl and wash each of the disciples' feet, wiping them with the towel that he had wrapped around his body. The act is offered as a specific demonstration of Jesus' love for his disciples, again anticipating the cross, where "having loved His own who were in the world, He loved them to the end." The reader is confronted, together with Peter and the rest, with the gift of naked transcendence. Here he lays down his clothes, but within the narrative the symbolism is clear, and the hermeneute is invited to conclude that Jesus is preparing to lay down his own life for his disciples.

Within the wider contemporary symbolism of the thesis of this book, the correlation between Jesus' nakedness and the loving activation of the potential power of naked life is impossible to avoid. At first, Peter recoils from the ensuing act of footwashing, perceiving it as marking the distance between him and the transcendent other. But Jesus' words reverse this hierarchical expectation of transcendent power. Unless he can serve Peter in this way, Peter can have no share in him, but he has no occasion to fear for greater times of intimate participation have already taken place. Peter replies, "then wash not only my feet, but also my hands and my head" for a share in this love is dependent on divine gift. Jesus then indicates that this transcendently immanent gift is also corporate. As a result the disciples can serve love to others in the same way, "For I gave you an example that you also should do as I did to you." The hermeneute is challenged to experimental participation in the kenarchic actions of Jesus by continuing them in the service of others.

The account of the gospel of John's narrative of this evocative episode consummates the reconfiguration of transcendence contemplated by the third and final part of this book. The God behind everything transpires to rule by the choice to lay down his life as a humble gift to human beings, who are thereby empowered to do the same for each other. In

101. Abbott-Smith, *A Greek Lexicon*, 216.

the context of the theological enquiry into the relationship of church and empire presented in the first two parts of this book, it embodies the antidote to the representation of sovereign power disclosed there. It concludes that the configuration of transcendence consequent on a fourth-century embrace of sovereign power amounted to a misrepresentation of the divine character of epic proportions. The identification of Constantine's *pax Romana* as the evident success of the church, secured by the application of the power of the cross understood as the resolution of God's offended transcendence, affirmed empire's strength as the upholding of its law, its violent defense, and the ongoing appeasement of transcendent sovereignty.

These instruments of empire have been pursued throughout the genealogy of Christendom to their present manifestation in terms of biopower. This has come to a fullness in terms of the commodification of the naked life of the multitude. However, this is now being met by the potential power of naked life, and the renewed revelation of transcendence, to offer a prospective *katargēsis* of empire's fullness. The consideration of future directions for theology and praxis set out in this third part of the book has begun to express this consummated fullness in a kenarchic perspective of the divine, configured directly from the Jesus of the gospel testimony. The experimental hermeneutic set out here has indicated that the narrative of the events of Passion week deliberately places Jesus in confrontation with the imperial powers, in a way that suggests that in the incarnation, and finally at the cross, the power of empire and its subsumptive association with transcendence in terms of law, monarchy, and temple was brought to an end.

From this perspective the fourth-century fall and subsequent genealogy of Christendom can be seen to have effectively reversed the intention of the incarnation and reintegrated transcendence and sovereignty. This has two particularly significant outcomes. Firstly, with the real possibility that the manifestation of this miscegenation of church and sovereignty is now at its fullness, the task of the radical *ecclesia* is to bring it to an end in true imitation of the gospel Jesus. This chapter has attempted to point towards a contemporary praxis that might accomplish this. The fuller theopolitical development of this in theology and praxis is a matter of real urgency. Secondly, seen in this light, it is likely that the Old Testament story of salvation can be recast as testimony to a God who showed himself in terms of kenosis while humankind insisted on law, monarchy, and temple. But, far from being the substance of the kingdom of God, these were in fact the very foundational structures of empire. Rather than renouncing people created in his image, he remained with them, inhabiting and ultimately reversing the very structures of empire in order to bring them to an end for the whole of humanity. The Old Testament story awaits further theological reinterpretation in this light. It may well appear that the same longsuffering, kenotic character of the divine displayed through the miscegenation of church and empire was displayed in bearing away their previous misalliances and subsumptive reinterpretations of his loving character. Then as now, permanently displayed in the trans-historical content of the incarnation event, was the unceasing desire of transcendent divinity to manifest peace among the multitude.

Conclusion

FOLLOWING THE CONTOURS OF the search for the occasion of a theological fall responsible for the dislocation of theology from contemporary Western life, the thesis of this book has exposed a much earlier fall than generally anticipated, to be found in the fourth-century partnership of church and empire. The nature of this fall has been identified as a crisis in the perception of transcendence leading to a subsumption of ecclesial form and theology by sovereign power. The book has explored the implications of this supposed lapsis for the Western church and embarked on its resolution, by venturing onto three crucial steps, derived from the direction indicated by Paul Fletcher, as a possible route towards the theological realignment called for in Part I.

1. THREE CRUCIAL STEPS

To recapitulate, these steps are the eschatological reconception of time, the cultivation of the eschatological instant to connect with the politics of Jesus, and an interrogation of the process by which faith became "beholden to the force of law."[1] Affirming the latter interrogation as central to the problem of dislocation, the attempt has been made to provide a compelling narrative of the genealogy of faith's obligation to the force of law from the supposed fourth-century fall to the present. The argument has deliberately stopped short of offering a cause and effect analysis, given that any such apparently objective explanation might be the consequence of the genealogy itself and neither advisable nor possible in tracking the supposed subsumption. Nonetheless, the conduits of Part II have hopefully succeeded in providing a sustainable account of the developing obligation of faith to juridico-political force through the partnership of church and empire. It is hoped that this book now offers a substantial trajectory of the relationship of church and empire through

---

1. Fletcher, *Disciplining the Divine*, 178.

the course of Western Christendom that will be a resource and catalyst for further exploration and study.

The thesis has focused from the start on the role of the cross in the supposed subsumption, tracing its pathway onwards from the fourth-century ecclesial identification of imperial sovereignty as the means to eschatological peace. It has attempted to demonstrate that the heart of the church's ability to maintain this peace was seen by Eusebius, and subsequent medieval and early modern rulers and clerics, to be embodied in a view of the atonement expressed in a soteriology of appeasement in which law and physical violence establish sovereign power. As the application of this soteriological strategy therefore became faith's task, it became increasingly obligated to it. Part II has delineated the process by which the application of the soteriological components of the cross was configured as the primary purpose of faith through the eventual medieval bifurcation of sovereignty, the shift of agency from the church and monarchy to the nation state, and the conjunction of sovereignty and money in contemporary Western biopower. The final conduit has attempted to show that, by the time of the culmination of the historical genealogy of the partnership of church and empire, faith was so deeply embedded in the soteriological transformations of law, war, and money that secured the persistence of sovereignty, that it had become inextricably beholden to juridico-political force. The interdependence of the affirmation of sovereignty as the nature of divine transcendence and the accompanying transformations of an appeasement soteriology of the cross are demonstrated to be the underlying legitimative mechanism of Western Christendom.

It follows that, to resolve the enduring genealogical problem behind the dislocation of theology from contemporary life, it is necessary to separate faith from its apparently inextricable bondage to imperial sovereignty and the accompanying soteriological transformations. It is this that Part III has endeavored to prepare the way for. Exploring the contemporary trend to make kenosis central to the understanding of the divine and offering a particular expression of kenotic theology characterized as kenarchy, it has presented an alternative approach to the general understanding of divine transcendence. Finally it has set out the components for a radical hermeneutic involving the eschatological reconception of time and the cultivation of the eschatological instant by which it expects to reconnect with an originary counterpolitical Jesus.

The anticipated outcome of the application of this hermeneutic is that it will enable the reconfiguration of the divine in terms of the gospel Jesus and so provide a new locus for the life of faith beyond any obligation to the requirements of empire. This has the effect of reversing the inversion of the *corpus verum* and giving renewed significance to the narratives presented as the alternative substratum running alongside the primary genealogy narrated in the four conduits. In order to give greater direction to future theopolitical development consequent on this thesis, a brief restatement of the contribution of these past promulgators of radical action to the future shape and praxis of the church in the world now completes the story.

2. STREAMS OF PAST ESCHATOLOGICAL HOPE

The subplots traced through the four conduits carry a resounding call for an alternative eschatological completion that can overcome the juridico-political captivity represented by Christendom, although they lacked the capacity to fully answer the summons in their own day. The ongoing presence of a different kind of power to imperial sovereignty in the early church tradition is clear from Irenaeus' gracious and flexible attitude to the celebration of Easter, and Dionysius' specific recognition of the reciprocal nature of human relationships in his permissioning of second baptisms, as described in the first conduit. The examples given portray both bishops demonstrating an open, egalitarian leadership that makes room for others, in distinction from the monarchical tendency to insist on uniformity of doctrine and practice. While perhaps not their mature custom, as is clear from the way in which Irenaeus anchors his writings against heresy in a strong affirmation of apostolic succession,[2] his opinions on Easter, and Dionysius' views on baptism, are examples of unity in diversity resonant with a more kenotic approach. The implications, had this way of leadership operated instead of sovereign rule, could have had epoch-changing consequences for the later acrimonious debate over Easter[3] or the violent responses to Anabaptists.[4] This evidence of an early collaborative leadership style resonates with the advice of the synoptic

---

2. Irenaeus, *Against Heresies*, Bk. 3, ch. 3.

3. See Bede, *A History of the English Church and People*, 101–3.

4. See Broadbent, *The Pilgrim Church*, 197–9.

gospels, "The kings of the Gentiles lord it over them . . . But it is not this way with you,"[5] and indicate a way forward for leadership today.

Joachim of Fiore's theological reconception of time and new monastic praxis of church, together with Francis of Assisi's embrace of the poor, similarly resonate with a kenotic way to peace. Joachim's innovatory proposals for a whole new form for the church, and, in turn, its agency to shape society, attempted a counterpolitical reconfiguration of church and world. Francis of Assisi provided the complementary kenotic praxis intimately felt by the poor and the leprous, and its integrity as an authentic representation of Christian discipleship led to the exponential growth of the three Franciscan orders. Together they could have provided an alternative direction for the future history of Christendom where church and gospel affirmed the revolutionary move of the emerging multitude at the Renaissance, rather than playing a part in the counterrevolutionary reassertion of sovereign power. Joachim's prophetic reconception of time and Francis' radical embrace of the gospel testimony likewise affirm the direction of the hermeneutic developed in the last part of this book.

The distinctive contribution of the seventeenth-century radicals, who form the subplot to the third conduit, is their deeply subversive attempt to redraw the relationship between sovereignty and land at a time when the new capitalism was about to disconnect the majority of the population from it by enclosure. In the case of Gerrard Winstanley and the Diggers on St George's Hill, it took the form of a challenge to private property, and with William Penn and the American colony of Pennsylvania, it related to the de facto right of imperial power to annexe foreign territory. These approaches confronted the developing multiplied sovereignty of the emerging nation state. Rejecting the hierarchical authority of the official church for the inner light of personal revelation, and donating labor and money for equality with the poor and strangers, both Winstanley and Penn attempted to reconnect the people with the subsistence wealth of the land. Penn went a stage further and attempted to transform colonization into a form of universal citizenship by purchasing territory several times over to secure a common constitutional context for all, including the Native Americans. Had their radical approach to land tenure overcome the imperial system, the enclosures of the eighteenth and nineteenth centuries and the consequent exploi-

5. Luke 22:25–26.

tation of peasant labor power might never have taken place. Together they point to the pressing need for land redistribution today where, in twenty-first-century Britain, less than one percent of the population continues to own seventy percent of the land.[6]

The emerging subplot of the prevailing narrative of contemporary biopower is the hopeful conjunction of immaterial labor and the loving abandon of living by faith. The deliberate dislocation of faith from sovereignty, and its reconnection with a kenotic transcendence able to revolutionize the life of the multitude, could thereby meet the contemporary dislocation of theology from life. The unconditional donation of naked life with its inherent gifts and skills, in consort with the gospel Jesus and encountered in the egalitarian transcendence of the century of the Holy Spirit, provides for the resurrection of the *corpus verum*. Coming together in a mutual empowerment with the new immaterial and cooperative creativity of the multitude, the reconfigured *ecclesia* joins the proposed posse of resistance against the biopolitical conjunction of power and money, irrespective of the ultimate consequences for personal or corporate autonomy. Such an advent of eschatological hope might yet complete the collaborative initiative in leadership that Irenaeus and Dionysius pointed towards, the new community suitable for a reconceived fullness of time such as Joachim reached for, the return to the originary gospel identification with the poor that Francis embraced, and the reconnection with the land that Winstanley and Penn modeled.

Each of the past counterpolitical examples of a possible break with sovereign power failed to overcome the enduring grip of the church's agreement with empire. Joachim's prophetic program faltered when it came to the monarchical formation of the *Arrangement of the New People of God* and the need to establish his innovative reordering of society around the imperial authority of the papacy. The Franciscans soon became an arm of authoritarian papal power and, while their radical poverty remained a prophetic sign, in the long term it was unable to prevent the economic developments of the advance of Christendom. As with Joachim, the source of the difficulty lay with the ontological commitment to ecclesiastical sovereignty, in Francis' case particularly the mediatory role of the ecclesiastical priesthood in the eucharist, which weakened both the poverty and the radicality of the order. While Winstanley and Penn rejected the imperial authority of church and state,

6. Cowley, "The coming battle over land and property."

both nonetheless looked to reconstitute a new relationship with the land through a form of sovereign law.

In the light of the lessons provided by these radical exponents of change, three issues stand out that it is necessary to deal with decisively today if their common experience is not simply to be repeated. Firstly, while each looked for a means of reconnection with originary aspects of the gospel testimony, it required more than this to undo faith's obligation to imperial power and mount a successful counter-imperial resistance. Rather it called for a complete reconfiguration of the nature of transcendent being, such as, by arguing directly from Jesus to God, Part III points the way towards. Secondly, in order to succeed in such deep structural endeavors, it was necessary to devise an eschatological hermeneutic that could escape predication on medievality, modernity, or both, re-conceive time divergently from imperial time, and reengage the Spirit and the gospel narratives. The increasing displacement of the *corpus verum* made this very difficult for them to do. Nevertheless, they point forward in hope to a fullness in the present time, along lines that the final chapter has attempted to set out. It is hoped that the immediacy of the egalitarian transcendence of the century of the Holy Spirit accompanied by a newly configured kenotic theology, such as that proposed by this project, will provide for the renewed availability of the *corpus verum*. Thirdly, the obstacle to success in the case of each substratum can be simply identified as hierarchical sovereignty. This then becomes the final, critical, albeit controversial, observation of this whole project. That is to say that, in order to avoid falling back to the traditional imperial partnership, there must be a courageous break with those ecclesiastical and theological components or representations that carry sovereign transcendence and the accompanying soteriology of appeasement. This has enormous implications for ongoing church practice and theology that will need to be worked through in a spirit of kenotic love and not in accusation, domination, or exclusion. Such is the challenge of kenarchy.

3. THE ZEITGEIST QUESTIONS

This brings us naturally to the zeitgeist questions with which this project began, and particularly the question of the persistent relapse to hierarchical domination and control. For it is in resolving this that the questions of progress, power, money, and marginalization may also be answered. From the perspective of the thesis set out here, it is now possible to see that unless the hierarchical position of pope and pastor, elders or church councils, and their authoritative role in presiding over liturgy, teaching, behavior, and vision are subverted by an egalitarian empowering and collaborative leadership among the people, radical initiatives will continue to be overcome by sovereign power. It follows that unless the assumed connection between sovereign power and eschatological peace is broken, the soteriological connection between poverty and war will continue unchanged. This means, in turn, that until the dependency of democracy on the already predefined agency for peace through the sovereignty of the nation state, or the global institutions to which it is giving way, can be renegotiated as peace through love and community along lines such as kenarchy suggests, power and money will continue to stifle democracy. Finally, without the public recognition by the church of its own responsibility for the subjection of faith to sovereign power and a thorough disengagement from it, it is difficult to see how the church can ever recover from its present marginalization and be trusted by the multitude. Nothing less than the recasting of transcendence and an accompanying, sustained counter-imperial reorientation of the *ecclesia* is the pressing task of twenty-first-century theology.

Bibliography

Abbott-Smith, George. *A Manual Greek Lexicon of the New Testament.* New York: Scribner, 1936.

Abulafia, David. *Frederick II: A Medieval Emperor.* London: Pimlico, 2002.

Agamben, Giorgio. *Homo Sacer. Sovereign Power and Bare Life.* Translated by Daniel Heller-Roazen. Stanford, California: Stanford University Press, 1998.

———. *Means Without End. Notes on Politics.* Translated by Vincenzo Binetti and Cesare Casarino. Minneapolis and London: University of Minnesota Press, 2000.

———. *State of Exception.* Translated by Kevin Attell. Chicago and London: The University of Chicago Press, 2005.

———. *The Time That Remains. A Commentary on the Letter to the Romans.* Stanford, California: Stanford University Press, 2005.

Anderson, Allan H. *An Introduction to Pentecostalism: Global Charismatic Christianity.* Cambridge: Cambridge University Press, 2004.

Andreades, A. *History of the Bank of England 1640–1903.* Translated by Christabel Meredith. London: Frank Cass & Co. Ltd, 1966.

Andrewes, Patience. *Frederick II of Hohenstaufen.* Oxford: Oxford University Press, 1970.

Armstrong, Regis J., OFM, CAP, and Ignatius Brady OFM. *Francis and Clare, the Complete Works.* London: SPCK, 1982.

Balthasar, Hans Urs von. *Theo-Drama: Theological Dramatic Theory,* vol. II. Translated by Graham Harrison. San Francisco: Ignatius Press, 1988–98.

Barnes, T.D. *Constantine and Eusebius.* Cambridge, Massachusetts: Harvard University Press, 1981.

Barrett, David. "The Worldwide Holy Spirit Renewal." In *The Century of the Holy Spirit. 100 Years of Pentecostal and Charismatic Renewal 1901-2001* by Vinson Synan. Nashville, Tennessee: Thomas Nelson, 2001.

Barth, Karl. *Church Dogmatics,* 4 vols. Edited by G.W. Bromley and T.E. Torrance. Edinburgh: T. & T. Clark, 1956–75.

Bartleman, Frank. *Azusa Street.* Plainfield, New Jersey: Logos International, 1980.

Beatrice, Pier Franco. "The Word 'Homoousios' from Hellenism to Christianity." *Church History* 71:2 (June 2002). The American Society of Church History, 2002.

Bell, Daniel. "A Theopolitical Ontology of Judgement." In *Theology and the Political, The New Debate,* edited by Creston Davis et al. Durham and London: Duke University Press, 2005.

Bede. *A History of the English Church and People.* New York: Barnes and Noble, 1993.

Benjamin, Walter. *One Way Street.* London: Verso, 1997.

Bett, Henry. *Joachim of Flora.* London: Methuen, 1931.

Bevan, Bryan. *King William III: Prince of Orange, The First European.* London: The Rubicon Press, 1997.

Binns, L. Elliot. *Innocent III*. London: Methuen, 1968.

Black, Jeremy. "The Revolution and the Development of English Foreign Policy." In *By Force or Default*, edited by Eveline Cruickshanks. Edinburgh: John Donald Publishers Ltd, 1989.

Boardman, John, et al. *The Oxford History of the Roman World*. Oxford: Oxford University Press, 1991.

Bolton, Brenda. *Studies in Church History, 31*. Oxford: Blackwell, 1994.

Borg, Marcus, and Wright N.T. *The Meaning of Jesus: Two Visions*. New York: HarperCollins, 1999.

Broadbent, E.H. *The Pilgrim Church*. Basingstoke, Hants: Pickering and Inglis, 1931.

Brown, David. *Divine Humanity: kenosis defended and explored*. London: SCM Press, 2011.

Brown, Raphael. "A Francis of Assisi Research Bibliography." In *St. Francis of Assisi Omnibus of Resources*, edited by Marion A. Habig. Chicago: Franciscan Herald Press, 1973.

Bulgakov, Sergius. *The Lamb of God*. Grand Rapids, Michigan: William B. Eerdmans Publishing Company, 2008.

Burnet, Gilbert. *History of His Own Time*, vol. I. Oxford: Clarendon Press, 1823.

———. *History of His Own Time*, vol. III. Oxford: Clarendon Press, 1823.

———. *History of His Own Time*, vol. IV. Oxford: Clarendon Press, 1823.

Cameron, Averil. *Christianity and the Rhetoric of Empire*. Berkeley: University of California Press, 1991.

Cameron, Euan. *The European Reformation*. Oxford: Clarendon Press, 1991.

Canning, Joseph. "Power and the Pastor." In *Pope Innocent III and his World*, edited by John C. Moore. Brookfield, Vermont: Ashgate, 1999.

Caputo, John. *The Weakness of God. A Theology of the Event*. Bloomington and Indianapolis: Indiana University Press, 2006.

Carter, Warren. *Matthew and Empire*. Harrisburg: Trinity Press, 2001.

Cavanaugh, William T. *The Myth of Religious Violence*. Oxford: Oxford University Press, 2009.

———. *Theopolitical Imagination*. London and New York: T. & T. Clark, 2002.

———. *Torture and Eucharist*. Oxford and Malden, Massachusetts: Blackwell Publishers, 1998.

Clapham, Sir John. *The Bank of England*, vol. I. Cambridge: Cambridge University Press, 1944.

Clarke, T.E.S., and H.C. Foxcroft. *A Life of Bishop Burnet*. Cambridge: Cambridge University Press, 1907.

Claydon, Tony. "Latitudinarianism and Apocalyptic History in the Worldview of Gilbert Burnet." In *The Historical Journal*. Cambridge: Cambridge University Press, 2008.

———. *William III*. London: Longman, 2002.

———. *William III and the Godly Revolution*. Cambridge: Cambridge University Press, 1996.

Cowley, Jason. "The coming battle over land and property." *The New Statesman*, October 18, 2010.

Crossan, John Dominic, and Jonathan L. Reed. *In Search of Paul*. New York: HarperSanFrancisco, 2004.

Crossan, John Dominic. *God and Empire*. New York: HarperSanFrancisco, 2007.

Cupitt, Don. "The Christ of Christendom." In *The Myth of God Incarnate,* edited by John Hick. London: SCM Press, 1977.

Davidson, Ivor J. *The Birth of the Church.* The Baker History of the Church, vol. I. Grand Rapids, Michigan: Baker Books, 2004.

Davies, Glyn. *A History of Money.* Cardiff: University of Wales Press, 1994.

Davis, Creston, et al., eds. *Theology and the Political, The New Debate.* Durham and London: Duke University Press, 2005.

Dayton, Donald W. *Discovering an Evangelical Heritage.* New York: Harper and Row, 1976.

———. *Theological Roots of Pentecostalism.* Peabody, Massachusetts: Hendrickson Publishers, 2007.

de Certeau, Michel. *The Mystic Fable.* Chicago: The University of Chicago Press, 1992.

de Lubac, Henri, SJ. *Corpus Mysticum.* Translated by Gemma Simmonds CJ. London: SCM Press, 2006.

De Vries, J., and A. Van Der Woude. *The First Modern Economy. Success, Failure, and Perseverance of the Dutch Economy, 1500-1815.* Cambridge: Cambridge University Press, 1997.

Dickson, P.G.M. *The Financial Revolution in England.* London: Macmillan, 1967.

Droogers, André. "The Normalization of Religious Experience." In *Charismatic Christianity as Global Culture,* edited by Karla Poewe. Columbia, South Carolina: University of South Carolina Press, 1994.

Duchesne, L.M. *The Beginnings of the Temporal Sovereignty of the Popes, A.D. 754–1073.* Translated by A.H. Matthew. New York and London: Benziger, 1908.

Durnbaugh, Donald F. *The Believers' Church.* Ontario: Herald Press, 1968.

Ecclesia. Online daily report for January 20, 2011. No pages. Online: http://www.ekklesia.co.uk/node/13967

Eusebius. *Demonstratio evangelica.* Translated by W.J. Ferrar. London: SPCK, 1920.

———. *The History of the Church.* Translated by G.A. Williamson. London: Penguin Books, 1965.

———. *The Church History.* Translated by Paul L. Maier. Grand Rapids, Michigan: Kregel Academic & Professional, 2007.

———. "The Life of Constantine." In *The Nicene and Post-Nicene Fathers,* vol. I. New York: Charles Scribner's and Sons, 1925.

———. "The Oration in Praise of the Emperor Constantine." In *The Nicene and Post-Nicene Fathers,* vol. I. New York: Charles Scribner's and Sons, 1925.

Evans, C. Stephan, ed. *Exploring Kenotic Christianity.* Oxford: Oxford University Press, 2006.

Feenstra, Ronald J. "A Kenotic Christology of the Divine Attributes." In *Exploring Kenotic Christianity,* edited by C. Stephan Evans. Oxford: Oxford University Press, 2006.

Fields, Darrel., with Lorrie Fields. *The Seed of a Nation.* New York: Morgan James Publishing, 2008.

Fletcher, Paul. *Disciplining the Divine.* Farnham, Surrey and Burlington, Vermont: Ashgate, 2009.

———. "The Political Theology of the Empire to Come." In *Cambridge Review of International Affairs,* vol. XVII, no. 1. Carfax Publishing, April 2004.

Forster, Roger T., and Paul T. Marston. *God's Strategy in Human History.* Bromley, England: Send the Light Trust, 1973.

Foucault, Michel. *The History of Sexuality,* vol. I. Translated by Robert Hurley. London: Penguin Books, 1990.

Fowden, Garth. *Empire to Commonwealth.* Princeton: Princeton University Press, 1993.

Gardner, Lucy, et al. *Balthasar at the End of Modernity.* Edinburgh: T. & T. Clark, 1999.

Giles, Kevin. *The Trinity and Subordinationism.* Downers Grove, Illinois: InterVarsity Press, 2002.

Gillespie, Michael Allen. *The Theological Origins of Modernity.* Chicago: The University of Chicago Press, 2008.

Giuseppi, John. *The Bank of England.* London: Evans Brothers Ltd, 1966.

Goodchild, Philip. *Theology of Money.* London: SCM Press, 2007.

Grant, Robert M. *Eusebius as Church Historian.* Oxford: Clarendon Press, 1980.

———. "Religion and Politics at the Council of Nicaea." *The Journal of Religion,* vol. LV. no. 1. The University of Chicago Press, January 1975.

———. *The Emperor Constantine.* London: Weidenfeld & Nicolson, 1993.

Greig, Martin. "Gilbert Burnet and the Trinitarian Controversy." *The Journal of Ecclesiastical History,* vol. XLIV. Cambridge University Press, 1993.

———. "Gilbert Burnet and the Problem of Nonconformity in Restoration Scotland and England." *Canadian Journal of History,* vol. XXXII (April 1997).

Grubb, Norman P. C. T. *Studd, Cricketer and Pioneer.* London: Lutterworth Press, 1965.

Habermas, Jurgen. "The European Nation-State: On the Past and Future of Sovereignty and Citizenship." In *Public Culture,* translated by Ciaran Cronin. Durham, North Carolina: Duke University Press, 1998.

Habig, Marion A., ed. *St. Francis of Assisi Omnibus of Resources.* Chicago: Franciscan Herald Press, 1973.

Halsall, Paul, ed. *Internet Mediaeval Sourcebook.* Fordham University Center for Medieval Studies 2006. No pages. Online: http://www.ewtn.com/library/COUNCILS/LATERAN4.HTM#list constitution 1.

Hardt, Michael, and Antonio Negri. *Empire.* Cambridge, Massachusetts and London, England: Harvard University Press, 2000.

———. *Multitude.* New York: Penguin Books, 2004.

Healy, Nicholas M. *Church, World and the Christian Life.* Cambridge: Cambridge University Press, 2000.

Heinze, Rudolph. *Reform and Conflict.* The Monarch History of the Church, vol. IV. Oxford: Monarch Books, 2006.

Hepden, Stephen. "The Impact of Racial Inclusivity in the Azusa Street Revival." MTh diss., University of Manchester, 2008.

Hick, John, ed. *The Myth of God Incarnate.* London: SCM Press, 1977.

Hill, Christopher. *Reformation to Industrial Revolution.* London: Penguin Books, 1969.

———. *The World Turned Upside Down.* London: Penguin Books, 1975.

Hocken, Peter. *The Challenges of the Pentecostal, Charismatic and Messianic Jewish Movements.* Farnham, Surrey and Burlington, Vermont: Ashgate, 2009.

Hollenweger, Walter J. *Pentecostalism: Origins and Developments Worldwide.* Peabody, Massachusetts: Hendrickson, 1997.

Hollerich, M.J. *Eusebius of Caesarea's Commentary on Isaiah.* Oxford: Clarendon Press, 1999.

Horsley, Richard. *Jesus and Empire.* Minneapolis: Fortress Press, 2003.

Howard-Brook, Wes, and Anthony Gwyther. *Unveiling Empire.* Maryknoll, New York: Orbis Books, 1999.

Israel, Jonathan, ed. *The Anglo-Dutch Moment*. Cambridge: Cambridge University Press, 2003.

Israel, Jonathan. *The Dutch Republic*. Oxford: Clarendon Press, 1995.

Jenkins, Philip. *The Next Christendom*. Oxford: Oxford University Press, 2002.

Johns, Jeremy. "Christianity and Islam." In *The Oxford History of Christianity*, edited by John McManners. Oxford University Press, 1990.

Kantorowicz, Ernst. *Frederick the Second*. London: Constable & Co., 1931.

———. *The King's Two Bodies*. Princeton: Princeton University Press, 1957.

Kärkkäinen, Veli-Matti. *Pneumatology*. Grand Rapids, Michigan: Baker Academic, 2002.

Lake, Kirsopp. *The Epistle to Diognetus*. A pamphlet from Kessinger Publishing, extracted from *The Apostolic Fathers*. London: Heinemann, New York: Macmillan, 1912–13.

Lidgett, John Scott. *The Biblical Doctrine of the Atonement*. Minneapolis, Minnesota: Klock & Klock, 1983.

Lester, Geoffrey. *The Earliest English Translation of Vegetius' De Re Militari*. Heidelberg: Carl Winter, Universitätsverlag, 1988.

Lossky, Andrew. "'Maxims of State' in Louis XIV's Foreign Policy in the 1680s." In *William III and Louis XIV*, edited by Ragnhild Hatton and J.S. Bromley. Liverpool: Liverpool University Press, 1968.

Löwith, Karl. *Meaning in History*. Chicago: The University of Chicago Press, 1949.

Macmullen, Ramsay. *Constantine*. London: Croom Helm, 1987.

Maier, Christoph T. "Mass, the Eucharist and the Cross: Innocent III and the Relocation of the Crusade." In *Pope Innocent III and his World*, edited by John C. Moore. Brookfield, Vermont: Ashgate, 1999.

Manent, Pierre. *An Intellectual History of Liberalism*. Translated by Rebecca Balinski. Princeton: Princeton University Press, 1994.

Mann, Michael. *Sources of Social Power: A History of Power from the Beginning to A.D. 1760*. Cambridge: Cambridge University Press, 1986.

Masson, Georgina. *Frederick II*. London: Secker and Warburg, 1957.

Mayhew, Ray. "Turning the Tables, Resurrection as Revolution." Review of N.T. Wright, *The Resurrection of the Son of God*. No pages. Online: http://tinyurl.com/659lokn.

McCormack, Bruce. "The Humility of the Eternal Son: A Reformed Version of Kenotic Christology." *International Journal of Systematic Theology* 8 (2006): 243–51.

McGiffert, Arthur Cushman. "Notes to the Church History of Eusebius." In *Nicene and Post Nicene Fathers*, edited by Philip Schaff, vol. I, 2nd series. Peabody, Massachusetts: Hendrickson Publishers Inc., 1995.

McGinn, Bernard. *Apocalyptic Spirituality*. London: SPCK, 1980.

———. "Apocalyptic Traditions and Spiritual Identity in Thirteenth-Century Religious Life." In *The Roots of the Modern Christian Tradition*, edited by E. Rozanne Elder. Michigan: Kalamazoo, 1984.

———. *The Calabrian Abbot*. New York: Macmillan Publishing Company, 1985.

Milbank, John. "Forgiveness and Incarnation." In *Questioning God*, edited by John D. Caputo et al. Bloomington and Indianapolis: Indiana University Press, 2001.

———. "Postmodern critical Augustinianism." In *The Radical Orthodoxy Reader*, edited by John Milbank and Simon Oliver. London and New York: Routledge, 2009.

———. *The Word Made Strange*. Oxford: Blackwell Publishers Ltd, 1997.

Moore, John C., ed. *Pope Innocent III and his World*. Brookfield, Vermont: Ashgate, 1999.

———. *Pope Innocent III.* Leiden and Boston: Brill, 2003.

Moorman, John R.H. *St Francis of Assisi.* London: SCM Press Ltd, 1950.

Murphy, Andrew R. *The Political Writings of William Penn.* Indianapolis: Liberty Fund, 2002.

Negri, Antonio. *Insurgencies.* Minneapolis and London: University of Minnesota Press, 2009.

O'Donovan, Oliver, and Joan Lockwood O'Donovan. *From Irenaeus to Grotius.* Grand Rapids, Michigan: William B. Eerdmans Publishing Co., 1999.

Partington, Kenneth. "The Making of a Decretal Collection. The Genesis of Compilatio Tertia." In *Proceedings of the Fifth Annual Congress of Medieval Canon Law.* London, 1995.

Partner, Peter. *The Lands of St Peter; the Papal State in the Middle Ages and the Early Renaissance.* London: Eyre Methuen, 1972.

Paterson, William. *The Writings of William Paterson,* vol. III. Edited by Saxe Bannister. London: Judd & Glass, 1859. Reprint, New York: Augustus M. Kelley, 1968.

Petersen, Erik. *Theologische Traktate.* Wurzburg: Echter Verlag, 1994.

Philips, D.Z. *The Problem of Evil and the Problem of God.* London: SCM Press, 2004.

Pickstock, Catherine. *After Writing.* Oxford: Blackwell Publishers, 1998.

Poewe, Karla, ed. *Charismatic Christianity as Global Culture.* Columbia, South Carolina: University of South Carolina Press, 1994.

Rawson, Elizabeth. "The Expansion of Rome." In *The Oxford History of the Roman World,* edited by John Boardman et al. Oxford: Oxford University Press, 1991.

Reeves, Marjorie. *Joachim of Fiore and the Prophetic Future.* Stroud, Gloucestershire: Sutton Publishing, 1999.

Ricoeur, Paul. *Time and Narrative,* vol. I. Chicago: University of Chicago Press, 1983.

Robson, Michael. *St Francis of Assisi, The Legend and the Life.* Cassell, London: Geoffrey Chapman, 1997.

Roger of Wendover. *Chronica, sive Flores historiarum,* 4 vols. Edited by H.O. Coxe. London: English Historical Society, 1831–44.

Ronquist, E.C. "Learning and Teaching in the Curia." In *Pope Innocent III and his World,* edited by John C. Moore. Brookfield, Vermont: Ashgate, 1999.

Sabatier, Paul. *Life of St Francis of Assisi.* Translated by Louise Seymour Houghton. London: Hodder and Stoughton, 1919.

Skinner, Quentin. *The Foundations of Modern Political Thought,* vol. II. Cambridge: Cambridge University Press, 1978.

Smith, Charles Edward. *Innocent III Church Defender.* Westport, Connecticut: Greenwood Press, 1971.

Smith, John Holland. *Francis of Assisi.* London: Sidgwick and Jackson, 1972.

Southern, R.W. *Western Society and the Church in the Middle Ages.* The Penguin History of the Church, vol. II. London: Penguin, 1970.

Stead, G.C. "'Eusebius' and the Council of Nicaea." *The Journal of Theological Studies* N. S., vol. XXIV, Pt. 1 (April 1973).

Stephenson, Carl. *Mediaeval History.* New York: Harper and Row, 1962.

Stockton, David. "The Founding of the Empire." In *The Oxford History of the Roman World,* edited by John Boardman et al. Oxford: Oxford University Press, 1991.

Stone, Lawrence. *The Crisis of Aristocracy.* Oxford: Clarendon Press, 1965.

Synan, Vinson. *The Century of the Holy Spirit. 100 Years of Pentecostal and Charismatic Renewal 1901-2001.* Nashville, Tennessee: Thomas Nelson, 2001.

Taylor, David C. *Gerrard Winstanley in Elmbridge.* Cobham, Surrey: Appleton Publications, 2000.

Tertullian. *Apology.* Translated by T.R. Glover. Loeb Classical Library. Cambridge, Massachusetts: Harvard University Press, 1931.

Thomson, David. *England in the Nineteenth Century.* London: Penguin Books, 1950.

Toulmin, Stephen. *Cosmopolis.* Chicago: Chicago University Press, 1992.

Traill, H.D. *William III.* London: Macmillan, 1921.

Troost, Wout. *William III, the Stadtholder King.* Translated by J.C. Grayson. Aldershot: Ashgate, 2004.

Ullmann, Walter. "The Development of the Medieval Idea of Sovereignty." *The English Historical Review,* vol. LXIV, no. 250 (January 1949).

Van Cleve, Thomas Curtis. *The Emperor Frederick II of Hohenstaufen.* Oxford: Oxford University Press, 1972.

Verduin, Leonard. *The Reformers and Their Stepchildren.* Grand Rapids: William B. Eerdmans, 1964.

Vilar, Pierre. *A History of Gold and Money.* Translated by Judith White. London: NLB, 1976.

Virno, Paolo. *A Grammar of the Multitude.* Cambridge, Massachusetts and London, England: MIT Press, 2004.

Wacker, Grant. *Heaven Below.* Cambridge, Massachusetts and London, England: Harvard University Press, 2003.

Waley, Daniel. *The Papal State in the Thirteenth Century.* London: Macmillan, 1961.

Wallace, Naomi. *Things of Dry Hours.* London: Faber and Faber, 2007.

Wallace-Hadrill, D.S. *Eusebius of Caesarea.* London: A.R. Mowbray & Co., 1960.

Ward, Graham. *Christ and Culture.* Oxford: Blackwell Publishing, 2005.

———. *Cultural Transformation and Religious Practice.* Cambridge: Cambridge University Press, 2005.

———. "Kenosis: Death, Discourse and Resurrection." In *Balthasar at the End of Modernity,* edited by Lucy Gardner et al. Edinburgh: T. & T. Clark, 1999.

Watt, F.W., ed. *Matthew Arnold Selected Poems and Prose.* Oxford: Oxford University Press, 1964.

Wells, Colin. *The Roman Empire.* London: Fontana Press, 1992.

Wessley, Stephen E. *Joachim of Fiore and Monastic Reform.* New York: Peter Lang Publishing, 1990.

West, Delno C., and Sandra Zimdars-Swartz. *Joachim of Fiore.* Bloomington and Indianapolis: Indiana University Press, 1983.

Williams, George Huntston. "Christology and Church-State Relations in the Fourth Century." *Church History,* vol. XX, no. 3 (Sept. 1951).

———. "Christology and Church-State Relations in the Fourth Century." *Church History,* vol. XX, no. 4 (Dec. 1951).

Williams, Rowan. *On Christian Theology.* Oxford: Blackwell Publishing, 2000.

Williamson, G.A. "Introduction." In *Eusebius: The History of the Church.* London: Penguin Books, 1965.

Winstanley, Gerard. *The Law of Freedom in a Platform, or True Magistracy Restored.* New York: Schocken Books, 1941.

Wood, Ellen Meiksins. *Empire of Capital.* London and New York: Verso, 2003.

Woodhead, Linda. *An Introduction to Christianity.* Cambridge: Cambridge University Press, 2004.

————. *Christianity: A Very Short Introduction.* Oxford: Oxford University Press, 2004.

Wright, N.T. *Jesus and the Victory of God.* London: SPCK, 1996.

————. *The Challenge of Jesus.* London: SPCK, 2000.

————. *The New Testament and the People of God.* London: SPCK, 1997.

Wright, Steve. "Mapping Pathways within Italian Autonomist Marxism: A Preliminary Survey." In *Historical Materialism*, 16. Brill Publishing, 2008.

Subject/Name Index

Note: those subjects so integral to the book that they appear in the title, such as church, gospel, empire, politics and sovereignty, occur throughout and are not included in the index.

A

Abulafia, David, 77, 78
Act of Accommodation, 103
Act of Seclusion, 112
Act of Settlement, 117
Act of Uniformity, 127
Acts of the Apostles, 105, 163, 225
Africa, 47, 158, 197
African American, 139, 154, 156
Agamben, Giorgio, ix, 16, 18, 19, 21, 24, 132, 136, 138, 142–144, 150, 175, 194
Althaus, Paul, 178
Altizer, Thomas J.J., 185
America, 127, 128, 139, 143, 147, 154–158, 167, 236
American Constitution, 128
Amos, 214
analogia entis, analogy of being, 7, 8, 10, 11, 13, 186–188
Anderson, Allan H., 153
Anglican Church, 103, 104
Ann, queen of England, 117
annuities, 118
Anselm, 57, 85
Antichrist, 63, 81, 88, 104, 123
Antioch, Council of, 49, 50
apocalyptic, 87, 104, 123, 211, 213–215, 220, 221
appeasement, 19, 41, 57, 85, 129, 140, 145, 204, 220, 230, 234, 238
Aquinas, Thomas. See Thomas Aquinas.

Aristotle, Aristotelian, 12, 44, 138, 207
Arius, Arian, 48, 49, 51, 52, 56, 58, 75
Arnold, Matthew, ix
Athanasius, 51
Augustine, Saint, Augustinian, 12, 160, 161, 187
Augustus Caesar, 79, 216, 217
autonomy, 12, 21, 72, 110, 134, 135, 139, 157, 158, 165, 167, 197, 237
Azusa Street, 152–154, 156

B

Balthasar, Hans Urs von, 180, 186–188, 200, 201
Bank of England, xiv, 25, 96, 100, 116–125, 129, 130, 133, 141
Bartleman, Frank, 153, 155, 156
Beatrice, Pier Franco, 51
Benedict, Saint, 27, 74, 87, 88
Benjamin, Walter, 138, 144, 150
biopolitics, biopolitical, ix, xi, xiv, 12, 13, 19, 20, 23, 135, 137, 139, 142–144, 152, 154, 163, 167, 171, 175, 205, 237
biopower, 130–152, 154, 157, 158, 163, 164, 166, 167, 174, 175, 185, 196, 218, 222, 230, 234, 237
Blumenberg, Hans, 6
Bogomils, 26
Bosch, Hieronymus, 8
Bourdieu, Pierre, 211

bourgeoisie, 121, 122, 129, 134, 184
Bradley, Arthur, 13
British Coalition Government, 140, 141
Broadbent, E.H., 27
Brown, David, 180–184, 186, 187
Bulgakov, Sergius, 180
Burnet, Gilbert, xiv, 96, 97, 99–109, 112, 114, 116, 122–125, 127
   sermons, books and political pamphlets
   History of His Own Time, 123, 124
   Four Discourses, 123, 124
   Mystery of Iniquity, 104
   Subjection, for Conscience Sake Asserted, 106
   Vindication of the Authority, Constitution and Laws of the Church and State of Scotland, 104–107
Burnet, Rachel, 101, 102
Burnet, Robert, 101

C

Calvin, Calvinism, 103, 110
Canning, Joseph, 70
capital, capitalism, capitalists, 119, 125, 129, 130, 133, 136–140, 155, 158, 164, 166, 175, 197, 203, 236
Cappadocians, 12
Caputo, John, 182, 189–193
Carlos II, king of Spain, 117
carmen Christi, 173, 174, 183, 192
Carolingian Empire, 24, 68, 77
Carter, Warren, 215, 216
Cavanaugh, William, 4, 7–10, 202–204
Cerinthus, 44
Chalcedon, 176, 179, 186
charismata, 202, 204
Charismatic. See Pentecostal-charismatic movement.
Charlemagne, 64, 68, 71, 77
Charles I, king of England, 97, 102, 108, 112
Charles II, king of England, 101–103, 106, 114, 117, 127

Charles V, Holy Roman Emperor 109, 111
Chile, 202
China Inland Mission, 166
Christendom, chapters 2–5, 120, 121, 128, 134, 140, 141, 143, 146, 152, 159, 160, 163, 171, 173, 175–177, 190, 191, 197, 202, 208, 209, 218, 230, 234–237
Christ, 8, 9, 16, 31, 34, 35, 38, 39, 41, 42, 44, 46, 48, 53, 55–58, 65, 73, 74, 76, 79, 81–86, 90, 91, 93–95, 98–100, 124, 129, 139, 145, 146, 159, 160, 173–179, 181–184, 187, 188, 199, 201, 204, 209, 215–217, 229
Christology, 20, 24, 28, 43, 45, 47, 48, 49, 53, 57, 58, 65, 75, 82, 83, 91, 95, 124, 140, 146, 160, 161, 171, 173, 177
Cistercians, 70
civil rights. See rights.
Clarke, T.E.S., 100
Claydon, Tony, 104, 122
cleresy, clergy, 67, 88, 89, 99, 102, 127, 179
coinage, 119, 120, 122
commodification, ix, 130–132, 134, 135, 141, 146, 174, 185, 197, 202, 230
Constance, Queen of Sicily, 70
Constantia, 49
Constantine, 9, 28–37, 39, 41, 45, 49–52, 54, 55, 77, 81, 145, 176, 230
Constantinius, 29
contentions, before the cross, 210, 218, 222, 226
Cook, Stephen L., 212
Copernicus, Copernican, 7, 9, 10, 12, 25
Corporation Act, 127
corpus mysticum, 7, 85, 179, 204
corpus verum, 7, 10, 65, 85, 95, 124, 144, 172, 179, 202, 204, 235, 237, 238
counterpolitical, 9, 24, 55, 59, 84, 95, 100, 153–155, 158, 161–163, 171, 172, 189, 192, 203–205,

210, 218, 220–222, 226, 234,
236, 237
creation, 6, 7, 11, 23, 38, 126, 128, 174,
178, 180, 184–188, 194, 200
critical realism, 194, 201, 205, 206–208,
210, 211
cross, 28, 35–41, 46–48, 52–54, 56, 57,
63, 64, 65, 69, 73–75, 77, 78,
83–85, 94, 95, 115, 117, 140,
145, 175, 192–194, 195, 197,
210, 218, 226, 228–230, 234
Crossan, John Dominic, 214
Cupitt, Donald, 43, 175–177
currency, 79, 100, 119, 120, 122, 125

D

Daniel, Book of, 33
Dante Alighieri, 5
Dayton, Donald, 27, 158
Death of God, 185
debt, 125, 127, 128, 130, 133, 141, 182
de Certeau, Michel, 4, 7–9, 13
Declaration of Reasons for appearing
in arms in the Kingdom of
England, 108
Declarations of Indulgence, 114, 115
de-eschatologization. See eschatology.
de Lubac, Henri, 4, 7, 13, 84
Descartes, René, 5, 148
devotio moderna, 109
de Witt, Johan, 112, 113
Diepold, 68–70, 72
Diet of Worms, 80
Diggers, 27, 125, 126, 129, 236
Dillon, Michael, 13
Diocletian, 29
Diognetus, Epistle to, 26
Dionysius, 26, 46, 47, 132, 235, 237
doctrine, 7, 8, 12, 13, 14, 23, 31, 58, 72,
76, 84, 85, 101, 102, 104, 105,
107, 122, 123, 154, 159, 166,
175, 189, 194, 226, 235
Donation of Pippin, 68
Donation of Sutri, 68
Droogers André, 157
Duns Scotus, 5, 6, 188

Durnbaugh, Donald F., 27
Dutch Golden Age, 108–110
Dutch Reformed Church, 111
Dutch States, 96, 108, 111, 112

E

Eastern Orthodox Church, 160, 161
Ebionites, 44
economy of response, 193, 201, 205,
208–210, 219, 221, 228
Edict of Nantes, 103
enclosure, 133, 236
England, 75, 78, 97, 107–115, 117, 121,
123, 125, 128
episcopacy, episcopal, episcopalian, 33,
44, 99, 101–103, 110
eschatology, eschatological, 164, 167,
171, 172, 176, 189–191, 196,
197, 199–202, 204–214, 218,
219, 221, 226, 227, 233–235,
237–239
anti-eschatological, 175
de-eschatologization, 161–163, 165,
200
eschatological peace, 8, 24, 47, 50, 53,
57, 64, 80, 90, 100, 129, 160,
162, 199, 211, 214, 234, 239
over-realized eschatology, 55, 226
realized eschatology, 162, 163
under-realized eschatology, 162
evangelical, 27, 202
eucharist, 47, 54, 56, 65, 84–86, 93, 95,
98, 99, 123, 124, 129, 179, 188,
202–204, 237
Eusebius of Caesarea, xiv, 9, 12, 19,
24–27, 28–59, 63, 74, 76, 81, 82,
87, 105, 145, 149, 162, 234
works
Commentary on Isaiah, 28–32,
36, 45, 48, 55
History of the Church, 28–30,
32, 33, 35, 42, 43, 45, 46,
48, 54
Life of Constantine, 30, 36, 37
Oration in Praise of
Constantine, 31, 40

Eusebius of Nicomedia, 48, 49, 51
Eustathius, 51
Event, 189, 190–193
exception, state of, power of, 16, 19, 85,
    142–147, 149, 150, 175, 185,
    195, 196, 226
Exclusion Bill, 107

F

Fagel, Gaspar, 113
faith. See living by faith.
Feenstra, Ronald J., 186
feminist thinkers, 208
filioque, 161
Finney, Charles, 158
First World War, 157
Fletcher, Paul, 4, 7–15, 21, 81, 171, 175,
    199–201, 221, 233
footwashing, 218, 222, 226–229
Fordist, 137
Foucault, Michel, 132, 134, 135, 147,
    149
Fourth Lateran Council, 72, 74, 86, 98
Fowden, Garth, 54
Foxcroft, H.C., 100
Francis of Assisi, xiv, 27, 63, 65, 86,
    90–94, 164, 236
    works
        Canticle to Brother Sun, 92
        Admonitions, 93
Frederick II, the Hohenstaufen, xiv,
    10, 12, 24, 63, 75–81, 93, 109,
    113, 139

G

Galerius, 29
Galilei, Galileo, 5
geminal, 83, 94
Geneva Convention, 143
Geoffrey of Villehardouin, 74
Giles, Kevin, 178, 183
Gillespie, Michael Allen, 4, 6, 8, 9
Giuseppi, John, 119, 120

God
    Eusebius's view of, 28, 32–34,
        39–45, 48, 50–58
    Innocent III & his contemporaries
        view, 72, 75, 77–80, 84–88,
        92–94
    from the beginning of the modern
        age, 98, 105, 106, 122–124, 126,
        127
    and biopower, 140, 141, 144, 145,
        148, 164, 165
    and the new transcendence, 153–
        155, 158, 160, 166, 167
    in kenotic theology, 172, 177, 178,
        180–188
    arguing from Jesus to God, 173,
        174, 177, 178, 179, 183, 185–
        195
Godfrey, Michael, 118
godly polity, 31, 32, 34–36, 39, 41, 42,
    54, 63, 67, 89
Goodchild, Philip, 119, 120
Gore, Charles, 176, 180, 184
Gospels
    Johannine, 198, 218, 226, 227
    John, 39, 222, 229
    synoptic, 194, 218, 222, 223, 226,
        227, 235
    Matthew, 216, 223–225
    Mark, 209, 218, 224, 225
    Luke, 223–225
Grand Alliance, 117
Great Treaty, 128
Gregory VII, Pope, Gregorian
    movement, 67, 76, 82
Gregory IX, Pope, 93
Greig, Martin, 124
Greimas, A.J., 207
Grotius, Hugo, 111, 113
Guantanamo, 143
Gwyther, Anthony, 211, 212

H

Habermas, Jürgen, 21, 22
habitus 211, 215, 218

Haggai, 212

Hanson, Paul D., 212

Hapsburgs, 110, 111

Hardt, Michael, x, xi, 5, 6, 18, 132–139,
    147–151, 163, 164

Hebblethwaite, Brian, 180

Hegel, 13, 148, 190

Heidegger, 190

Henry VIII, king of England, 78

hermeneutics, vii, viii, 20, 86, 87, 171,
    185, 188, 190, 191, 194–196,
    198, 199, 201, 205, 207–210,
    213, 218, 219, 221, 227, 228,
    230, 234–236, 238

Hermetic philosophy, 52

Herodians, 222–224

hierarchy, ix, x, xiii, 7, 11, 12, 14, 16–18,
    21, 22, 26, 41, 42, 45, 47, 49, 52,
    54, 64, 89, 92, 93, 95, 98, 101,
    134, 148, 150, 154, 156, 161,
    162, 174, 175, 177, 179, 180,
    183, 189, 193, 199, 202–204,
    215, 221, 226, 229, 236, 238, 239

High Priests, 43, 81, 216

Hilberath, Bernd Jochen, 159, 161

Hill, Christopher, 27

Hobbes, Thomas, 5

Hollenweger, Walter J., 153

Hollerich, M.J., 30, 31, 35, 36

Holy Experiment, 125, 128

Holy Spirit, 43, 84, 88, 89, 93, 131, 151,
    156, 159–163, 166, 191, 197,
    198, 237, 238

homoousios, 48, 51, 52, 58, 76, 161

Honorius III, Pope, 82

Hooker, Richard, 103

Horsley, Richard, 215, 216

House of Hanover, 117

Howard-Brook, Wes, 211

Huguenots, 114

human rights. See rights.

I

imago dei, image of God, 6, 42, 185,
    187, 231

immanence, xi, 3–7, 9–14, 17, 18, 21,
    44, 55, 65, 94, 95, 121, 129, 134,
    136, 139, 148, 149, 177, 180,
    184, 197, 198, 200, 204, 205,
    209, 210, 213, 221, 226–229

immaterial labor, 137, 138, 166, 167,
    196, 197, 237

incarnation, incarnational, x, 9, 10, 14,
    23, 34–36, 38, 41, 43, 45, 48, 49,
    52, 53, 55, 58, 59, 81, 83–86, 90,
    171–181, 183–190, 192–196,
    198–202, 204, 205, 218, 221,
    226, 230, 231

Innocent III, Pope, xiv, 10, 24, 63,
    65–80, 82, 84–89, 92, 113

interactive labor, 137

Ireland, 115, 117, 127

Irenaeus, 26, 46, 47, 132, 235, 237

Isaiah, 28–32, 36, 39, 45, 48, 55, 191,
    212, 220, 222

Islam, 54, 64, 72

Israel, 31–34, 40, 41, 43, 63, 67, 81, 123,
    212, 213, 216, 217

J

James II, king of England, 97, 101, 102,
    104, 106–108, 114, 115, 117

Jenkins, Philip, 152

Jeremiah, 212, 214, 220, 222

Jesus, 15, 35, 43, 52, 57–59, 65, 75, 83–
    86, 93, 95, 129, 150, 160, 165,
    171–186, 188–194, 196–199,
    201, 203–205, 208–211, 214,
    216, 218, 219–230, 233, 235,
    237, 238

Jews, 31, 33, 34, 42, 63, 220

Joachim of Fiore, xiv, 27, 63, 65, 86–90,
    92, 95, 125, 132, 236, 237

    works
        Arrangement of the New People
            of God, 88, 237
        Book of Figures, 87, 88
        Eternal Gospel, 87
        Life of Benedict, 87

John, king of England, 75

Johnston, Archibald, 102

John the Baptist, 223
Judaism, 164
Julius Caesar, 215, 217

K

Kant, Immanuel, 148
Kantorowicz, Ernst, 77–79, 83
Kärkkäinen, 159–161
katargēsis, 24, 139, 140, 230
Kautsky, Karl, 215
Kennedy, Lady Margaret, 106
kingdom of God, 33, 52, 55, 154, 197,
        203, 211, 214, 218, 231
kingship
    Christ's earthly kingship, 76, 82,
        83, 105
    the king's two bodies, 76
Kierkegaard, 200

L

labarum, 37, 49, 74, 145
labor power, 129, 133, 134, 137, 138,
        197, 237
Lactantius, 26
land, 32, 33, 63–71, 73, 74, 80–82,
        93, 100, 108, 126, 128, 133,
        146, 157, 213, 215, 216, 219,
        236–238
lapsis, xi, 3, 4, 6, 8–11, 13, 15, 17, 27, 84,
        94, 145, 147, 161, 167, 171, 176,
        186, 188, 190, 233
Latitudinarian, 25, 96, 99, 100, 102, 104,
        106, 108, 116, 123–125, 134,
        140, 142, 173
Laud, William, Archbishop of
        Canterbury, 102
Lauderdale, Lord, First Secretary of
        Scotland, 101–103, 105, 106
law
    canon, 65–67, 82, 94, 99
    Old Testament, 33, 34, 36, 56, 128,
        213, 220, 225, 226
    parliamentary, 99, 105, 108, 115,
        123, 130, 132, 134, 140–145

Roman, neo-Roman, 75, 78–80, 83,
        94, 99, 216, 230
League of Augsburg, 115
Leighton, Bishop, 102–104
Leo III, Pope, 64
Leopold I, Holy Roman Emperor, 114
Leopold VI, Duke of Austria, 73
Levellers, 27, 125
Liber Augustales, 79
Licinius, 29, 37, 49, 50
Liddon, H.P., 176
Lidgett, John Scott, 85
liturgy, 34, 64, 76, 101, 102, 105, 202,
        204, 239
living by faith, 132, 155, 158, 166, 167,
        190, 196, 197, 199, 205, 210,
        218, 226, 237
Locke, John, 122
Louis XIV, king of France, 97, 103, 106,
        110, 112–114, 117
love, x, xii, 11, 14, 18, 19, 53, 146,
        151, 153–155, 161, 163–167,
        173–175, 177, 179, 182–187,
        189, 191–198, 202, 204, 205,
        208, 210, 222, 223, 227–229,
        238, 239
Löwith, Karl, 198
Lupold, bishop of Worms, 71
Luther, 98, 105, 178, 179, 183, 184
Luxembourg, 114

M

Maccabaean Revolt, 213
Machiavelli, 5
Maier, Christopher T., 73
Mammon, 116
Mann, Michael, 217
Marcion, 44
Markward of Anweiler, 63, 67–70
Mary, wife of William III, joint
        monarch of England, 101, 107,
        108, 114, 115, 121, 123
Mass, 56, 98, 99, 140, 203,
mathēsis, 6
Maurice, of Orange, 111
Maxentius, 29

Maximian, 29
Maximinus, 29
Mayhew, Ray, 226
McCormack, Bruce, 179
mediation, 8, 35, 54, 75, 78, 162, 179,
    203, 204
medievality, x, 4, 15, 23–25, 65, 124,
    132, 148, 189, 205, 238
Messianic, 31, 116, 122, 124, 125, 144,
    158, 184
Methodist, 158
Michelangelo, 5
Middle East, 64, 197
Milbank, John, 3, 6, 8, 9, 178
Milvian Bridge, Battle of, 37
mimesis, 207, 209, 227
modern, modernity, x–xiii, 3–7, 9–14,
    17, 18, 20, 21, 23–25, 65, 77,
    81, 90, 94, 96, 97, 108, 114, 118,
    123, 129, 131, 132, 134, 137,143,
    148–150, 152, 159, 166, 173,
    176, 184, 185, 190, 198, 200,
    205, 207, 208, 219, 234, 238
Mohammed, 64
Moltmann, Jürgen, 12, 178
monarchy, 16, 20–22, 70, 114, 127, 215,
    221, 230, 231
    universal, 34, 47–54, 58, 65, 99, 108
    limited, 101, 108, 109, 111, 112,
    115, 116, 122, 131, 234
money, 91, 95–97, 100, 113, 116,
    118–123, 125, 127–134, 137,
    139–143, 145, 146, 154, 157,
    158, 173, 182, 185, 191, 196,
    197, 199, 202, 219, 221, 222,
    234, 236–239
monotheism, monotheistic, 12, 34, 53,
    54, 2134
Montanism, 162
Montaigne, 5
Moses, 35, 43, 225, 226
multitude, ix–xi, xiii, 14, 21, 22, 57, 129,
    132, 135–140, 147–149, 151,
    154, 158, 163–167, 172, 177,
    185, 193, 194, 196–198, 200,
    202, 204, 219, 220, 223, 230,
    231, 236, 237, 239
Muslim. See Islam.

N

naked life, 132, 136, 138–140, 147,
    149–151, 163, 175, 196, 229,
    230, 237
Naked Truth, 104
Native American, 128, 236
Negri, Antonio, x, xi, 5, 6, 18, 132–139,
    147–151, 163, 164, 165
negotium crucis, 65, 69, 72, 73, 75, 78,
    91, 94, 99, 109, 140
Nehemiah, 212
neo-Marxists, x, xi, xii, 18, 21, 133, 134,
    140, 147, 149, 163, 165, 166, 196
Nepos, 44
New Deal, 135
New Testament, 44, 98, 160, 199, 200,
    216, 217
Nicaea, Council, formulations, 26, 28,
    47–52, 56–58, 75, 83, 161, 179,
    186
Nietzschean, 6, 78
nominalists, nominalism, 6, 8, 9, 25,
    188
Norman Anonymous, 83, 84

O

Ockham, William. See William of
    Ockham.
O'Donovan, Oliver, and Joan
    Lockwood, 26, 35
Old Testament, 43, 63, 82, 95, 128, 140,
    160, 199, 212, 230, 231
Origen, 28
Otto of Brunswick, 71, 72, 77

P

Pamphilius, 28, 29
Papacy, 25, 63, 66–69, 72, 76, 78–83, 86,
    89, 93, 98, 99, 140, 147, 237
papal lands, 65–69, 71, 73, 82
Papal States, 66, 67, 69, 70, 72, 80
Parham, Charles, 154, 156

parliament, parliamentarian, 102, 105, 106, 108, 111, 112, 117, 118, 120, 121

Paterson, William, 116, 118, 120–122, 133, 139

patristic, 12, 51, 199

Paulicians, 26

Paulinus, 51

Paul of Samosata, 44

Paul, the apostle, 105, 165, 174, 191–194, 200, 201, 224, 225, 228
    epistles, 173, 174, 193, 199, 224

pax Romana, 9, 31, 36, 39, 47, 48, 57, 73, 99, 100, 161, 162, 215, 230

peace, ix, 8, 9, 16, 24, 25, 30–34, 36, 39–42, 47, 49, 50, 53–55, 57, 64–67, 76, 79–81, 85, 90, 94–96, 99–101, 104, 105, 107, 108, 110, 112–114, 116, 117, 121, 123, 124, 129–133, 135, 141, 146, 148, 151, 160–162, 167, 179, 197, 199, 202, 211, 212, 214, 231, 234, 236, 239

Pennsylvania, 128, 236

Penn, William, 27, 100, 125, 127–129, 132, 236, 237

Pentecostal-charismatic movement, 132, 139, 151–158, 160, 163, 166, 167, 172, 196, 197, 202, 204

Pentecostal churches and networks, 155

people, ix, 16, 21, 22, 33, 34, 79, 96, 104–107, 109, 121, 136, 137, 165, 179, 185, 219, 220, 236, 239

Persian Empire, 212

persona mixta, 83

Peter, apostle, 82, 93, 94, 225, 227, 229
    epistle, 224

Petersen, Erik, 12, 54, 58

Petty, Sir William, 97

Pharisees, 222, 223

Philip Augustus, king of France, 71

Philip of Anjou, 117

Philip of Swabia, 69–71, 75, 76

Philip II, Holy Roman Emperor, 109

Phillips, D.Z., 191

Pickstock, Catharine, 6

Pinochet, General Augusto, 202

Platonic, Platonists, 103, 190

plenitudo potestatis, 66, 82, 84

Poewe, Karla, 155, 158, 166, 167, 196

polis, x, 31

poll tax, 224

postmodern, postmodernity, ix, x, xii, 3, 24, 90, 96, 132, 134, 150, 152, 164, 185, 205, 198

power
    constituted, 18, 19, 142, 144, 145, 165
    constituent, 18, 19, 125, 132, 137, 140, 142, 144, 145, 151, 155, 164, 165, 167
    imperial, x, 4, 8, 13, 19, 20, 24–27, 36, 41, 53, 54, 72, 97, 108, 116, 129, 173, 180, 177, 184, 192, 194, 204, 210, 217, 224, 226, 228, 230, 236, 238
    papal, 63–75
    potential, xi, 19, 132, 134, 138, 139, 146, 149, 151, 166, 167, 172, 174, 175, 185, 197, 198, 229, 230
    sovereign, x, 4, 9, 19, 21–23, 27, 34, 52, 75, 84, 85, 87, 94, 95, 111, 117, 123, 126, 131, 134, 135, 140, 142, 147, 151, 155, 162, 166, 171, 172, 174, 179, 183, 184, 187, 191, 203, 222, 228, 230, 233, 234, 236, 237, 239

preaching, 74, 104, 106, 127, 201, 202, 204, 221

predication, 3, 4, 10–14, 18, 21, 66, 177, 198, 205, 207, 208, 219, 238

presbyterian, 101–103, 107, 110

proletariat, 137

prophetic, 30–32, 55, 87, 95, 126, 160, 162, 211–215, 218–221, 223, 236, 237

Propp, Vladimir, 207

Protestant, 11, 85, 94, 98, 103, 104, 114, 117, 202, 204

Q

Quakers, 27, 125, 127–129

R

Reed, Jonathan L., 215, 217
Reformation, 7, 11, 25, 27, 94, 96, 98, 103, 109, 122
Renaissance, xi, xii, 5, 25, 78, 79, 136, 148, 236
republic, 16, 20–22, 26, 103, 108, 111–117, 199, 215
réunions, 114
rights, 17, 20–23, 99, 122, 125, 126, 128, 200
Roman Catholic Church, 11, 66, 98, 104, 110, 114, 123, 124, 152, 204, 222
Ronquist, E.C., 89
Russell, Lord, 107
Rye House Plot, 107

S

Sabatier, Paul, 92, 93
Sadducees, 223, 225, 226
Sandy Foundation Shaken, 127
Schmitt, Carl, 12, 19, 142, 144
Scotland, 102, 103, 105, 106, 115
Scotus, Duns. See Duns Scotus.
Second Vatican Council, 159
secular, secularism, xi, xiii, 4, 13, 17, 65–67, 82, 83, 88, 89, 98, 148, 209, 217
Severus, 29
Seymour, William, 154, 156
Shakespeare, William, 5
society, ix, 4, 7, 8, 31, 40, 73, 75, 92, 97, 99, 119, 122, 142, 156, 158, 164, 167, 182, 197, 204, 220, 236, 237
    of discipline, 132, 134, 146, 147
    of control, 134, 136
Socinian, 124
Solemn League and Covenant, 102
soteriology, soteriological, 24, 53, 56, 57, 59, 64, 65, 73–76, 85, 94, 95, 99, 100, 105, 109, 115, 116, 120–124, 129–132, 140–142, 144–146, 156, 157, 175, 234, 238, 239

Spanish Netherlands, 114
stadtholder, 111–113
standpoint theology, 194, 205, 208
Stanislavsky, Konstantin, 181
States-General, 108, 111–115
Stillingfleet, Edward, 104
Studd, C.T., 197
subsumption, xi, xiii, xv, 4, 11, 13, 15, 17–20, 26, 27, 58, 59, 84, 132, 135, 136, 138, 147, 159, 161, 163, 172, 180, 188, 190, 202, 211, 230, 231, 233, 234
surplus value, 133
Sweden, 114
Swinburne, Richard, 181

T

Taylor, Mark C., 185
tax, x, 109, 118, 119, 122, 126, 130, 133, 215, 216, 223, 224
Tertullian, 162
theology
    dislocation, 3, 4, 7, 9–11, 27, 233, 234, 237
    kenotic, 171–195
    of the event, 189, 190
Things of Dry Hours, 139
Thirty-Nine Articles, 103
Thirty Years War, xi, 25, 148
Thomasius, Gottfried, 184
Tiberius, Roman Emperor, 33, 84
Tillotson, John, 104
tontine loans, 118
Toulmin, Stephen, 5
trade, 97, 110, 119, 121, 126, 130, 215, 221, 222, 224
transcendence, xi, xii, 4, 8, 10–14, 17–19, 46, 53, 95, 131, 132, 136, 139, 140, 144–153, 155, 158, 159, 163, 165–167, 171–177, 180, 183–186, 188, 191, 193–195, 198, 201, 205, 210, 211, 217–219, 226, 228–230, 233, 234, 237–239

transubstantiation, 72, 76, 84, 85, 95, 98, 204
Treaty of Nantes, 103
Treaty of Nijmegen, 114
Trinity, trinitarian, 12, 13, 51, 54, 58, 87, 88, 122–124, 172, 178, 180, 186, 188
Truce of Regensburg, 114
True Freedom, 112
Tudor, 122

U

univocal, univocity, 6, 8, 188

V

Van Cleve, Thomas Curtis, 78
Vegetius's De Re Militari, 74
Verduin, Leonard, 27
Virno, Paolo, 136–138
Volksgeist, 21

W

Wacker, Grant, 155–157
war, ix–xii, 5, 7, 25, 33, 34, 41, 53, 56, 65, 73–75, 78, 95, 99, 102, 108–110, 112–114, 116–119, 123, 124, 128–133, 139, 145–148, 154, 156, 157, 182, 234, 239
Wallace, Naomi, 139
Walter of Brienne, 63, 69, 74
Walter of Palear, 69, 70
Ward, Graham, 183–188, 194, 201, 205, 208–211, 221, 227
Wellhausen, 212
Wikileaks, 147
William of Ockham, 6, 8, 9, 25, 188
William III, of Orange, xiv, 97, 103, 108–125
William I, 111
William II, 112
Williams, George Huntston, 48, 56
Williams, Rowan, 159

Winstanley, Gerrard, 27, 100, 125–128, 132, 236, 237
Wood, Ellen Meiksins, 23
Woodhead, Linda, xii, xiii, 58
Word, the, 33–43, 45, 47, 48, 53, 54, 56, 74, 160
World Council of Churches, 160
worldview, 158, 206–211, 213, 217
Wright, N.T., 178, 194, 201, 205–211, 213, 214, 221, 226

Z

Zadokites, 212
Zechariah, 212
zeitgeist, ix, 238